T0271138

THE SERVICE SECTOR IN INDIA'S DEVELOPMENT

A striking aspect of India's recent growth has been the dynamism of its services sector. In 2010, it accounted for 57 per cent of the country's GDP and 25 per cent of its total employment. The results do not conform to the growth experience of currently industrialized countries or other developing economies. Is the increasing share of the service sector in India's total output simply notional, as several activities that were earlier classified in the industrial sector are now subsumed in services' value added, or perhaps because the relative price of services has increased over time? The answer is: neither. The sector's growth is real – linked to household final demand, policy reforms and increased service exports. Is this service-led growth process sustainable? That remains an open question because the service sector is highly heterogeneous, ranging from software services and business process outsourcing to wholesale and retail trade and personal services. These sub-sectors vary considerably in the context of different economic characteristics that are important for development.

Gaurav Nayyar is an economist in the Economic Research Division of the World Trade Organization, Geneva, Switzerland. Previously, he was a college lecturer at St Catherine's College, University of Oxford. He holds a PhD in Economics from the University of Oxford, where he was a Dorothy Hodgkin Scholar. His other alma maters include the London School of Economics and Political Science, the University of Cambridge and St. Stephen's College, University of Delhi. Dr Nayyar's research interests lie primarily in the area of development economics, and he has published in academic journals on issues relating to the service sector, economic growth and poverty reduction. He was a co-author of the 2010 World Trade Report Trade on Natural Resources and the 2011 World Trade Report on Preferential Trade Agreements.

The Service Sector in India's Development

GAURAV NAYYAR

World Trade Organization, Geneva

CAMBRIDGE
UNIVERSITY PRESS

CAMBRIDGE
UNIVERSITY PRESS

Shaftesbury Road, Cambridge CB2 8EA, United Kingdom

One Liberty Plaza, 20th Floor, New York, NY 10006, USA

477 Williamstown Road, Port Melbourne, VIC 3207, Australia

314–321, 3rd Floor, Plot 3, Splendor Forum, Jasola District Centre, New Delhi – 110025, India

103 Penang Road, #05–06/07, Visioncrest Commercial, Singapore 238467

Cambridge University Press is part of Cambridge University Press & Assessment, a department of the University of Cambridge.

We share the University's mission to contribute to society through the pursuit of education, learning and research at the highest international levels of excellence.

www.cambridge.org
Information on this title: www.cambridge.org/9781107019898

© Gaurav Nayyar 2012

First published 2012

A catalogue record for this publication is available from the British Library

Library of Congress Cataloging-in-Publication data
Nayyar, Gaurav, 1981–
The service sector in India's development / Gaurav Nayyar.
p. cm.
Includes bibliographical references and index.
ISBN 978-1-107-01989-8 (hardback)
1. Service industries – India. I. Title.
HD9987.I42N39 2012
338.40954–dc23 2011047840

ISBN 978-1-107-01989-8 Hardback

For my mother and father
with love

Contents

Figures

Tables

Preface

This book is a modified version of my doctoral dissertation at the University of Oxford. It is a product of research carried out at the University's Department of Economics between 2005 and 2009. First and foremost, I would like to acknowledge the generous support of the Dorothy Hodgkin Scholarship, without which it would not have been possible for me to take up the opportunity to carry out doctoral research at Oxford. The Chellgren Scholarship, awarded by University College, Oxford, also made a valuable contribution in this regard. Second, I would like to thank both my fellow doctoral students and faculty members in the Department of Economics for an intellectually stimulating environment. But my greatest debt is to John Knight, without whose constant help, guidance and advice, this book would have been difficult to complete. At the very outset, he clarified many of my ideas to help balance ambition and feasibility.

Conversations with Amit Bhaduri, who was researching a certain aspect of India's service sector growth at the time, provided the starting point for the study. The wide coverage of India's 'services revolution' in the media, alongside the relatively thin academic literature on the subject, provided a further impetus. Subsequently, for elaborate discussion on different aspects of the work, I am extremely grateful to Sudhir Anand, Ajit Singh, Anjan Mukherji and Bilal Siddiqi. I am also grateful to Francis Teal, John Muellbauer, Frances Stewart, Christopher Adam, Andrew Glyn, Pronob Sen and Dipak Mazumdar for valuable comments, criticisms and suggestions. For advice and insight on the available household survey data relevant for the book, I would like to thank Alakh Sharma and Sandip Sarkar. But special thanks are due to Balwant Singh Mehta for helping me sift through, organise and interpret mountains of unit-level household survey data collected by India's National Sample Survey Organisation. Moreover, I am grateful to Savita Sharma for her advice on India's National Accounts Statistics as well as Gaurav Shreekant and Moonis Shakeel for their help with databases compiled by the Centre for Monitoring the Indian Economy.

The objective of this book is to analyse the role of the service sector in development, with reference to the Indian experience. Much of the analysis covers the period from the early 1990s to 2004–2005. This is due to two reasons. First, the period from 1990 to 1991 saw a dramatic increase in the share of the services sector in India's GDP, while the share of the industrial sector in GDP remained largely constant. Second, there are constraints imposed by the availability of data. In particular, when this research was undertaken, the last complete household survey on employment and consumer expenditure – conducted by India's National Sample Survey Organisation approximately every 5 years – for which unit-level data were available was carried out for the period between July 2004 and June 2005. The unit household level data from the 2009–2010 surveys were not available at the time.

The key overview statistics on employment in 2009–2010, however, were available and hence are included in the study. Furthermore, wherever else possible, the most recent data available have been analysed. In the case of India's National Accounts Statistics, for example, data on aggregate output extends to 2009–2010 while that on a host of other variables goes to 2008–2009. Of late, unit-level household data for the 2009–2010 surveys on employment and consumer expenditure have become available. While the major conclusions emerging from the book are unlikely to be affected (in any notable way) by the inclusion of these new data, some follow-up research may be a useful exercise.

It should also be said that I have got several new ideas on the subject since the manuscript was completed. These ideas have been posed in the concluding chapter. Hopefully, this additional set of questions sheds some light on future research topics in the area, perhaps even laying the ground for a new book.

I would like to acknowledge the fact that certain portions of the book – in somewhat different forms – have been published as papers in refereed journals. First, one section of Chapter 3 appeared as a paper entitled 'Growth of the Services Sector in India: Notional or Real', in *Economics Bulletin*. Second, a sub-set of Chapter 6 was published in *Applied Economics* as a paper entitled 'The Quality of Employment in India's Services Sector: Exploring the Heterogeneity'. Third, a sub-set of Chapter 5 is forthcoming in the *Cambridge Journal of Economics* as a paper entitled 'Inside the Black Box of Services: Evidence from India'.

I would like to thank my wife, Naira, for coming up with solutions to all kinds of problems that I faced during the writing of this book – her comments as a non-specialist audience, her (relative) prowess in the use of word-processors and her patience with my stress-induced idiosyncrasies were all equally valuable. In fact, she patiently read through an entire earlier draft of the book even when we were not bound in holy matrimony! And last, but not least, this book would be incomplete without an acknowledgement of my parents, Rohini and Deepak Nayyar, who have been a constant source of inspiration, support and guidance.

ONE

Introduction

A striking aspect of India's recent growth has been the dynamism of its services sector, which accounted for 57 per cent of the country's gross domestic product (GDP) in 2010. The object of this book is to analyse the role of the services sector in economic development with reference to the Indian experience. The introduction aims to situate the book in its wider context with reference to the available literature on the subject, thereby providing its motivation. However, it does not attempt to provide an exhaustive enumeration of the related issues, let alone a survey of the literature on the broader subject, which is vast even if it is limited or incomplete in important respects. The introduction outlines important stylized facts as well as the objective, scope and structure of the book. It also seeks to state clearly what the book sets out to do and what it does not attempt to do.

1.1. The Services Sector: Structural Change in Economies

1.1.1. The Early Literature

The process of economic development has been historically associated with structural changes in national economies. The pioneering work of Fisher (1935), Clark (1940), Chenery (1960) and Kuznets (1971) postulates a set of stylized facts from empirical evidence relating to the now industrialized countries. They suggest that in the early stages of economic development, the share of agriculture in both output and employment is overwhelmingly large. Subsequently, as industrialization proceeds, the share of the agricultural sector falls, with the decline being greater in output than in employment. At the same time, the share of the industrial sector rises. Once countries have industrialized and reached an advanced stage of economic

1

development, the share of industry declines while the share of the services sector increases.

This literature attributes the aforementioned pattern of structural change to the income elasticity of demand – which for industrial goods is higher than that for agricultural goods, whereas that for services is even higher than that for industrial goods. With rising levels of income, the demand for agricultural goods will increase at a proportionally lower rate than income because the income elasticity of demand for agricultural goods is less than one, meaning they are 'necessities'. On the other hand, the demand for industrial goods will grow at a proportionately higher rate than income as the income elasticity of demand for industrial goods is greater than one. This leads to the growth of the industrial sector. However, after an economy reaches a sufficiently high level of income, the rate of increase in demand for services increases sharply as the services have an even higher income elasticity of demand than industrial goods. Fisher (1935) refers to this transformation in patterns of demand as a 'hierarchy of needs', where the growth of the services sector is defined by saturation of demand for manufactured goods. Of course, the increase in the rate of change of demand for services could be from both domestic and foreign consumers.

Rowthorn and Wells (1987) provide a similar description of the patterns of structural change in present-day advanced economies, focusing on employment. They argue that modern economic growth is associated with a decline in the share of agriculture in total employment, thereby resulting in an increase in both the proportion and number of people engaged in non-agricultural activity. This includes the industrial sector as well as commercial, government and domestic personal services. In the first stage of development, which the authors term the 'industrialization phase',[1] this refers to the rising share of industry in total employment. As the development process advances, some of the aforementioned trends continue, whereas others change. The share of agriculture in total employment continues to decline, and domestic personal services follow suit. Importantly, so long as there is plenty of labour still employed in agriculture and domestic personal services, non-domestic services can increase their share of total employment at the expense of these two sectors, leaving the share of industry unaffected. Hence, for a period of time, the share of industry may actually rise along with that of non-domestic services. Eventually, however, any significant increase in the share of non-domestic services will be at the

---

[1]   Rowthorn, R.E. and Wells, J.R. (1987), *De-Industrialization and Foreign Trade*, Cambridge University Press, Cambridge.

expense of the industrial sector. This decline in the share of industry and a corresponding increase in the share of services in total employment are referred to by Rowthorn and Wells (1987) as 'de-industrialization'.[2]

Furthermore, using stylized facts for the present-day industrialized countries, Rowthorn and Wells (1987) show that real output of services did not rise significantly faster than that of manufactured goods, and that output per worker increased faster in industry than in services. This suggests that owing to its slower productivity growth, the services sector absorbs an even greater fraction of total employment to keep notional output rising parallel to that of industry. Baumol (1967) provides a theoretical framework for analysing this assertion. He argues that unlike manufacturing, the relatively labour-intensive nature of many service-sector activities implies that their productivity cannot be readily increased through capital accumulation, innovation or economies of scale. As a corollary, this suggests that owing to its slower productivity growth, the increasing share of services in total output may be attributable not to demand-side arguments, but to increasing relative prices of services. It is referred to as Baumol's 'cost disease' hypothesis.

1.1.2. The More Recent Literature

The importance of service-sector activity is highlighted in a more recent literature on the stylized facts of structural change. For instance, analysing a sample of 123 non-socialist countries for the period from 1970 to 1989, Kongsamut, Rebelo and Xie (2001) show that the decline in the share of the agricultural sector in output and employment as an economy matures goes more to the services sector and less to industry than the Kuznets-Chenery work had suggested. In other words, over time, the share of services in output and employment grows along with a decline in agriculture. By contrast, the share of industry first increases modestly and then stabilizes or declines. Hence, in sum, as countries develop, there is an inevitable increase in the importance of service-sector economic activity. This is reflected in the data which show that the services sector constituted 70 per cent of world GDP in 2008.[3]

Using data on a cross section of developed and developing economies over the period from 1950 to 2005, Eichengreen and Gupta (2009) identify

---

[2] Rowthorn, R.E. and Wells, J.R. (1987), *De-Industrialization and Foreign Trade*, Cambridge University Press, Cambridge.

[3] World Bank, *World Development Indicators*, online database; 2008 is the latest year available.

two waves of service-sector growth: a first wave as a country moves from 'low' to 'middle' income status, and a second wave as it moves from 'middle' to 'high' income status. According to them, the first wave consists primarily of traditional services, whereas the second wave comprises modern – financial, communication and business – services. Eichengreen and Gupta (2009) also show that while countries experience the first wave of service-sector growth more or less at the same level of income as they did in earlier years, the second wave, in the post-1990 period, starts at earlier stages of economic development than before. Furthermore, they note that this greater importance of the second wave in medium- to high-income countries is most evident in economies which are relatively open to trade.

The early literature on structural change did not address this issue because unlike manufactured goods, services at the time were largely non-tradeable across borders. More recently, however, the rapid development of information and communication technologies and the formulation of the General Agreement of Trade in Services (GATS) at the World Trade Organisation (WTO) have led to a rapid increase in international trade in services. Hence, whereas exports of labour-intensive manufactured goods may result in an industrial sector whose share rises further and for longer than the average, the increasing service-sector share at higher income levels may reflect increased opportunities for producing and exporting financial, communications and business services. Naturally, in countries which are in a position to specialize and export services in which they have a comparative advantage, international trade in services may be an important explanation for the increasing importance of the services sector. In addition, Eichengreen and Gupta (2009) show that the second wave of service-sector growth is more evident in democracies and in countries close to major financial centres. They attribute this to the fact that democracies are less likely to suppress the diffusion of information and communications technologies, whereas countries in proximity to a financial hub are more likely to have a comparative advantage in the provision of financial services.

Of late, the share of services in output may also have been boosted by a change in production methods resulting from increasing specialization. For instance, industrial firms may make greater use of specialist subcontractors to provide services – such as legal, accounting and transport – which were previously provided from within the firm. In the literature, this process of specialization, whereby enterprises in the industrial sector 'contract out' certain activities to the services sector is referred to as 'splintering' (Bhagwati, 1984; Kravis et al, 1982). It may result in an increase in the share of services in GDP, even when GDP is not growing itself.

Table 1.1. *Sectoral shares in GDP in 2008: Global averages*

	Agriculture	Industry	Services	Stage of development
Low-income countries	27	28	45	Stage 1
Lower-middle-income countries	13	40	47	
Upper-middle-income countries	6	34	60	Stage 2
High-income countries	1	25	74	

Source: World Bank, *World Development Indicators*, online database.

1.2. The Services Sector in India: Patterns of Structural Change

In the context of both the early and more recent literature on structural change, cross-country data on sectoral shares in GDP – presented in Table 1.1 – suggest two stages of development.[4] In the first, as countries move from low-income to lower-middle-income status, the share of both industry and services rises, the rise in the former being greater than that in the latter. In the second stage, as the economy moves to upper-middle- and high-income levels, the share of industry declines and that of services increases. Importantly, the nature of development may influence the transition from one stage to another. For example, exporters of labour-intensive manufactured goods may have an industrial sector the share of which rises further and for longer than the average.

1.2.1. Sectoral Shares in Output

In 1950, the Indian economy showed structural characteristics similar to most developed countries of today at the time when they embarked on the process of industrialization. Agriculture accounted for approximately 56 per cent of GDP, industry contributed around 14 per cent and services about 30 per cent. The fact that the share of the service sector in GDP fits the global trend is shown in Figure 1.1 which relates the share of the services sector in GDP to per capita income in 1960 using data for various countries. It shows that the size of India's service sector equalled the average for its level of GDP per capita.

---

[4] We do not use time-series data as the composition of countries in the different groups may change over time.

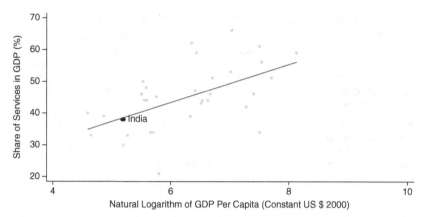

Figure 1.1. Per capita income and services share in GDP (1960).
Note: The scatter points represent other countries in the sample; the line is a fitted regression line.
Source: World Bank, *World Development Indicators*, online database.

Table 1.2 outlines the changes in the sectoral composition of output in India since independence. It shows that between 1950–51 and 2009–10, the share of the agricultural sector in GDP fell from 55.9 per cent to 14.6 per cent, whereas that of the industrial sector rose from 14.3 per cent to 28.1 per cent and that of the services sector rose from 29.8 per cent to 57.3 per cent.

This comparison, over a period that spans more than half a century, does not reveal that the changes were uneven over time. During the period from 1950–51 to 1980–81, the share of the agricultural sector in GDP declined by 17 percentage points, whereas that of the industrial sector increased by 10 percentage points and that of the services sector increased by 7 percentage points. Between 1980–81 and 2009–10, the share of the agricultural sector in GDP declined, once again, by about 24.3 percentage points. In contrast with the previous period, however, the share of the industrial sector in GDP increased by a modest 3.6 percentage points, whereas that of the services sector increased by 20.7 percentage points.

The decline in the share of the agricultural sector in GDP throughout the period conforms to the stylized facts that emerge from the experience of the now industrialized countries. From 1950–51 to 1980–81, the increase in the share of the industrial sector in GDP, which was greater than that of the services sector in GDP, also conforms to the conventional wisdom about structural change. This is reflected in the fact that even in 1980, for its level of GDP per capita, the size of the services sector in India was about the same as the cross-country average (Figure 1.2).

Table 1.2. *Sectoral shares in India's GDP: 1950–51 to 2009–10*

	1950–51	1960–61	1970–71	1980–81	1990–91	2000–01	2004–05	2009–10	Change between 1950–51 and 2009–10
Agriculture	55.9	46.7	46.0	38.9	31.3	24.6	21.1	14.6	–41.3
Industry	14.3	19.0	20.3	24.5	27.6	26.6	27.2	28.1	13.8
Services	29.8	34.3	33.7	36.6	41.1	48.8	51.7	57.3	27.5

Source: Central Statistical Organisation, National Accounts Statistics.

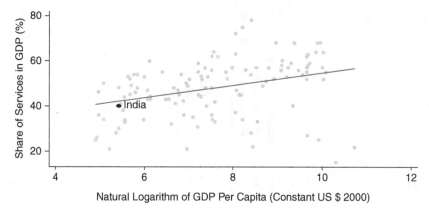

Figure 1.2. Per capita income and services share in GDP (1980).
Note: The scatter points represent other countries in the sample; the line is a fitted regression line.
Source: World Bank, *World Development Indicators*, online database.

From 1980–81 to 2009–10, however, the increase in the share of the industrial sector in GDP was, at best, modest, whereas the increase in the share of the services sector in GDP was so substantial that it picked up more than 85 per cent of the decline in the share of the agricultural sector in GDP. This does not conform to stylized facts about structural change in the process of development in the now industrialized countries. These facts are striking for two reasons. First, the expansion of the services sector in India has been very rapid during the past three decades. Second, the services sector now appears to dominate economic activity in India.

It may be argued that India's pattern of structural change conforms to the "two-wave" findings of Eichengreen and Gupta (2010), where the second wave – comprising the growth of financial, communication and business services – starts at lower levels of income after 1990 than it did before. In particular, they show that at a level of per capita income of about US $4,000 (in year 2000 US purchasing-power-parity dollars), the share of the service sector begins to rise again in a second wave, before eventually levelling off. But India, which has experienced a dramatic growth of its services sector during the decades since 1980, had a per capita income level of about US $3,300 (in year 2000 US purchasing-power-parity dollars) in as late as 2009. Importantly, the dramatic increase in the share of the services sector in India's structural shift is in sharp contrast to other major developing economies. For example, in 2009, although the services and industrial sectors accounted for about 57 per cent and 28 per cent of India's GDP, respectively,

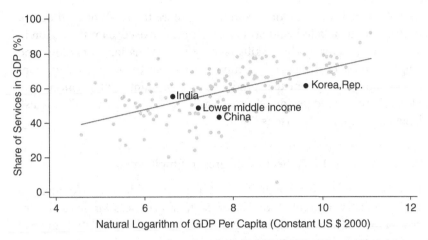

Figure 1.3. Per capita income and services share in GDP (2009).
Note: The scatter points represent other countries in the sample; the line is a fitted regression line.
Source: World Bank, *World Development Indicators*, online database.

they constituted about 43 per cent and 46 per cent of China's GDP, respectively. The relatively low share of the services sector in China's total output is indicative of its manufactured-exports-led growth process. In fact, in 2009, the share of the services sector in India's GDP nearly equalled that of a newly industrialized country such as Korea.[5] This contrast can be seen in Figure 1.3, which, using data for various countries, relates the share of the services sector in GDP to the level of per capita income. Figure 1.3 shows that in 2009, the size of India's services sector, relative to GDP per capita, was higher than the average for a large cross section of countries. In addition, it shows that for its level of GDP per capita in 2009, the size of the services sector in India was notably bigger than even the average of lower-middle-income (LMI) countries – the group in which India was classified[6] at the time.

At the same time, Figure 1.3 shows that for its level of GDP per capita, the size of the service sector in India in 2009 was by no means an outlier. According to Basu and Maertens (2009), the little parallel to India's structural change experience that exists, either in the historical experience of the now industrialized countries or in the contemporary world, is the growing importance of the services sector in the rest of South Asia. For instance,

[5] Sixty-one per cent – The World Bank, *World Development Indicators*, online database.
[6] The World Bank, *World Development Indicators*, online database.

in 2009, the services sector accounted for more than half of total output in Pakistan, Bangladesh and Sri Lanka.[7] This relative edge for the region in the services sector – where skills relating to information technology and language are of relatively greater importance – may be attributable to a top-heavy education system that produced a large number of engineers and other highly trained personnel, as well as the colonial legacy of the English language (Basu and Maertens, 2009).

1.2.2. Sectoral Shares in Employment

In 1950, agriculture accounted for 75 per cent of total employment in India, industry accounted for 10 per cent, and services for about 15 per cent. Table 1.3 outlines the changes in the sectoral composition of total employment in India since independence.

During the period from 1951 to 2009–10, the share of agriculture in total employment declined by about 21 percentage points, while that of the industrial and services sectors increased by 11 and 10 percentage points, respectively. Even during the period from 1983 to 2009–10, while the share of agriculture in total employment declined by about 16 percentage points, that of the industrial and services sectors increased by about 8 percentage points each. This is in sharp contrast to the case of total output, where the increase in the share of the services sector was significantly more than the corresponding increase in the share of the industrial sector. It implies that during the last three decades, the sharp increase in the share of the services sector in output in India has not been accompanied by a corresponding increase in the share of services in employment.

These data set India apart from its South Asian neighbours – Pakistan, Bangladesh and Sri Lanka – which exhibited similar patterns of structural change in terms of output as measured by GDP. For instance, in 2005, whereas the services sector accounted for about 25 per cent of India's total employment, it constituted as much as 40 per cent of total employment in these other South Asian countries.[8] Furthermore, East Asia, with a smaller share of its GDP in services compared to India, has a substantially larger share of its employment accounted for by the sector (Bosworth and Maertens, 2010). In fact, Figures 1.4 and 1.5 reveal that this asymmetry makes India somewhat unusual in the context of the rest of the world. Relating the share of the services sector in GDP to the share of the services sector in total

---

[7]   The World Bank, *World Development Indicators*, online database.
[8]   The World Bank, *World Development Indicators*, online database.

Table 1.3. *Sectoral shares in India's total employment: 1951 to 2009–10*

	1951	1961	1972–73	1977–78	1983	1987–88	1993–94	1999–00	2004–05	2009–10	Change between 1951 and 2009–10
Agriculture	74.7	76.2	73.9	71.1	68.6	65.0	64.7	59.9	56.4	53.1	–21.6
Manufacturing	10.1	10.7	11.3	12.6	13.8	15.9	14.8	16.2	18.8	21.5	11.4
Services	15.2	13.1	14.8	16.3	17.6	19.1	20.5	23.9	24.8	25.4	10.2

Source: National Sample Survey Organisation, Surveys on Employment.

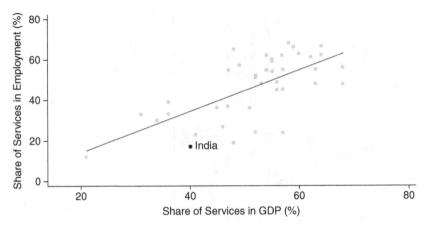

Figure 1.4. Services output versus employment shares (1980).
Note: The scatter points represent other countries in the sample; the line is a fitted regression line.
Source: World Bank, *World Development Indicators*, online database.

employment in 1980 and 2005,[9] respectively, using data for various countries clearly shows that India is an outlier. In part, an increase in services employment not commensurate with the increase in services output may reflect substantial underemployment in agriculture, which in 2005 accounted for only a fifth of the country's GDP but more than half of total employment. It may also be because output per worker or labour productivity of services in India may have risen relative to agriculture and industry. This is illustrated in Table 1.4 which shows that during the period from 1983 to 2009–10, the average annual rate of growth of output per worker was notably higher for services, compared to both agriculture and industry. This is unlike several other advanced and developing economies where the rate of growth of real output per worker in the services sector has been much lower than in manufacturing (Kim and Kim, 2003; Triplett and Bosworth, 2000).

The discordance between changes in the service-sector's share in GDP and its share in employment has created perceptions of the sector's limited ability to absorb labour, thereby delivering jobless growth. This, in turn, leads to the larger question of whether, given the large supply of unskilled labour, this lack of employment generation will have an adverse impact on welfare (Bosworth and Maertens, 2010).

---

[9]   The latest year for which data on employment is available for a large number of countries in the *World Development Indicators*.

Table 1.4. *Output per worker (rupees per person at 1993–94 constant prices): 1983 to 2009–10*

	1983	1987–88	1993–94	1999–00	2004–05	2009–10	Average annual rate of growth of output per worker between 1983 and 2009–10 (%)
Agriculture	12,488	12,343	14,962	16,042	14,994	15,198	0.9
Industry	36,048	38,481	51,951	59,779	60,665	63,981	2.3
Services	39,065	47,351	55,653	73,664	87,254	109,441	3.9

Source: Central Statistical Organisation, National Accounts Statistics and National Sample Survey Organisation, Surveys on Employment.

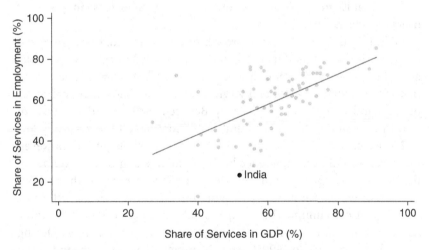

Figure 1.5. Services output versus employment shares (2005).
Note: The scatter points represent other countries in the sample; the line is a fitted regression line.
Source: World Bank, *World Development Indicators*, online database.

1.2.3. Sectoral Shares in Economic Growth

Given the possibility of increasing levels of productivity or output per worker, it is likely that the recent surge in service-sector activity has positively affected the supply side potential output of the economy. Moreover, like manufacturing, the services sector may be a potential 'engine of growth'

Table 1.5. *Rate of growth of sectoral output in India: 1960 to 2010*

	1960–80	1980–2010	1980–90	1990–2010
Agriculture	1.9	2.8	2.9	2.6
Industry	4.7	6.4	6.4	6.5
Services	4.9	7.5	6.6	8.2

Source: Central Statistical Organization, National Accounts Statistics.

because as a result of technological progress, certain service activities may be characterised by static and dynamic economies of scale, spillover effects and high potential for tradeability in international markets (Dasgupta and Singh, 2005). In fact, using cross-country data, Dasgupta and Singh (2006) show that Kaldor's third law of economic growth holds true for the services sector – that is, growth of services output leads to an increase in growth of overall productivity.

Table 1.5 outlines the rate of growth of output in India, disaggregated by sector. It shows that during the period from 1960 to 1980, whereas the annual rate of growth of output of the agricultural sector was 1.9 per cent, that of the industrial sector and services sector was almost identical, at 4.7 per cent and 4.9 per cent, respectively. Between 1980 and 2010, the rate of growth of output of the agricultural sector continued to be relatively low at 2.8 per cent per annum. In contrast to the previous period, however, there was a significant difference between the rate of growth of output of the industrial sector and of the services sector. The rate of growth of output in the former was 6.4 per cent per annum whereas that in the latter was 7.5 per cent per annum. This comparison, over a period that spans three decades, does not reveal that the changes were uneven over time. During the period from 1980 to 1990, the rate of growth of output of the industrial sector was almost the same as that of the services sector. Services-sector growth showed the most significant upward trend during the period from 1990 to 2010, exceeding industrial growth by 1.7 per cent per annum. On a similar note, Rakshit (2007) argues that while there was a deceleration of industrial growth during the 1990s, especially in the period from 1995 to 2005, the services sector showed a significant upward trend during the same period.

This upward trend is usually interpreted to represent rapid strides made by communication, financial and business services such as business process outsourcing, software services, accounting and research. For instance, comparing growth rates of various service activities in the 1990s with their previous trend growth rates (computed for the period from 1954 to 1990),

Table 1.6. *Sectoral contribution to GDP growth in India: 1970–71 to 2004–05*

	1970–71 to 1980–81	1980–81 to 1990–91	1990–91 to 2004–05
Rate of Growth of GDP	3.44	5.51	5.92
Agriculture	0.67	1.07	0.69
Industry	1.01	1.81	1.62
Services	1.65	2.71	3.66

Source: Rakshit (2007).

Gordon and Gupta (2004) show that these were three of five service sub-sectors that experienced an 'acceleration'. Similarly, in more recent empirical work, Bosworth et al. (2007) and Eichengreen and Gupta (2010) show that business, communication and financial services were the fastest-growing segments of the sector during the last decade and a half. All these studies, however, outline the fact that the growth of the services sector has been very broad-based, not limited to these few sub-sectors. Other fast-growing services include hotels and restaurants, transport and community services.

Higher rates of growth of output, relative to industry and agriculture, together with the sector's rising share in GDP, naturally imply that the contribution of the services sector to GDP growth has been significantly higher than that of the other two sectors since the early 1980s. This is analysed formally by a section of the literature through growth accounting exercises for India (Balakrishnan and Parameswaran, 2007; Bosworth et al., 2007; Rakshit, 2007).Table 1.6 outlines the changes in the sectoral contribution to GDP growth for the last three and a half decades. These figures suggest that services have been leading India's economic growth over the last two decades.

In a departure from conventional wisdom, the general conclusion of these growth accounting studies is that service-producing industries have been the primary source of India's growth surge, consistently outperforming the industrial sector. For instance, Bosworth, Collins and Virmani (2007) show that growth in total services output accounts for 1.4 percentage points of the 3.8 percent per of annual GDP growth during the period from 1980 to 2004, versus 0.7 percentage points each for agriculture and industry and 1 per cent for reallocation.[10]

---

[10] Such decomposition exercises do not rule out the possibility that industrial-sector growth may have stimulated service-sector growth. To overcome this shortcoming, Balakrishnan and Parameswaran (2007) show that the growth of the service sector is statistically significant for the growth of the manufacturing sector, but not vice versa.

In sum, the changing structural composition of India's economy sets it apart from the historical experience of the now industrialized countries. The service sector appears to be an important driver of India's recent growth story. But the world is very different from what it was when the authors associated with the early literature on structural change wrote. Services are no longer confined to public administration, hairdressing, tailoring, lodging and housekeeping. They are being increasingly supplemented by modern financial, telecommunication and professional business services. These services can be produced on a large scale. They can readily incorporate technological advance to increase efficiency in provision. Over the last two decades, rapid advancement in information and communication technologies has meant that services can now even be traded in international markets. All of this suggests that several services can now be organized in ways that resemble the modern manufacturing sector. In fact, over the last three decades, labour productivity – measured by output per worker – has grown faster in India's service sector, relative to its manufacturing sector. This is very different even from the growth experience of newly industrialized countries, such as Korea, as well as other developing economies, such as China. It suggests that India's services-led growth process is perhaps sustainable. But is it really, given the sector's relatively low contribution to employment creation? In a country with a large uneducated workforce, can the service sector create employment traditionally associated with the expansion of labour-intensive manufacturing?

1.3. Outline

1.3.1. Background

The agricultural and industrial sectors have been the subject of extensive study and intensive debate in the literature on development economics. Historically, economists have largely ignored the role of the services sector in the process of development. India, which has become one of the fastest-growing economies in the world over the last three decades, is no exception to this rule. But India's development experience over the past fifty years suggests that the increasing importance of the services sector deserves attention, in terms of explanation and analysis.

Reflecting this reality, a literature on the growth of India's services sector has emerged of late. However, most of the studies in this literature are limited to an examination of the following issues. First, they document and analyse relevant trends in output, employment, productivity and international trade (Banga, 2005; Basu and Maertens, 2009; Bosworth and Maertens, 2010; Chanda, 2006; Dasgupta and Singh, 2006; Ghani, 2010; Gordon and Gupta, 2004; Rakshit, 2007; Singh, 2006) and carry out growth accounting exercises (Balakrishnan and Parameswaran, 2007; Bosworth et al., 2007). Second, using data at the macroeconomic level, the studies analyse the factors which may help to explain the ensuing services-sector growth in India (Banga, 2005; Eichengreen and Gupta, 2010; Gordon and Gupta, 2004). Third, they explore possible interrelationships between the manufacturing and services sectors (Banga and Goldar, 2004; Hansda, 2001). Fourth, they identify policies and institutions necessary to sustain the service-led growth process (Ghani, 2010). The academic literature on the growth of the services sector worldwide – in developed and other developing countries – is also limited to the presentation of sectoral output, employment and productivity trends (Eichengreen and Gupta, 2009; Kravis et al., 1982; OECD, 2005; World Bank, 2000), the examination of possible interrelationships between the agricultural, manufacturing and services sectors (Blunch and Verner, 1999; Gemmell et al., 1998; Lee and Wolpin 2006) and an analysis of the impact of services trade liberalization on economic growth (Kim and Kim, 2003; Mattoo et al., 2001). Hence, the literature on the services sector is limited not only in India but also elsewhere.

1.3.2. Objective, Scope and Structure

The stylized facts described in Section 1.2 highlight the dynamism of India's services sector as a striking aspect of its recent growth – something which sets it apart from the development experience of the now industrialized countries as well certain developing economies. But what has contributed to the increasing share of the services sector in the country's total output? Is it simply that several activities which were earlier classified in the industrial sector are now classified as services because of the emergence of specialist service providers? Or has the relative price of services increased over time? Or rather, is it factors relating to the real economy – for instance, have economic reforms relating to increased deregulation and privatization increased the supply of services? Or is the real driving force India's comparative advantage in software exports? But several services are still non-traded. So has domestic demand – both household and government consumption – played an important role? Explaining the growth of India's service sector, in a composite empirical framework, forms the basis for the first substantive chapter of the book. In doing so, it first reviews the existing literature on the subject and then analyses available data at the macroeconomic level. But National Accounts Data, in its estimation of final consumption expenditure, cannot precisely distinguish between the goods and service components of different economic activities. Hence, to establish the significance of household final demand as an explanation for the increasing importance of the services sector, the second substantive chapter uses household survey data to estimate Engel curve-type relationships for six categories of services – education, health, entertainment, personal, communication and transport.

The remarkable success of India's services sector has led people to believe that India is unusual in that it has in significant part been able to 'skip' the usual stage that comes when the manufacturing sector's relative importance rises in the growth process. But does the service sector possess growth-promoting characteristics traditionally associated with manufacturing – can its productivity be readily increased by capital accumulation, economies of scale and improved technology? Can it improve the country's balance of payments through international trade? Can it be an engine of India's economic growth? The often cited experiences of India's software industry and business process outsourcing suggest that services can be organized like modern manufacturing. But the services sector is much more than this visible dimension of the country's recent growth story. It consists of, for example, wholesale and retail trade, transport, public administration and several domestic personal services. They may differ considerably from business services and even from each other. They may not be drivers of productivity growth, and may not be tradable in international markets, thereby raising questions about the sustainability of a services-led growth process. The sustainability question may also hinge on the employment that different segments of the service sector create.

Unfortunately, in the literature on the subject so far, economists have treated the services sector as a black box in much the same way as they treated technology for a long time. The third substantive chapter of the book develops a taxonomy that disaggregates the services sector in India with reference to a set of ten attributes so as to provide an analysis of its economic characteristics, which may differ significantly across sub-sectors. It reveals considerable heterogeneity, which is indicative of sub-sector-specific implications for economic growth, employment, balance of payments, the sustainability of services-led growth, poverty and inequality. This is important for advancing significant research questions because it suggests that economic analysis which considers services as a composite category may conceal more than it reveals.

The stylized facts presented in Section 1.2 showed that the productivity of services over the last three decades in India has increased relative to industry (and agriculture). Does that mean individuals employed in the service sector earn relatively higher incomes? Can you simply move an individual from the industrial sector to the services sector and make him or her better off? Or can educational requirements constrain such movement of labour? The logical answer would be that it is relative. For example, business services may be quite different from wholesale and retail trade. Certain sub-sectors of services may be capital and skill-intensive, whereas other may not be. Similarly, some service sub-sectors are likely to benefit – in terms of income – from productivity increase, but others are unlikely to do so. Furthermore, it may be the case that those sub-sectors which are skill-intensive and experience productivity increases do not create large-scale employment opportunities. All of the aforementioned could have implications for poverty reduction and income inequality in the country. The fourth substantive chapter attempts to find answers by analysing the heterogeneity in the nature of employment being generated in different service sub-sectors – relative to the industrial sector – and subsequently juxtaposing it with data on the quantity of employment. In a developing country such as India, whether services-led economic growth can fundamentally change the pattern of development is likely to be a function of the sector's role in job creation – both quality and quantity – especially for a large pool of unskilled and semi-skilled labour.

So it may be the case that individuals employed in different service sub-sectors are better or worse off, in terms of wages for example, than those employed in the industrial sector. But how do they compare to those employed in agriculture? This is especially interesting for the informal sector which is likely to be a significant component of wholesale and retail trade, hotels and restaurants, transport services, real estate and renting and personal services. Typically, much like agriculture, the urban informal service sector is likely to be associated with low levels of labour productivity owing to substantial underemployment. In fact, the Harris-Todaro model of rural-urban migration predicts that wages in the urban informal sector must lie below wages in the rural agricultural sector. But the fifth substantive chapter shows that the numbers from India contradict this prediction. So does this mean that the informal services sector offers productive employment, thereby making it a pathway out of poverty for individuals migrating from rural to urban areas – those for whom the high skill and education requirements make several modern service-sector jobs unattainable? This chapter constructs a system of equations for the Indian economy in order to compare labour productivity levels in the agricultural and urban informal service sectors. In particular, it traces the dynamic effects of an increase in urban infrastructure and consequent changes in rural-urban migration on labour productivity in these two surplus labour sectors.

The object of this book is to analyse the role of the services sector in India's economic development. In doing so, its scope is defined by an analysis of the previously presented questions in five substantive chapters, each of which endeavours to make an original contribution to the literature on the subject. Furthermore, although each substantive chapter of the book is a self-contained piece of research, they are closely interrelated. For instance, the results of one chapter set the stage for the analysis in the next chapter, or a set of results from one chapter validate important assumptions in as subsequent chapter. In addition, there is a background chapter that reviews the conceptual problems, statistical limitations and measurement difficulties in analysing output and hence productivity of the services sector, both in general and in the context of India's National Accounts Statistics. This is important to set the stage because it is underscores an important reason for the paucity of academic research in this area. The scope of the book does not include detailed case studies on individual service sub-sectors.

The structure of the book is as follows. Chapter 2 provides a discussion on the estimation of services-sector output in the context of India's National Account Statistics in order to review the conceptual problems, statistical limitations and measurement difficulties associated with analysing output, and hence productivity, in the services sector. Using data at the macro-economic level, Chapter 3 analyses the importance of a range of factors in explaining India's services sector growth. Chapter 4 delves deeper into analysing one of those potential factors – domestic household demand. In doing so, it uses household survey data to estimate Engel curve-type relationships for six categories of services and these services in the aggregate. Chapter 5 develops a taxonomy that disaggregates the services sector in India with reference to a set of economic characteristics. Chapter 6 analyses the observed heterogeneity in the services sector, relative to the industrial sector, with respect to one characteristic – employment. In doing so, it examines the nature of employment – in terms of wages for example – being generated in the different service sub-sectors in India and juxtaposes it with data on quantity of employment. Chapter 7 presents an empirical puzzle in the context of observed differences in labour productivity between agriculture and urban informal services. Subsequently, it constructs a theoretical framework for India to analyse these observed differences. Chapter 8 presents conclusions. Given the paucity of rigorous research on the role of the services sector in economic development – both theoretical and empirical – it is hoped that this book would fill an important gap in the literature, thereby contributing to our understanding and furthering our knowledge of the subject.

TWO

Services

Concepts, Measurement and India's
National Accounts

2.1. Introduction

Services constitute a highly heterogeneous category of economic activity
that has become increasingly difficult to define over time. For classical
economists such as Adam Smith, services were products of labour that per-
ish the moment the labour is performed, seldom leaving any trace or value
behind them, and thereby amounted to unproductive economic activities.
Smith's conception of 'unproductive labour' included servants of wealthy
individuals, government employees, the military, the clergy, lawyers, doctors, writers and musicians (Smith, 1776). Similarly, on the other end of the
ideological spectrum, the Material Product System (MPS) of accounting,
based on the Marxist-Leninist theory of social production, distinguished
between 'material' and 'non-material' production, where the former represented productive economic activities and the latter represented unproductive economic activities. In fact, until very recently, the National Accounts
Statistics of socialist or centrally planned economies considered all services
that catered to social and personal needs of people as part of non-material
production and hence unproductive. The only exceptions were services
such as trade and transportation that contributed directly to material production (Lequiller and Blades, 2006).

In more recent times, economists have given due importance to a wide
range of services in light of their potential contribution to economic growth
and productivity increase. National Accounts Statistics the world over
include services as productive activities that contribute to value added in
an economy. Under the UN International Standard Industrial Classification
(ISIC), the broad categories of services include the following: electricity, gas
and water, construction, wholesale and retail trade, hotels and restaurants,
transport, storage and warehousing, post and telecommunication, financial

services, real estate, business services, machinery and equipment rental and leasing, public administration and defence, education and research, medical services, entertainment services, sanitary and social services and personal services (United Nations, 1993). Collectively, they constitute the services sector as distinct from agriculture and industry.

The object of this chapter is to provide an overview of the services sector in terms of concepts and measurement, situating the discussion in the context of India's National Accounts Statistics. The scope of the chapter is limited to a brief review of the literature on the subject and a detailed examination of the services sector in India's National Accounts Statistics. The structure of the chapter is as follows. Section 2.2 presents a discussion on a possible definition of services. Section 2.3 reviews characteristics that could distinguish services from goods. Section 2.4 discusses the problems associated with measuring output of the services sector. Section 2.5 summarizes the methods used to estimate output in national income accounting. Section 2.6 introduces India's National Accounts Statistics and provides certain key definitions. Section 2.7 describes the methodology used in India's National Accounts Statistics to estimate output of the different sub-sectors of services. Section 2.8 highlights the problems associated with the estimation methods described in the previous section. Section 2.9 presents conclusions.

2.2. Services: A Definition

Both goods and services must be capable of being the subject of transaction between two or more economic units.[1] But, in order to define characteristics of goods and services, it is important to identify exactly what one economic unit hands over to the other. Unlike goods, however, services are not physical objects which are easily observable and hence appropriable. The earliest attempt to define services was made by Hill (1977) who argues that 'a service is the activity of an economic unit which brings about a change in the condition of a person, or of a good belonging to some other economic unit, with the prior agreement of that person or economic unit.'[2]

---

[1] The fact that goods and services can be transacted does not mean that they necessarily have to be marketed. They are often produced and consumed by the same economic unit.

[2] Hill, T.P. (1977), "On Goods and Services", *Review of Income and Wealth*, Volume 23, Number 4, pp. 315–338.

Hill (1977) makes an important distinction between two different types of services in his seminal paper: 'services affecting goods' and 'services affecting persons'. According to him, 'services affecting goods' consist of producer activities that transform goods which already belong to some economic unit. Examples of such services include transportation, postal deliveries, repairs, cleaning and maintenance. Most often, such services transform goods that were originally produced in previous periods. 'Services affecting persons', on the other hand, comprise producer activities that change the consumer's physical or mental condition, at the latter's request. Services such as transportation, hair dressing and various forms of medical treatment involve changes in the physical condition of the consumer, whereas services such as education and communications involve changes in the mental condition. It is worth noting that there is very little correspondence between 'services affecting persons' and 'personal services' as conventionally understood in economics. For example, while the services of valets or personal maids are classified as 'services affecting persons', domestic personal services such as house-cleaning, cooking and gardening are classified as 'services affecting goods'.

Following Hill (1977), who argues that services and goods belong in separate logical categories, many studies in the literature adopt a simple and broad definition of services that helps to distinguish services from goods. One such broad definition is that services form a diverse group of economic activities not directly associated with the manufacture of goods, mining or agriculture. They typically involve the provision of value added in the form of labour, advice, managerial skill, entertainment, training, intermediation and so forth.

2.3. Characteristics Distinguishing Services from Goods

2.3.1. Simultaneity of Production and Consumption

Producers of a service work either on goods belonging to consumers or directly on consumers themselves. Hence, Hill (1977) argues that services must be consumed as they are produced. The consumption of a service cannot be detached from its production in the way that the acquisition of a good by a consumer in an exchange transaction may take place sometime after the good is produced. However, subsequent to this early conceptualization, many studies have highlighted the restrictiveness of Hill's definition. For instance, Melvin (1989) points out that Hill's definition simply relates to 'contact' services, and that there are a range of services that allow for a separation of the location of production and consumption across space. Such criticism is not entirely fair to Hill (1977); although his arguments rule out the possibility of a separation of production and consumption over time, they do not preclude the possibility of a separation of production and consumption across space.

Bhagwati (1984) argues that services can be divided into two categories: those that necessarily require the physical proximity of the consumer and producer, and those that do not essentially require this, although it may be useful. Importantly, physical proximity between the consumer and producer is becoming less important for several services, such as banking and insurance, owing to rapid technological progress, especially in the realm of communications and information technology.

2.3.2. Non-Storability and Perishability

The need for simultaneity in the production and consumption of services implies that they cannot be stored. In contrast, the production of most goods precedes their consumption. The only exception to this norm in the case of goods is highly perishable commodities, which cannot be put in stock and must be consumed as they are produced. Given this, classical economists argued that services might be classified as being similar to highly perishable commodities (Smith, 1776).

However, Hill (1977) disagrees with this approach, emphasizing that the fact that services cannot be put into stock has nothing to do with their physical durability as many services such as education are not only permanent but also irreversible. He argues that the erroneous classification of services as highly perishable commodities creates the illusion that the benefits derived from the services must be confined to the period in which they are produced. Hence, like the distinction between durable and non-durable goods, a distinction must also be made between permanent and transitory services.

2.3.3. Intangibility

Griliches (1992) defines services as anything that is a result of labour which does not produce a tangible commodity. He argues that it is fundamentally the lack of tangibility that leads to non-storability, and to non-transferability. However, given the advent of information technology, intangibility must be interpreted with caution. For example, software programmes and other forms of digital electronic content have only limited tangibility, but are storable and transferable. And importantly, the creation of these digital products may often be classified as a service, as also their delivery.

2.3.4. The Role of Labour

In a study of unbalanced growth models, Baumol (1967) argues that economic activities can be classified into two groups: technologically progressive activities characterized by innovations, capital accumulation and economies of scale, and activities which, by their very nature, permit only sporadic increases in productivity. According to him, the basic difference lies in the role played by labour in a particular activity. Baumol argues that whereas labour is simply an incidental requisite for the attainment of the final product in manufacturing, it is an important end in itself for a number of services. Hence, because of their relatively labour-intensive nature, the productivity of many service-sector activities cannot be increased through capital accumulation, innovation or economies of scale. However, given technological progress over the last few decades, it is inappropriate to classify all services as activities which permit only sporadic increases in productivity.

2.3.5. International Trade

The conceptual distinction between goods and services has often been emphasized in the literature on international trade. In the past, physical proximity between the producer and consumer of a service was generally viewed as a requirement for the provision of several services. More recently, however, significant reductions in transport costs, rapid technological progress in communication and information technology and fewer restrictions on the movement of labour across national boundaries have made location characteristics less relevant for international trade.

In the literature on international trade in services, service transactions are classified into four broad analytical categories (Nayyar, 1988; Sampson and Snape, 1985; Sapir and Winter, 1994): those in which the producer moves to the consumer (establishing a commercial presence abroad), those in which the consumer moves to the producer (consumption abroad), those in which either the producer or the consumer moves to the other (cross-border movement of people) and those in which neither the consumer nor the producer moves to each other (cross-border supply).[3]

---

[3] The phrases in the parentheses refer to the terminology adopted by the World Trade Organization under the General Agreement on Trade in Services (GATS) for the analytical distinctions described.

2.3.6. Contractual Nature of the Market Transaction

In the marketing literature, the distinction between goods and services is often based on the contractual nature of the market transaction (Singh, 2006). At the most fundamental level, consumer durables or physical assets yield a stream of services over time. Consumers can either buy the goods that provide a service or buy the service if demand is occasional rather than continuous. For example, an automobile is purchased as a durable good, but its value is based on the stream of services that it will provide over time. Hence, consumers can either buy a car, which provides them with transport services, or buy transport services directly by using taxis, buses or trains. All such durable products may be leased or rented, in which case the service is more explicitly contracted for than in the case of a product transaction.

In sum, consumer durables and services provided by specialist service providers may be possible substitutes as the former yield a stream of services over time. Hence, the distinction between goods and services is often a function of market conditions, as opposed to the intrinsic characteristics of what is being exchanged – that is, whether consumers buy a good which provides a service or simply lease the same service directly from a specialist service provider.

2.4. Output of the Services Sector: Issues of Measurement

In the context of measuring output, services are not very different from goods at a basic level. Most of the problems affecting the measurement of commodity output also affect the measurement of services output. To measure the output of any economic activity, we need information on its total receipts as well as an appropriate price index for it. In addition, we need to know the relevant unit of transaction. Finally, we need to deal with the problem of quality change, which arises from the underlying heterogeneity of outputs, the emergence of new products and varieties and the disappearance of old ones. Problems of measuring services output, however, are more serious because of conceptual problems, non-availability of price data and relatively greater heterogeneity (Griliches, 1992).

In several service sectors, conceptual problems arise because it is not very clear as to what is being transacted, what the output is and what services correspond to the payments made to their providers – in other words, the 'quantity' of services is difficult to capture. This is because, unlike goods, services are not necessarily quantifiable in physical terms as they often represent a process by which a consumer is charged (Melvin, 1995).

For example, in several service sectors such as health, business and legal services, the 'object' of transaction is a delivery and exchange of information. Furthermore, Hill (1977) notes that in the case of services, the process of production is often mistaken for the output of that process. The process of producing a service is the activity which affects the person or goods belonging to some economic unit, whereas the output itself is the change in the condition of the person or good affected. Thus, output cannot be clearly distinguished from the benefits or utility that the consumer expects to derive from the service.

Historically, far more data were collected on agricultural and manufacturing commodities and their prices than on services (Griliches, 1992). Censuses and annual surveys of services industries are a very recent development and much less detailed in their coverage. Moreover, these are limited to present-day advanced countries. In most developing countries, the wholesale price index or the consumer price index, which are the primary source of deflators for GDP (by sector) data, do not collect information on the price of services. Owing to this lack of data, the output series of a number of sub-sectors of services are deflated by makeshift deflators (Griliches, 1992). Furthermore, for publicly provided services such as public administration and defence, there are no available market prices. This implies that real output is often presumed to grow proportionally to some measure of input.

It is also difficult to account correctly for quality changes in services (Griliches, 1992). Intuitively, quality changes within a service should lead to adjustments in the output measure to account for the fact that these services are no longer the same homogenous unit. Output measures should then ideally incorporate data on the number of services provided, differentiated by unit labour requirements and in sufficient detail to account for quality differentials. However, such data are generally not available. Consequently, approximations based on alternative approaches that utilize a variety of assumptions are used. Of course, this problem of accounting for quality change is a general one that extends to manufactured goods as well as construction. However, relative to goods, services are characterized by a greater degree of heterogeneity owing to the underlying nature of transactions, thereby making it difficult to aggregate them (Griliches, 1992).[4] This implies that the difficulty of making comparisons across space and over time is even greater in the case of services. For instance, in many sub-sectors of services, output depends on interaction with the user and hence is

---

[4]   The various units must be expressed in some common basis for aggregation.

more difficult to standardise. Finally, the problem of accounting for quality change in services is further complicated by makeshift deflators – those which do not collect information on prices of different services.

2.5. National Income Accounting

2.5.1. Methods of Estimating Output

In national income accounting, there are three possible approaches to estimate income or output of any economy: the production approach, the income approach and the expenditure approach (CSO, 2007a). The production or value-added approach argues that value is added in the process of production. The income approach implies that the production process generates income, which is paid to the different factors of production. The expenditure approach assumes that production within the economy for a given period of time is meant for domestic consumption or domestic investment. By definition, the three alternative approaches give an identical estimate of income or output of an economy. This is because the three methods of estimating output or income are circular in nature. It begins at the production process where production units engage labour and capital to produce goods and services, the total measure of which gives the domestic product. Thereafter, this production process generates a given amount of income, which is distributed to the different factors of production. Finally, the income thus received by the factors of production is spent in two ways: by persons in terms of consumption goods and services or by producers in acquiring more capital and increasing the physical assets of their productive units. Hence, although national income can be measured by any of the three approaches outlined earlier, it should be measured by all three for a complete analysis of the economy. In an open economy, output and income figures have to be adjusted for transactions with the rest of the world in the form of exports, imports, gifts, loans and factor income flows.

2.5.2. Estimating Services Sector Output

Unlike the commodity or goods-producing agricultural and industrial sectors, the use of the production or value-added approach for estimating services sector output is not straightforward because the 'quantity' of services is difficult to capture. Given the limitations, value added in services under this approach is measured as the difference between the total amount of money paid in return for services received and the cost of material and other inputs used in the process of production.

Under the income approach, however, the services sector is not very different from other sectors. Value added for each unit of production is equal to the amount of total income earned by different factor owners involved in the process of production. This consists of labour income and capital income. Labour income takes the form of wages and salaries, payments in kind or supplementary contribution of employers to social security, pension and other welfare funds. Capital income has different components. A part of it is retained by producers for further investment that increases their capital assets. This is referred to as undistributed profits. On the other hand, a part of it is distributed to the owners of capital in the form of dividends, interest on bonds and rent on land. In addition, there is a category of 'mixed income' to the self-employed who employ their own capital and labour for production. This income consists partly of profits and partly of labour income (CSO, 2007a). Hence, the total income generated in the form of factor shares consists of: wages and salaries, interest, rent, dividends, undistributed profits and mixed income of self-employed.

Finally, under the expenditure approach, like for agriculture and industry, services sector output is computed by estimating the utilization of income available (labour income, capital income, mixed income) in the form of household consumption expenditure, government consumption expenditure and capital formation. Naturally, under all three methods, output estimates of the service sector have to account for transactions with the rest of the world.

2.6. India's National Accounts Statistics: Some Basic Definitions

2.6.1. The Services Sector

In India's National Accounts Statistics, the service sector consists of the following economic activities: wholesale and retail trade,[5] hotels and restaurants, transport services, storage services, communication services, financial services, real estate, ownership of dwellings and renting services, business services and other social, community and personal services. This is broadly similar to the classification of services sector activity in the UN International Standard Industrial Classification (ISIC), but there is one important point of distinction. In contrast to the UN ISIC, India's National

---

[5]   Not necessarily consistent with the definition of services provided by Hill (1977).

Accounts Statistics consider electricity, gas and water supply and construction activity to be part of the industrial sector rather than the services sector (CSO, 2008).

2.6.2. Organized versus Unorganized Economic Activity

In the literature, the 'informal sector' usually refers to production units that do not constitute separate legal entities independent of the household or household members that own them, and for which no complete set of accounts are available. Typically, these enterprises operate on a small scale, and labour relations, where they exist, are based on kinship, social relationships and casual employment rather than market-based contractual agreements. India's National Accounts Statistics, however, does not use the term 'informal sector'. Instead, it distinguishes between 'unorganised' and 'organised' economic activity. 'Unorganised' economic activity in the Indian context has been used to represent the informal sector, as defined in the System of National Accounts (SNA), although the two are not identical.

The unorganized segment of any sector of the Indian economy includes operating units whose activity is not regulated under any legal provision (NSSO, 2001). In the manufacturing sector, all factory units not registered under the 'Factories Act of 1948' constitute the unorganized segment. In the different sub-sectors of services, all non-public-sector operating units that do not maintain and submit regular accounts of their activity constitute the unorganized segment[6] (NSSO, 2001). Furthermore, for survey and estimation purposes, the unorganized segment of any services sub-sector is divided into three categories based on the size of the workforce: 'directory establishments' that employ more than five workers with at least one worker hired on a fairly regular basis; 'non-directory establishments' which employ one to five workers with at least one hired worker; and 'own account enterprises' which employ no hired worker (CSO, 2007a).

2.6.3. Public versus Private Provision

The public sector in India consists of administrative departments of the government, departmental enterprises and non-departmental enterprises (CSO, 2007a). Administrative departments comprise government departments, offices and other bodies of the central, state and local authorities.

---

[6] An exception to this norm is the education services sector where, despite the non-availability of regular accounts, educational institutions are included under the organized sector.

They govern the socio-economic policy of the country and provide goods and services, which others may not have an incentive to provide. The economic activities carried out include general administrative services such as police, external affairs, defence services, law and justice, fiscal services such as tax collection and debt servicing, and social services such as education, health and housing.

Departmental enterprises are enterprises owned, controlled and run directly by public authorities. Unlike administrative departments, they charge for the goods and services they provide on a commercial basis. Moreover, they control productive capital in the form of equipment such as machines, plants and stocks. At the same time, they normally do not hold or manage financial assets and liabilities.[7] Departmental enterprises operate in the following sub-sectors of services: railways, civil aviation, road and water transport, communication and radio and television broadcasting (CSO, various issues).

Non-departmental enterprises are government companies in which at least 51 per cent of the stake is held by the central government, or a state government, or partly by the central government and partly by one or more state governments. Statutory corporations set up under special enactments of Parliament or State Legislatures are also included in this category. Unlike departmental enterprises, these enterprises hold and manage financial assets and liabilities as well as tangible assets involved in their business. Moreover, they have separate Boards of Directors and profit and loss accounts as in the case of the private corporate sector. Non-departmental enterprises operate in the following sub-sectors of services: banking and insurance, wholesale and retail trade, hotels and restaurants, storage and road, air and water transport services (CSO, National Accounts Statistics, various issues).

2.7. India's National Accounts Statistics: Estimating Output of the Services Sector

In the context of collection and analysis of data, each sub-sector of services in India is divided into three segments: public, private organized and private unorganized (CSO, 2007a). For the public-sector segment, estimates of gross value added are based on data on output (total money earned for services rendered) and intermediate inputs from budget documents and

---

[7] Working balances and payables and receivables on their business accounts are the exceptions.

annual reports of government-owned corporations. Usually, value added is obtained as the sum of compensation of employees and operating surplus, which is also equal to gross output less intermediate consumption of goods and services, consumption of fixed capital and indirect taxes (minus subsidies). These are 'direct' estimates that reflect the situation in the year to which they refer. For the private organized segment, three alternative methods are used (Saluja and Yadav, 2007). In several sub-sectors of services, estimates of gross value added are usually based on an analysis of data on output (total money earned for services rendered) and intermediate inputs from annual accounts of private companies. In others, value added is estimated through certain sample surveys. For a few sub-sectors, value added is computed by the 'labour-input' method. This involves multiplying the estimates of value added per worker (VAPW) in a benchmark year by the estimated number of workers. The information on VAPW in a benchmark year is usually obtained from the results of relevant enterprise surveys, while the estimates of workforce are prepared using the results of population censuses and large-scale sample surveys on employment carried out by the National Sample Survey Organisation (NSSO). For the unorganized segment in each sub-sector of services, estimates of value added are computed using the 'labour-input' method described above. This method of estimating value added is 'indirect' in the sense that some benchmark estimate,[8] based on a periodically carried-out sample survey, is derived for some base year and extrapolated backwards and forwards to other years (Kansal, 1992; Kulshreshtha et al., 2002).

A detailed description of the sources and methods used to estimate value added in the different sub-sectors of services is provided in Appendix A, Table A.1. Importantly, the estimation of output or value added in certain sub-sectors is relatively more problematic. The following is a brief synopsis.

2.7.1. Transport by Railways

Similar to the public-sector segments of other sectors, gross value added at current prices for railways (owned by the government) is obtained as the sum of compensation of employees and gross operating surplus. This figure, however, includes value added pertaining to manufacturing, construction and other service activities. Hence, these are subtracted from the overall

---

[8] The benchmark estimate itself is a product of the estimated number of workers multiplied by value added per worker which is estimated independently from a sample survey.

figure to obtain estimates of value added for government railway transport services only.

2.7.2. Public Administration and Defence

The expenditure on services produced by administrative departments is mainly financed by the government itself. In other words, the government is considered to be the final consumer of these services except for a minor part sold to other sectors (Griliches, 1992). These services include the wage bill of employees, the rental value of several buildings occupied by administrative departments that are owned by the government, rent paid for hired premises, interest paid on capital borrowed and the purchase of goods and services which serve as inputs. There are no profits as this is the non-profit arm of the government sector. The cost of inputs is not included in the output of the sector as they represent intermediate purchases, while interest paid on capital borrowed by the government is included under interest on public debt and hence does not form a part of factor payments. Therefore, value from the activities of public administration and defence consists only of compensation of employees and consumption of fixed capital (Saluja and Yadav, 2007).

Given that output of the services sector is often estimated on the basis of employee compensation, it may be argued that an increase in real wages or salaries would imply an increase in real output even with the same actual activities. However, this argument can be refuted to an extent by the following. Producers of goods as well as services are said to generate value added – that is, compensation of employees and other factor payments. It is only for the sub-sector of public administration that value added is restricted to compensation of employees. Moreover, persons employed in different sub-sectors of services are involved in consumption, saving and investment in the same way as persons employed in agriculture or manufacturing. Hence, whether we look on the production and distribution side or at the consumption side, the national accounts aggregates remain the same in service sectors as in the other sectors. If remunerations of some categories of employees rise without an increase in output or productivity, it has to be at the cost of some other categories of employees, thus bringing about redistribution. This is also true for profits of entrepreneurs and remunerations of government employees. In the context of productivity, this sector presents a serious measurement problem as well. Usually, we can either assume that the output of the sector grows proportionately to some measure of inputs implying that productivity of individuals remains constant, or that the wage rate measures the rise in productivity. The latter would only hold true in a perfectly competitive setup.

2.7.3. Financial Services

The gross output of banks and other financial institutions consists of two components: actual service charges and imputed service charges (Srimany and Bhattacharya, 1998). The first relates to direct or auxiliary services that the sector provides to its customers. An example of such services is banks maintaining accounts for individuals. Measuring such services involves no real conceptual problem as customers are charged explicitly for them. The second component of the banking sector output relates to financial inter-mediation services rendered by banks to their customers; out of the deposits collected, banks provide loans to borrowers, where the interest they earn on such transactions is higher than the payments made to depositors. This positive net return accruing to banks is usually large enough to meet their expenses and to earn a profit. In National Accounts Statistics, however, interest is primarily a transfer payment and hence does not constitute value added. Hence, if financial institutions are treated like any other productive enterprise, their output would be limited to charges made on customers for the provision of auxiliary services. Given these charges are nominal, this would result in banks having a negative operating surplus and perhaps even negative value added (Chakraborty and Das, 2007).

To circumvent this problem, the output of intermediation services provided by financial corporations is measured using the concept of Financial Intermediation Services Indirectly Measured (FISIM).[9] It is an imputed service charge which equals the interest rate spread between loan rates and depositor rates. This implies that output of financial institutions includes interest received from borrowers who are producers. However, as the interest paid by the producers is already accounted for in the output of their respective industries, its inclusion in the output of financial institutions amounts to double counting. To avoid this duplication, FISIM is allocated as intermediate consumption by industries or businesses, final consumption by government, households and non-profit institutions and exports to the rest of the world. Importantly, it is only FISIM attributed to households, government and the rest of the world that is part of final demand and hence part of GDP (Hill, 1996). In sum, gross value added of financial institutions is based on actual service charges and the concept of imputed service

---

[9] This is in accordance with the UN System of National Accounts.

charge, which is equivalent to interest and dividend receipts, net of interest paid to depositors.

2.8. India's National Accounts Statistics: Limitations of Services-Sector Data

2.8.1. Organized Sector

Estimates of value added for the public-sector component are based on budget documents and annual accounts of different enterprises. The data are current and reflect the situation in the year to which they refer. This also holds true for certain parts of the private organized sector where estimates of value added are based on the annual reports and accounts of private companies. On the other hand, for parts of the private organized sector where estimates of value added are based on data from sample surveys on finances of medium and large private limited companies, data are only available with a considerable time lag. In the absence of current data, estimates are usually computed on the basis of growth in paid-up capital (Shetty, 2007). In addition, for parts of the private organized sector where valued added is computed using the 'labour-input' method, there are a number of limitations that are discussed later.

2.8.2. Unorganized Sector

For the unorganized segment, value added is computed by the 'labour-input' method – that is, by using benchmark estimates of value added per worker multiplied by the number of workers in the respective sector. These benchmark estimates are thereafter carried forward with some physical indicator of economic activity in that particular sub-sector. Hence, changes in the GDP contributions of the unorganized segment of a given service sub-sector from year to year are taken to be proportional to the movements in the physical indicator used. In this context, questions have been raised on both crucial components involved in the end results: estimates of value added per worker (based on periodic enterprise surveys as follow-up of the quinquennial Economic Censuses, which are used to estimate the benchmark estimates) and estimates of the work force (Tendulkar, 2007). First, studies reveal that the precision of estimated gross value added per worker for activities of storage, real estate, business services, health services and other services is relatively low (Manna, 2007). What is more, there are no methods of validating estimates of value added per worker that are based

on the various enterprise surveys (Kar et al., 2003). Second, workforce estimates computed by applying the worker-population ratio to population
projections are not entirely satisfactory. Moreover, there is an impression
that the residual method pushes up the labour force engaged in unorganized service-sector activity (Shetty, 2007).

2.8.3. The Issue of Deflation

The absence of suitable price deflators for the services sectors is a weakness
in the estimation of output in these sectors. The recommended method
for computing constant price estimates is the double deflation procedure,
whereby the value of output and value of inputs are deflated separately by
their appropriate price indices. Thereafter, gross value added is simply the
difference between outputs and inputs. Unfortunately, there is no services-
sector price index in the country, let alone appropriate price indices for
inputs and outputs or various components of gross value added such as
wages and salaries or operating surplus (Shetty, 2007). This is unlike several
advanced countries where methods used by national accounts to adjust for
price change with regard to service-sector output are much better defined
and more elaborate. In the United Kingdom, for example, services-sector
deflation is based on two approaches. First, services sold directly to consumers use components of the consumer prices index (CPI) or the retail prices
index (RPI) that include price information on both goods and services.
This is in sharp contrast with India, where consumer price indices include
price information on agricultural and manufactured goods only. Second,
for services sold to firms for further production, services-sector output is
deflated by specially constructed corporate service price indices (CSPI). It
is now referred to as the services producer price index (SPPI). In addition,
an overall index of prices for corporate services has been developed as well
(Tilly, 2006).

In the absence of any direct estimates of 'prices' of services, India's National
Accounts Statistics estimate constant price estimates of value added in
most service sub-sectors by moving forward base year estimates with some
physical indicator of volume of activity. This holds true for public, private
organized and private unorganized segments. For certain segments in a
few sub-sectors, constant price estimates are obtained by deflating current
price estimates using the consumer price index for agricultural labourers,
the consumer price index for industrial workers or even an implicit GDP
deflator (of GDP excluding that particular sector) (CSO, 2007a). A detailed
description of the precise methods used in deflating output in the different

sub-sectors of services is provided in Appendix A, Table A.2. Hence, given these methods of deflation (where there is widespread use of commodity price indices), the pricing of services may not be appropriately captured (Nagaraj, 2009; Saluja and Yadav, 2007).

2.9. Conclusion

In sum, there are conceptual problems, statistical limitations and measurement difficulties in attempting an analysis of the services sector. But this cannot and should not lead to the conclusion that any such exercise is impossible. The services sector accounts for an increasing proportion of output, and even employment, everywhere, particularly in developing countries. Therefore, it is important to recognize the problems, limitations and difficulties and to resolve them as much as possible, in an attempt to understand the role of the services sector in the process of growth and development.

THREE

Explaining the Growth of India's Services Sector

3.1. Introduction

There is a wide consensus in the literature that, as an economy grows, both demand-side and supply-side factors lead to an increasing share of the services sector in output. These factors comprise high-income elasticity of demand for services, increasing relative prices of services, structural changes within the manufacturing sector – which make contracting out services more efficient than producing them in the firm – and increased international trade in services. There is a growing literature analyzing the growth of India's services sector in recent years, which explores several of the aforementioned factors.

The object of this chapter is two-fold. It first reviews the relevant literature in order to identify a set of supply and demand factors that are potentially important explanations for the growth of India's services sector. In doing so, it draws on seminal theoretical contributions as well as country-specific studies. It also presents relevant descriptive statistics. Subsequently, following a couple of studies in the literature, the chapter combines the different factors in a comprehensive regression framework – rather than examining them in isolation – in order to capture their relative importance in explaining the growth of India's services sector. In this exercise, it uses more recent data as well as alternative measures for certain variables. The scope of the empirical exercise is limited to an analysis of data for the period from 1990–91 to 2008–09.

The structure of the chapter is the following. At the very outset, Section 3.2 analyses whether the growth of India's services sector has been notional or real or a bit of both. Thereafter, Section 3.3 explores a number of supply and demand factors that are potentially important in explaining the sector's real growth in India. Section 3.4 brings together the different factors – affecting the sector's notional and real growth – in a comprehensive regression framework. Section 3.5 presents conclusions.

3.2. Notional or Real?

It may be argued that the rapid growth of the services sector in India is notional rather than real. This can be explained by two factors: an increase in the relative price of services or a statistical artifice whereby what was earlier subsumed in manufacturing or agriculture value added is now accounted for as service-sector contributions to GDP. Let us analyse the two, in turn.

3.2.1. Relative Prices

Chapter 1 alluded to a seminal paper by Baumol (1967) where he argues that unlike manufacturing, the relatively labour-intensive nature of service-sector activities implies that their productivity cannot be readily increased through capital accumulation, innovation or economies of scale. It suggests that the increasing share of services in total output may be attributable to increasing relative price of services.

Computing implicit GDP price deflators from India's National Accounts Statistics, Table 3.1 shows that during the period from 1993–94 to 2009–10, the relative price of services did not increase notably.[1] This reinforces the findings of Bosworth et al. (2007) who show that the price of services in India, relative to industrial goods, has not increased notably during the period from 1980 to 2005. It suggests that increasing relative prices of services is not likely to be an important explanation for the increasing share of the services sector in total output.[2]

3.2.2. Contracting Out

In a seminal article on the nature of the firm, Coase (1954) argues that 'as a firm becomes larger, costs of organizing additional transactions within the firm may rise'. According to Coase, this may be explained by the following. First, as transactions increase, an entrepreneur fails to place factors of production in the uses where their value is greatest. Second, as the size of the

---

[1]   Assuming arbitrary weights for agriculture and industry
[2]   A conclusive answer would depend on the price elasticity of demand.

Table 3.1. *Implicit GDP deflators (at 1993–94 constant prices)*

Year	Agriculture	Industry	Services
1993–94	100	100	100
1994–95	110	111	109
1995–96	112	121	118
1996–97	131	127	127
1997–98	144	135	134
1998–99	155	146	145
1999–00	161	148	152
2000–01	163	154	158
2001–02	167	158	165
2002–03	179	164	169
2003–04	185	172	174
2004–05	173	186	190
2005–06	194	205	202
2006–07	212	221	212
2007–08	232	233	222
2008–09	258	250	239
2009–10	301	257	257

Note: Base year for index numbers is 1993–94.
Source: Author's Estimates based on National Accounts Data, Central Statistical Organisation.

firm increases, there is a waste of resources resulting from duplication of tasks performed. Third, the supply price of one or more factors of production may increase because the "other advantages" of small firms are greater than those of a large firm. For example, managers may prefer to be heads of small independent businesses rather than heads of departments in a large business.

For the purpose of our analysis, the essential point to take away from Coase (1954) is that a firm will tend to expand until the costs of organizing an additional transaction within the firm equal the costs of carrying out the same transaction by means of exchange in the open market. In other words, firms would reach a stage where it would be more profitable for them to contract out certain activities to other firms as opposed to producing them in-house. This argument may be relevant for explaining the growth of the service sector in an economy as production on a large scale and the application of new technologies increase the complexity of manufacturing production and distribution. Given this, manufacturing firms may see potential advantages in procuring certain services from specialist service producers.

In the more recent literature, Bhagwati (1984) and Kravis, et al. (1982) refer to this process as 'splintering'.

Importantly, if the service components of manufacturing activity such as distribution, transport, accounting and logistics are outsourced to other firms, they will be accounted for as service-sector contributions to GDP, as opposed to being subsumed in manufacturing value added. Hence, increased externalisation of activities or splintering alters aggregate accounting, whereby even when economic growth is not associated with rising share of services in final demand, growing final demand for industrial or agricultural products will tend to raise the share of services in GDP. This implies that the rapid growth of the services sector in India may be a statistical artifice, as opposed to being real.

3.2.2.1. The Empirics

Gordon and Gupta (2004) estimate the importance of splintering to services growth in India by measuring the increase in the input usage of services in other sectors of the economy. They measure this through changes in input-output coefficients, which are constructed using National Accounts Data (see Table 3.2).[3] The authors show that during the 1980s, input-output coefficients for services input in agriculture and industry increased by 0.03 and 0.04, respectively. These coefficient changes would have increased demand for services (as a first round, partial equilibrium effect) by:

$$\Delta Y_S = 0.03 Y_A + 0.04 Y_I \tag{3.1}$$

where Y_A is agricultural output, Y_I is industrial output and ΔY_S is the change in services sector output during the period under consideration.

Dividing Equation (3.1) throughout by total output Y, we get:

$$\Delta Y_S / Y = 0.03 (Y_A / Y) + 0.04 (Y_I / Y) \tag{3.2}$$

Next, dividing Equation (3.2) throughout by services sector output, Y_S, we get:

$$(\Delta Y_S / Y) / Y_S = [0.03 (Y_A / Y) + 0.04 (Y_I / Y)] / Y_S \tag{3.3}$$

---

[3] Input-output coefficients are derived from the absorption matrix (which records the inputs from industry 'i' to industry 'j') as the ratio of (the value of) a set of inputs to the total output of the industry.

Table 3.2. *Input-output coefficients for the Indian economy (1979–80 to 2006–07)*

		Agriculture	Industry	Services
1979–80	Agriculture	0.160	0.130	0.039
	Industry	0.068	0.345	0.105
	Services	0.020	0.149	0.096
1989–90	Agriculture	0.166	0.042	0.035
	Industry	0.144	0.373	0.172
	Services	0.047	0.188	0.185
1993–94	Agriculture	0.145	0.035	0.034
	Industry	0.140	0.365	0.150
	Services	0.048	0.213	0.195
1998–99	Agriculture	0.117	0.081	0.019
	Industry	0.075	0.397	0.145
	Services	0.050	0.173	0.144
2006–07	Agriculture	0.156	0.046	0.021
	Industry	0.097	0.482	0.137
	Services	0.075	0.165	0.131

Sources: Pre-2006–07, Singh (2006); 2006–07, author's calculations.

Rearranging the above equation, we get:

$$\Delta Y_S / Y_S = [0.03\ (Y_A / Y) + 0.04\ (Y_I / Y)] * (Y / Y_S) \tag{3.4}$$

$$=> \Delta Y_S / Y_S = [0.03\ (Y_A / Y) + 0.04\ (Y_I / Y)] / (Y_S / Y) \tag{3.5}$$

In Equation (3.5), (Y_A / Y), (Y_I / Y) and (Y_S / Y) represent the shares of agriculture, industry and services in GDP, respectively. Hence, evaluating at the average sectoral shares during the 1980s (0.35, 0.25 and 0.40 for agriculture, industry and services, respectively) yields:

$$\Delta Ys / Ys = [(0.03*0.35) + (0.04*0.25)]/0.4 = 0.051 \tag{3.6}$$

This implies that outsourcing or splintering added about 0.5 per cent to annual services growth over the decade. The authors show that a similar calculation for the period 1989–90 to 1993–94 yields a splintering effect on annual services growth of about 0.25 per cent. Thus, the increase in the use of services inputs is less during the early 1990s than in the1980s. Singh (2006) uses the same methodology to obtain essentially no contribution of splintering between 1989–90 and 1998–99. In doing so, Singh (2006) argues that the aforementioned methodology does not permit an analysis of the extent to which cross-country splintering – which became important in the 1990s – through offshore outsourcing of business services for example, would explain the observed patterns of service-sector growth. This is because the input-output coefficients are derived from an input flow (absorption) matrix in India's National Accounts Statistics, which does not include data on foreign producers. But Singh (2006) also argues such splintering would imply a real shift in economic activity to India, rather than an accounting change. Using more recent data and different methodology, Eichengreen and Gupta (2010) show that the share of value added in services accounted for by intermediate demand from industry and agriculture declined from 40 per cent and 5 per cent, respectively, in 1991 to 31 per cent and 2 per cent, respectively, in 2007.

3.2.2.2. An Extension

We use the methodology provided by Gordon and Gupta (2004) to extend the analysis beyond 1998–99, using the latest data available for 2006–07. This is important as during the period from 2000 to 2009–10, the share of the industrial sector in GDP remained more or less unchanged, whereas that of the services increased by about 9 per cent (see Chapter 1). The input-output coefficients for 2006–07 are derived[4] from the input flow (absorption) matrix in India's NAS (Table 3.2).

Table 3.2 reveals that during the period from 1979–80 to 2006–07, the input-output coefficient for services input in agriculture and industry increased by 0.055 and 0.016, respectively. These coefficient changes would have changed the demand for services (as a first round, partial equilibrium effect) by:

$$\Delta Y_S = 0.055 Y_A + 0.016 Y_I \qquad (3.7)$$

Dividing Equation (3.7) throughout by total output, Y, we get:

$$\Delta Y_S / Y = 0.055 (Y_A / Y) + 0.016 (Y_I / Y) \qquad (3.8)$$

Next, dividing Equation (3.8) throughout by services sector output, Y_S, we get:

$$(\Delta Y_S / Y) / Y_S = [0.055 (Y_A / Y) + 0.016 (Y_I / Y)] / Y_S \qquad (3.9)$$

---

[4]   They are derived as the ratio of the value of a set of service inputs to the total output of the industry.

Rearranging the above equation, we get:

$$\Delta Y_S / Y_S = [0.055 \, (Y_A / Y) + 0.016 \, (Y_I / Y)] * (Y / Y_S) \quad (3.10)$$

$$=> \Delta Y_S / Y_S = [0.055 \, (Y_A / Y) + 0.016 \, (Y_I / Y)] / (Y_S / Y) \quad (3.11)$$

Evaluating Equation (3.11) at the average sectoral shares during the period (0.30, 0.26 and 0.44 for agriculture, industry and services, respectively) yields:

$$\Delta Ys / Ys = [(0.055*0.30) + (0.016*0.26)]/0.44 = 0.047 \quad (3.12)$$

This calculation implies that during the twenty-seven-year period from 1979–80 to 2006–07, splintering increased annual services growth by about 0.17 percentage point – in other words, it had a negligible contribution. This is intuitive given that some of the fastest-growing services during this period were oriented towards final consumption. For instance, communication services, hotels and restaurants and community services grew at 12.8 per cent, 8.2 per cent and 5.3 per cent per annum, respectively, between 1980 and 2006–07. However, at the same time, growth in financial services and wholesale and retail trade – services not exclusive to final consumption – was also important, with the sectors growing at 10.5 per cent and 6.8 per cent per annum, respectively, between 1980 and 2006–07. This suggests that while splintering of services out of the manufacturing sector may have contributed little to the growth of the services sector, in the aggregate, during the last two and a half decades, it may have been significant for the growth of certain sub-sectors. Hence, we carry out the analysis presented earlier at a disaggregated level. In doing so, we compute input-output coefficients using primary data from the input flow (absorption) matrix in India's NAS, which unfortunately is not available for before 1993–94. Such an exercise has not been attempted in the literature.

Table 3.3 shows that during the period from 1993–94 to 2006–07, input usage of storage, communications, hotels and restaurants, public administration and defence and education and health services in producing agricultural and industrial output has remained more or less constant. In part, this is because many of these services cater almost exclusively to final demand. Strikingly, use of transport services as an input for agricultural and industrial production has reduced, whereas splintering increased the growth of wholesale and retail trade by only 1.5 percentage points during this twenty-seven-year period. Similarly, splintering increased the growth of financial

Table 3.3. *Changes in service input-output coefficients: 1993–94 to 2006–07*

	Agricultural output	Industrial output	Share of sector in GDP (average over the period)
Wholesale and Retail Trade	0.014	−0.008	0.137
Hotels and Restaurants	0.000	0.000	0.010
Transport	0.000	−0.016	0.055
Storage	0.000	0.000	0.001
Communications	0.000	0.003	0.031
Banking and Insurance	0.000	0.008	0.065
Public Administration and Defence	0.000	0.000	0.055
Education, Research and Health	0.000	0.000	0.053
Other Services (Business, Real estate, Renting and Personal Services)	0.001	0.012	0.087

Note: Figures are rounded off to the third decimal place.
Source: Author's calculation based on Central Statistical Organisation of India, National Account Statistics.

services and 'other services' (business, real estate and personal services) by only 3.2 and 3.9 percentage points, respectively.[5] Therefore, over a thirteen-year period, the increase in the use of these two services as inputs in other sectors plays a very small part in explaining their increasing share in GDP.

On the basis of this, we can conclude that the increase in the use of services inputs in other sectors over time cannot explain the recent surge in the growth of the services sector. The growth of the services sector in India has largely been real rather than notional. This real growth of the services sector may be attributable to a range of supply and demand factors. In fact, in an accounting exercise analyzing the contribution of different uses to services value added growth, Eichengreen and Gupta (2010) conclude that it is not intermediate demand for service inputs from other sectors, but private final demand and exports that are the major drivers of service-sector output. These and other real economy factors affecting the growth of India's services sector are analysed in the section that follows.

---

[5] The relevant data for business services as an independent category are not available for 1993–94.

3.3. Real Factors: Supply and Demand

3.3.1. Human Capital

Kochhar et al. (2006) show that both in 1981 and 2000, controlling for a country's GDP and size, the contribution of skill-intensive industries (both in manufacturing and services) to total value added in India was higher than the world average. It was higher than that in China and comparable to that in much richer countries such as Malaysia and South Korea. Using panel data for the fourteen major states of India over the period from 1980 to 2000, Amin and Mattoo (2008) find that the endowments of highly skilled labour had a statistically significant, positive impact on per capita output of the services sector, but no significant impact on agriculture or manufacturing. This finding suggests that the growth of skill-intensive segments of the services sector may be associated with the relatively greater availability of skilled workers.

Consider, for instance, business services – a skill-intensive sector based on information technology. Kochhar et al. (2006) argue that the sector's extraordinarily high rate of growth took root in India because of the relatively abundant supply of cheap high-skilled labour. This supply, in turn, may be attributable to the country's prior emphasis on tertiary education, relative to comparable developing countries. For example, in terms of purchasing-power-parity (PPP) adjusted dollars per student in tertiary education, India spent more than China and even South Korea or Indonesia in 2000 (Kochhar et al., 2006). The best-known examples of this large-scale investment in tertiary education for a country of its per capita income are the Indian Institutes of Technology and the Indian Institutes of Management. Their establishment created a large pool of engineers, computer scientists and managers that laid the foundation for India's emergence in the field of business services such as software, where a large export market was waiting to be exploited.[6] At the same time, India also made rapid strides in other, non-high-tech business services, such as business process outsourcing and call centres. This may have been attributable to the supply of a large pool of English-speaking young individuals with some basic education. Once again, this can be traced India's historical background (Amin and Mattoo, 2008).

---

[6] It is possible that the reputation of Indian engineers in the United States helped to create a brand name that is normally not associated with a developing country's foray into a high-tech activity.

3.3.2. Economic Reforms

Policy changes have influenced service-sector activity in India, especially economic reforms relating to deregulation, privatization of government-owned services and the liberalization of trade and foreign direct investment (FDI). Measuring the extent of liberalization of by the FDI cap and restrictions on movement of people across borders during the period from 1997[7] to 2003, Banga (2005) finds that services which have been liberalized typically experienced higher growth rates, whereas those that have seen limited or no liberalization experienced lower growth rates. The former comprises business – including software, call centres and business process outsourcing – telecommunication and financial services.

The services sector has gained from economic reforms both directly and indirectly. The direct impact came from the opening-up of certain service sub-sectors – telecommunications, for instance – to private ownership and foreign direct investment. The literature provides some preliminary support for the effect of reform-related measures on growth of the services sector. The participation of the private sector in service activities increased in the 1990s. In fact, for some service activities, the share started increasing as early as the 1980s. Furthermore, the data reveal a positive association between the private sector's share in GDP and the average growth rate during the 1990s in different services segment (Gordon and Gupta, 2004).[8]

Similarly, during the 1990s, there was a notable increase in FDI inflows to the services sector – the share of services in FDI rose from 10 per cent in the early 1990s to nearly 30 per cent in the second half of the decade (Joshi, 2006). In fact, growth in FDI flows during this period was the highest in telecommunications (especially the cellular phone segment), consultancy services, financial services and hotels and tourism (Joshi, 2006). But FDI is still restricted in some sectors, the most prominent of them being retail trade. In 2006, the government allowed FDI up to 51 per cent in 'single-brand retailing' – subject to certain conditions. Foreign ownership in the multi-brand retailing segment is still out of bounds (Mukherjee, 2006).

A section of the literature shows a strong correlation between services-sector growth and cumulative flow of FDI during the 1990s – a time when there was a discernable shift from FDI in the agricultural and industrial

---

[7] The period considered for the extent of liberalization is post-1997 as many services were liberalized since.

[8] The relationship is likely to be stronger if business services – for which the data on private and public shares are not available – were included.

sectors to FDI in services (Gordon and Gupta, 2004).[9] At the same time, other studies show that feedback effects between FDI and output are transitory in the services sector. If at all, long-run causality in the services sector runs from output to FDI and not vice versa (Chakraborty and Nunnenkamp, 2008). Yet, according to this literature, concluding that FDI in the services sector has failed to promote India's economic growth may be somewhat premature. This is because evidence indicates that output growth in manufacturing has been stimulated by FDI in the services sector. Moreover, offshoring of higher value-added services by foreign investors to India is a fairly recent phenomenon, the output effects of which may take considerable time to materialize.

The indirect impact of economic reforms on services-sector growth resulted from easier and cheaper access to factor services (N. Murthy, 2004). For instance, import de-licensing facilitated the immediate import of computers, financial liberalization enabled firms to raise capital through market-determined public offerings and current account convertibility made it easier for individuals to travel as well as for firms to hire foreign consultants and establish sales offices abroad. N. Murthy (2004) also credits FDI by software majors as a major reason behind the adoption of world-class quality processes, tools and methods. In fact, in a sectoral growth accounting exercise, Verma (2008) finds that increases in total factor productivity, driven to large extent by the inception of market-based liberalization policies in the 1990s, was an important source of service sector value-added growth in India.

3.3.2.1. Telecommunication Services: An Illustrative Example

Until the early 1990s, telecommunication services were regarded as a public utility, where inefficient government provision led to a situation of effective rationing (Gordon and Gupta, 2004). As part of the wide-ranging economic reforms initiated in 1991, the government opened the sector to private ownership, relinquishing its monopoly control. In 1992, it began with a pilot project in basic telecommunication services and cellular operations in India's four largest cities. In 1994, the "New Telecommunications Policy" was adopted, whereby one private operator was allowed to compete with the Department of Telecommunication (DOT) in each of the twenty regional divisions of the country (Chakraborty and Nunnenkamp,

---

[9] The positive and significant association survives even if we exclude the fastest-growing communication segment.

2008). The introduction of private competition in the sector was extended to foreign ownership, which – at present – ranges from 49 per cent to 100 per cent across its different segments. For instance, the government allows FDI up to 49 per cent in basic, cellular and other voice telephone services – subject to licensing and security requirements – with no restrictions on the number of providers. For Internet service providers (ISPs) with gateways, radio-paging and end-to-end bandwidth, the limit for FDI is set at 74 per cent with FDI beyond 49 per cent requiring government approval (Joshi, 2006).[10]

This high foreign equity participation ceiling in telecommunication services has been associated with massive FDI inflows into India. During the period from 1991 to 2005, telecommunications accounted for 7 per cent of cumulative FDI inflows – the highest among all service sub-sectors (Joshi, 2006). This includes the entry of some of the largest global telecom operators – AT&T, US West, Bell Atlantic, Nynex, Swiss Telecom, NTT and Bell Canada – into the Indian market, as well several small foreign firms that have established ties with some of the biggest Indian business groups, such as Reliance, Birla, Tata and Essar (Chakraborty and Nunnenkamp, 2008). Within the telecommunications sector, the cellular mobile telephone service segment was the largest recipient of FDI during this period (Joshi, 2006).

Deregulation, increased private-sector participation and greater FDI inflows since the 1990s have coincided with rapid growth of telecommunication services. Evidence suggests that it was one of the fastest-growing sub-sectors of services with an average annual growth rate of 21 per cent per annum during the period from 1993 to 2004 (Kotwal et al., 2010). In fact, the liberalization of the telecommunications sector has resulted in an increase in India's teledensity from 4 per 1,000 persons in 1986 to 45 per 1,000 persons in 2002 (Chakraborty and Nunnenkamp, 2008). Importantly, this growth in telecommunication services – cellular phones and the Internet – resulting from the aforementioned reforms in the sector are associated with positive externalities for other service sub-sectors. For example, the efficiency of the largest component of India's service sector – wholesale and retail trade – depends on the quality and timeliness of information flows between producers and consumers. The rapid growth in telecommunication services has facilitated that and hence is likely to have propelled its growth. Similarly, the large expansion of telecommunication services has played an important role in preventing supply bottlenecks and hence enhancing growth, especially in information-technology-enabled

---

[10] For ISPs not providing gateways, the limit for FDI is 100 per cent.

services such as business process outsourcing (Murthy, 2004), but also in financial services and community services such as education and health (Kotwal et al., 2010).

3.3.3. International Trade in Services

Chapter 2 showed that international trade in services is divided into four categories: establishing a commercial presence abroad, consumption abroad, cross-border movement of people and cross-border supply. There is considerable overlap between "establishing a commercial presence abroad" and FDI. Hence, India's economic reforms, which resulted in a large flow of FDI into the country, could have boosted the country's imports of services to the extent that profits of the foreign subsidiary were repatriated to the home country. At the same time, inward FDI could have also boosted India's service exports if the foreign subsidiary established a presence in the country's domestic services sector – tourism and hospitality, transport, telecommunication and banking services, for example. India's growing exports of services may also be attributable to outward FDI. In 2005–06, the service sector constituted about one-third of the country's outward FDI (Banga, 2006).

The sudden increase in the growth of international trade in services, however, is primarily attributable to rapid progress in the development of information and communication technologies, which has increased the ability of individuals to deliver services over long distances – in other words, cross-border supply. The offshoring of software and information-technology-enabled services, such as call centres and business process outsourcing, to firms in India is a prominent example in this regard. Hence, the increasing share of the services sector in India's total output growth may be associated with the liberalization of trade and the consequent emergence of foreign demand as a potential source of growth, which Indian firms have been able to exploit.

The increasing importance of the services sector in India, both in terms of its share in GDP and its contribution to economic growth, has been accompanied by the country's emergence as a major exporter of services. Gordon and Gupta (2004) show that exports of services grew by an average of 15 per cent a year in the 1990s, compared with 9 per cent in the 1980s, cumulatively having increased four-fold in the 1990s. In fact, during the period from 1990–91 to 2008–09, India's services exports grew faster – at 16.4 per cent per annum – than either GDP or services GDP – at 6.3 per cent and 8.2 per cent, respectively.

Table 3.4. *India's exports of goods and services: 1990 to 2008*

	India's share in world merchandise exports	India's share in world services exports	Exports of services as a % of GDP	Exports of services as a % of services GDP	Exports of services as a % of total exports
1990	0.5	0.6	1.9	5.0	21.6
2008	1.2	2.7	8.5	16.6	36.4

Source: World Bank, *World Development Indicators*, online database.

Table 3.4 shows that since the early 1990s, India's share in both world merchandise exports and world services exports has increased. The increase in the latter, however, has been much greater. A quantum leap in the country's share in world services exports, from 0.6 per cent in 1990 to 2.7 per cent in 2008, suggests major efficiency gains in India's services sector vis-à-vis agriculture and industry. This may be attributable to the fact that services are much less capital-intensive and many of them were relatively new, thereby implying that, unlike in the industrial sector, entrepreneurs were not burdened with inefficient capital equipment and hence found it easier to adopt the most efficient technology in a post-liberalization competitive environment. In addition, because of the relatively low financial requirement of the services sector, capital market imperfections were not a major hindrance for entrepreneurs to adjust their production according to changing market conditions (Rakshit, 2007).

India's increasing share in world service exports is also indicative of the country's strong competitive edge in the sector relative to the rest of the world. The success of India firms in this regard is attributable to the country's endowment of skilled (and relatively low-cost) labour resources which are, in turn, a product of the emphasis of government policy on tertiary education over the years. In addition, the stellar contribution of expatriate Indians in the software industry abroad is likely to have been a contributing factor (Balasubramanyam and Balasubramanyam, 1997). In fact, according to Chanda (2008), India is far ahead of other countries in the context of services outsourcing, and this is likely to remain so in the near future. At the same time, India's services exports are quite broad-based. They include sub-sectors as varied as transport, travel, software, business, communication and financial services. The composition of India's services exports, however, has changed over the years. Relative shares of traditional services such as travel and transportation have fallen, whereas those of software and other business services have increased (Figures 3.1 and 3.2).

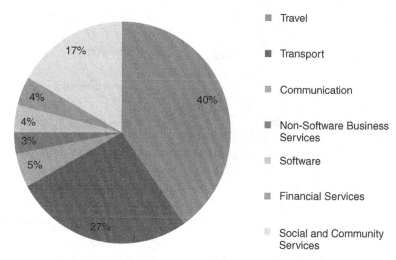

- Travel
- Transport
- Communication
- Non-Software Business Services
- Software
- Financial Services
- Social and Community Services

Figure 3.1. Composition of India's service exports in 1990–91.
Source: Reserve Bank of India.

The most noticeable feature in this regard has been the remarkable expansion of its exports in the fields of software and information-technology-enabled services such as business process outsourcing and call centres since the early 1990s. This may have been attributable to economic liberalization, educated manpower and growing international demand for these services. Classified under 'business services', software services grew at the rate of 22 per cent per annum between 1990–91 and 2008–09 and constituted almost half of India's total service exports in 2008–09. The correlation between exports and output growth is evident given that business services was one of the fastest-growing sectors, growing at about 16 per cent per annum during the period from 1990–91 to 2008–09. Given the nature of economic activity, professional service outsourcing is likely to be carried out almost entirely through cross-border supply. In the case of the software service exports, however, the movement of people across national boundaries could also play an important role. This refers to remittances sent back to the country by those who migrate – especially those who migrate permanently. The temporary movement of persons may even have a positive effect on software exports in the future owing to relevant knowledge and experience that the returning migrants bring with them (Commander et al., 2008).

Figures 3.1 and 3.2 also show that as a percentage of total service exports, India's exports of financial services have grown somewhat over the last two decades. This is largely attributable to the establishment of subsidiaries

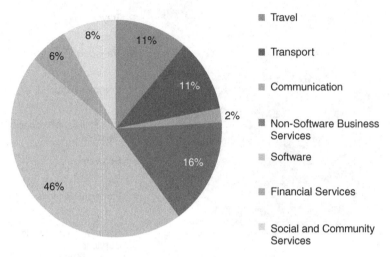

8%
11%
6%
11%
2%
16%
46%

- Travel
- Transport
- Communication
- Non-Software Business Services
- Software
- Financial Services
- Social and Community Services

Figure 3.2. Composition of India's service exports in 2008–09.
Source: Reserve Bank of India.

and representative offices by Indian banks abroad. Overall, however, India is not a major exporter of financial services. This may be attributable to the inability of Indian service providers to meet international prudential norms, such as minimum capital requirements and data protection requirements (Chanda, 2005). In certain segments, such as financial consulting, however, Indian exports can expand in the future. At the same time, India's imports of financial services are constrained by domestic policies that limit foreign participation in this sector, both in terms of FDI ceilings and on the type of foreign legal entity that is permitted (Chanda, 2005).

Of late, export opportunities in education and health services have emerged. There is increased interest among Indian higher-education institutions to establish offshore campuses as well as partnership arrangements through distance learning. Moreover, the cross-border movement of a large number of well-educated, world-class researchers, teachers and trainers would constitute exports to the extent that remittances flow back into the country. For a developing country like India, "consumption abroad" is important for imports of education services. This is because large numbers of Indian students complete their higher education in developed countries – at institutes with world-class infrastructure and international curricula (Bhushan, 2004). In the realm of health services, there are efforts underway to establish India as a medical tourism hub, both in modern and traditional forms. Health services could also be exported via telemedicine, although this mode of supply may be constrained by inadequate power infrastructure. In addition, the establishment of overseas health consultancy establishments and the movement of health personnel abroad could facilitate health service exports. The latter would constitute an export to the extent that migrants sent remittances back home. Furthermore, the transfer of knowledge and skills from migrants to health professionals in the home country could help to upgrade skills, thereby having a positive impact on future health service exports (Chanda, 2001).

Despite the increasing importance of international trade in services, however, exports of services constituted only about 8 per cent of India's GDP, 16 per cent of India's services GDP and a third of India's total exports in 2008 (see Table 3.4). In fact, the existing literature demonstrates that the contribution of exports to annual average services growth during the 1990s was about 0.6 per cent, being significant only for business services (Gordon and Gupta, 2004). Health and education services, for example, have a low share in total exports despite being liberalized. Banga (2005) attributes this to domestic constraints relating to infrastructure inadequacies, poor quality and standards and lack of effective regulation. The increased growth of India's services exports in the future may be hindered by such domestic constraints. In addition, in other sectors, external trade barriers such as limits on foreign equity participation, labour market regulations and discriminatory treatment with respect to taxes, subsidies and other policies may be a hindrance. For example, there has been a recent backlash against outsourcing in key markets like the United States and introduction of regulations such as data privacy laws which could affect India's business process outsourcing exports. The recent economic downturn which surfaced in late 2008 has constrained the prospects of exports of such services from India even further. But market diversification as well as an increased focus on services during trade negotiations at the WTO is likely to preserve their tradeability in international markets (Chanda, 2009; Dasgupta and Singh, 2005).

3.3.4. Domestic Demand

Changing patterns of household demand as an explanation for the increasing importance of the services sector has received special emphasis in the literature. Chapter 1 highlighted the early writings of Fisher (1935) and Clark (1940), who argue that the income elasticity of demand for agricultural goods is less than one, that for industrial goods is greater than one, whereas that for services is even higher than that for industrial goods. Hence, with rising levels of income, the demand for services increases at

Table 3.5. *Private final consumption expenditure*
on services in India

Year	As a percentage of total private final consumption expenditure
1950–51	12.5
1960–61	12.5
1970–71	14.6
1980–81	16.8
1990–91	20.9
1999–00	27.2
2008–09	44.3

Source: Estimates based on National Accounts Statistics, Central
Statistical Organisation.

a proportionally higher rate than income, thereby taking up larger share
of the household budget. Analyzing data at the macroeconomic level, the
high-income elasticity argument appears to have some merit in explaining
the rapid growth of the services sector in India.

Table 3.5 indicates that the share of services in private final consumption expenditure has increased almost four-fold during the period from
1950–51 to 2008–09. Furthermore, Table 3.6 shows that during the 1980s,
1990s and 2000s, which were periods of rapid growth of the services sector
in India, private final consumption of services grew at almost the same rate
as value added in services.

This evidence is striking given that value added in services may also be
influenced by government final consumption expenditure and exports.
Reinforcing the findings of Gordon and Gupta (2004) and Rakshit (2007), it
suggests that household demand patterns may be important for explaining
the increasing share of the services sector in total output. Domestic household demand is likely to have been a particularly important factor in the
growth of wholesale and retail trade, transport, public administration, education, health, personal and entertainment services.

The other component of domestic final demand for services is public
consumption. Table 3.7 shows that there was a sharp rise in government
final consumption expenditure in the second half of the 1990s compared
with that in the first half – while its average annual growth rate was only
5.6 per cent per annum between 1990–91 and 1994–95, the corresponding figure between 1995–96 and 1999–2000 was 11.4 per cent per annum.

Table 3.6. *Rates of growth in India (per cent per annum)*

	Private final consumption of services	Value added for the services sector	Gross domestic product
1980–81 to 1989–90	5.4	6.6	5.8
1990–91 to 1999–2000	7.7	7.7	6.0
2000–01 to 2008–09	8.7	10.2	7.6

Note: Rates of growth for the three variables are computed by running Ordinary Least Squares regressions of the logarithm of each variable on a time trend.
Source: Estimates based on National Accounts Statistics, Central Statistical Organisation.

Table 3.7. *Government final consumption expenditure*

	Rate of growth (per cent per annum)
1990–91 to 1994–95	5.6
1995–96 to 1999–2000	11.4
2000–01 to 2008–09	5.7

Note: Rates of growth for the three variables are computed by running Ordinary Least Squares regressions of the logarithm of each variable on a time trend.
Source: Estimates based on National Accounts Statistics, Central Statistical Organisation.

During the period from 2000–01 to 2008–09, however, growth of government final consumption expenditure declined to the 1990–95 level. This suggests that the sudden increase in public consumption during the second half of the 1990s – which Rakshit (2007) attributes to the implementation of the Fifth Pay Commission award – is unlikely to have been a significant factor behind the growth of the services sector over the two decades since 1990.

In addition, Table 3.8 shows that as a percentage of the total final consumption expenditure of government administrative departments, compensation of employees increased by little during the period between 1990–91 and 2008–09. In fact, between 2000–01 and 2008–09, this figure actually declined. The government's wage bill is a relevant proxy for government final consumption expenditure on services as it excludes purchases of good and depreciation of fixed capital.

Table 3.8. *Compensation of employees*

Year	As a % of total final consumption expenditure of administrative departments
1990–91	55
2000–01	63
2008–09	62

Source: Estimates based on National Accounts Statistics, Central Statistical Organisation.

3.4. Combining the Different Elements

3.4.1. The Existing Literature

Gordon and Gupta (2004) test for the significance of different factors in explaining India's services-sector growth in two alternative regression models. In the first approach, using time series data for the period from 1952 to 2000, they estimate individual regression equations for nine service sub-sectors – business, communication, financial, hotels and restaurants, distribution, transport, public administration and defence and community and personal services. In doing so, they regress growth of service-sector output on the rate of growth of GDP, growth rate of external trade volume of goods, growth rate of service exports, and two dummy variables to capture the influence of economic reforms relating to liberalization. The first dummy variable equals one for the 1990s and zero otherwise. The second dummy variable does the same for the 1980s. The authors attribute this to the fact that a majority of the reforms in the services sector were carried out in the 1990s, whereas some were initiated in the preceding decade.

Results show that for all the fast-growing segments – business, communication, financial, hotels and restaurants and community services – the dummy variable for the 1990s is positive and highly significant. For business, financial and community services, even the dummy variable for the 1980s is statistically significant. In the case of financial services, this may be attributable to deregulation in the sector, which began in the 1980s. The value of service exports appears to have a positive and significant effect only for the business-services segment – comprising software services, call centres and business process outsourcing, among others. The growth of external trade in goods expectedly has a statistically significant positive effect on transport and distribution services. Domestic demand appears to be a uniformly strong factor as the growth rate of GDP is positive and statistically significant for most service sub-sectors.

The second approach entails the use of panel data for the nine service activities (listed earlier), where the observations are averaged over five-year intervals during the period from 1970 to 2000.[11] Here, growth of service-sector activity is regressed on growth of agricultural output, growth of industrial output, growth in external volume of trade in goods, growth in service exports and a dummy variable for economic liberalization. Moreover, instead of a general dummy variable for the 1990s or 1980s, the authors construct sector-specific liberalization dummy variables which equal one for activities that were liberalized (in terms of FDI openness, external trade openness or private ownership) significantly in a given period. It is worth noting that even these dummy variables neither capture the precise timing, type or extent of reforms nor isolate the effects of reforms on growth from other simultaneous events.

The dummy variable for reform measures is found to be the most significant. This suggests that the service sub-sectors which were opened up to FDI, trade or private ownership were the ones which experienced faster growth. As a robustness check, Gordon and Gupta (2004) include a dummy variable for the 1990s. Its coefficient is statistically insignificant, thereby suggesting that the acceleration of the 1990s is largely attributable to economic reforms. The value of service exports[12] and the growth rate of industrial output are also significantly positively correlated with the growth of the services sector, albeit with smaller coefficients. The relatively small coefficient on service exports may be attributable to the fact that business services – software, business process outsourcing and so forth – constituted a relatively small part of GDP at the end of the 1990s. In 2008–09, however, they accounted for about 6 per cent of India's GDP. Given that exports of business services have grown rapidly of late, the inclusion of more recent data may reflect a greater contribution to the growth of India's services sector.

In a more recent study, using annual data for nine service sub-sectors – trade, hotels and restaurants, transport and storage, communication, banking and insurance, business services, public administration and defence, education and health services – over the period from 1980 to 2006, Eichengreen

[11] 1970s, 1981–85, 1986–90, 1991–95 and 1996–2000.
[12] The inclusion of a dummy variable for the 1990s renders the coefficient on service exports statistically insignificant. This should come as no surprise as service exports – primarily in the business services segment – took off in the 1990s.

and Gupta (2010) analyse the determinants of India's services-sector growth in a panel data regression framework. In doing so, the authors regress the real growth rate of different services on per capita income, the square of per capita income, a sector-specific index of liberalization, the tradability of the service in question, its skilled-labour intensity and the correlation of the service activity with industrial growth (a proxy for contracting out). The results show that while per capita income and per capita income-squared are not statistically significant individually, they are jointly significant in their positive impact on services sector growth. The tradability of services, as well as the extent of their liberalization, also has a statistically significant positive effect on services-sector growth. In fact, the authors show that tradable services grew 4 percentage points a year faster than non-tradable services (other things being equal), whereas service segments which were both liberalized and tradable grew about 7 percentage points higher than services that were neither tradable nor liberalized. This suggests that there are likely to be substantial future gains in economic growth from encouraging exports of IT, communication, financial and business services while also liberalizing activities like education, health care and retail trade.

3.4.2. Going Beyond

3.4.2.1. Empirical Specification

To identify the potential determinants of India's services sector growth, we follow the existing literature in using a regression framework that exploits variations over time and across service sub-sectors at the all-India level. In doing so, we consider the period between 1990–91 and 2008–09 and eleven service sub-sectors – wholesale and retail trade, hotels and restaurants, transport, storage, communication, financial services, real estate and renting services, business services, public administration and defence, social and community services and personal, cultural and recreational services. Hence, relative to the existing literature, we include data from more recent years and at a level of disaggregation that allows us to consider two more service sub-sectors.

We first estimate Equation (3.13):

$$SHAREGDP_{it} = \alpha + \beta_1 GDP_{t-1} + \beta_2 TRADE_{it-1} + \gamma_1 LIBZ_i$$
$$+ \gamma_2 ENROL_{t-4} + \mu_1 IOCOEFF_{it-1}$$
$$+ \mu_2 RELPRICES_{it-1} + \varepsilon_{it}$$

where *SHAREGDP* is the share of service sub-sector in GDP, *GDP* is the gross domestic product of the country, *TRADE* is sum of the value of exports and imports by service sub-sector, *LIBZ* is an index of liberalization which identifies the degree of liberalization in a service sub-sector, *ENROL* is the total enrolment of students in higher education (lagged by four years),[13] *IOCOEFF* is a coefficient which measures the intensity of the use of different services in producing industrial output and *RELPRICES* is the price of a service sub-sector output relative to industrial output.

It is worth noting that the values of the explanatory variables are lagged. This is to ensure that these explanatory variables are predetermined, relative to the dependent variable. For example, it is not clear whether a higher level of GDP is leading to an increased share of the services sector in GDP or vice versa. Similarly, it may be the case that both international trade in services and the share of services in GDP are being driven by an omitted variable such as telecommunications infrastructure. A departure from the existing literature, the use of lagged explanatory variables reduces the possibility of the estimated coefficients being biased. However, it was not possible to find good instrumental variables which would ensure that the associations we find represent causal effects.

The aforementioned exercise also entails other points of departure from the existing literature in terms of the choice of variables used. First, in explaining the increasing importance of the services sector in India's total output, we use the share of a service sub-sector in GDP – rather than the rate of growth of its output – as our dependent variable. Second, we use actual data on services trade as opposed to a dummy variable which classifies a service as being tradable in international markets or not. While data on international trade in services in India are subject to problems of coverage and classification, the recent availability of information from balance-of-payments statistics at a sufficiently disaggregated level facilitates this inclusion. Third, we also use continuous time series data for student enrolment in higher education – as opposed to a dummy variable for skill intensity – to analyse the availability of skilled labour. Fourth, instead of using the growth of industrial output or the correlation between service-sector output growth and industrial-sector output growth as a proxy for the outsourcing of economic activity from industry to the service sector, we use input-output coefficients that measure the intensity of the use of services as inputs in producing industrial output. Fifth, we include a variable tracking

---

[13] Assuming that it takes about four years for an individual to be employed from the time he or she enrols in higher education.

the increase in the price of service output, relative to industrial output, over time. This is not done in the aforementioned studies in the literature.

In a second specification, we estimate Equation (3.14):

$$SHAREGDP_{it} = \alpha + \beta_1 PFCE_{t-1} + \beta_2 GFCE_{t-1} + \beta_3 EXPORTS_{it-1}$$
$$+ \gamma_1 LIBZ_i + \gamma_2 ENROL_{t-4} + \mu_1 IOCOEFF_{it-1}$$
$$+ \mu_2 RELPRICES_{it-1} + \varepsilon_{it}$$

where *PFCE* is an estimate of private final consumption expenditure on services, *GFCE* is government final consumption expenditure and *EXPORTS* is exports by service sub-sector.

Here, instead of using GDP or per capita GDP as a measure for final demand, we consider three of its components individually – private household demand, government demand and exports. This also marks a point of departure from the existing literature. Once again, the values of the explanatory variables are lagged to get around the problem of reverse causality and omitted variable bias.

3.4.2.2. Results

Table 3.9 shows that the levels of GDP, services trade and service liberalization have a statistically significant positive impact on the share of services in GDP. In contrast, the relative price of service output, the coefficient measuring the intensity of services used as input in producing industrial output, and enrolment rates in higher education do not have any such statistically significant effects. Table 3.9 also shows that in the second specification – when considering three different components of GDP – private household demand and service exports appear to have a statistically significant positive impact on the share of services in GDP, whereas government final consumption expenditure does not. The signs and statistical significance of the coefficients of the other variables remain unaffected.

The set of aforementioned results are largely consistent with the trends in the data described earlier for each variable under consideration. The statistical insignificance of the coefficient on supply of skilled labour may be attributable to the fact that this variable is highly correlated with service exports. Final demand – that arising from domestic households and exports to the rest of the world – and policy liberalization appear to be important for explaining the increasing share of the services sector in India's total output. Of these, the value of service exports has the smallest coefficient.

Table 3.9. *Explaining the service sector's increasing share in India's GDP*

Dependent Variable → Explanatory Variables ↓	Share in GDP (1)	Share in GDP (2)
GDP	0.043***	
	(0.007)	
	[0.000]	
Trade (Exports plus Imports)	0.003***	
	(0.001)	
	[0.000]	
Index of Liberalization	0.023***	0.024***
	(0.003)	(0.006)
	[0.000]	[0.000]
Enrolment in Higher Education	0.006	0.003
	(0.005)	(0.008)
	[0.177]	[0.709]
Input-Output Coefficient	0.034	0.040
	(0.755)	(0.095)
	[0.656]	[0.670]
Relative Price of Services	0.022	0.021
	(0.015)	(0.015)
	[0.153]	[0.162]
Private Final Consumption Expenditure on Services		0.016***
		(0.001)
		[0.000]
Government Final Consumption Expenditure		0.019
		(0.023)
		[0.414]
Service Exports		0.002*
		(0.001)
		[0.051]
Observations	209	209
R-Squared	0.83	0.53

Note: Standard errors in brackets; ***p<0.01, **p<0.05, *p<0.1.

3.5. Conclusion

The rapid growth of the services sector in India, which constituted 57 per cent of GDP in 2010, is now well documented. First and foremost, evidence suggests that this growth has been real rather than notional – an increase in the relative price of services was negligible, while the 'outsourcing' of services from firms in the industrial sector was not significant enough to support the claim that services growth was simply disguised manufacturing activity. On the supply side, greater deregulation and privatization induced growth in sectors – such as communication services – that were state monopolies in the pre-reform period. This implies that the liberalization of sectors such as retail trade and education and health services is likely to enable producers to meet growing domestic household demand. The greater availability of skilled labour may also have been a contributing factor to the growth of certain skill-intensive services, through its positive impact on the exports of business services for instance.

On the demand side, government final consumption does not appear to be a significant factor explaining the growth of the country's services sector over the last two decades. But the growth of India's services exports does – although the overall size of this effect is still relatively small, being concentrated in the business services segment. The above suggests that exports of software, business process outsourcing, communication and financial services must continue to be encouraged.

In contrast, according to data at the macroeconomic level, the high-income elasticity of household final demand for services appears to have had a significant impact on the growth of India's services sector. In fact, Rakshit (2007) shows that private consumption is by far the largest component of final demand for both goods and services. Similarly, in a growth accounting exercise, Eichengreen and Gupta (2010) conclude that growth of private final demand accounts for about half of the growth of service-sector output since 1991. The other half is split between exports and outsourcing by the industrial sector, with the former accounting for a growing share in recent years. Unfortunately, these data, based on National Accounts, do not permit a precise split of private final consumption expenditure into a goods and a services component (Gordon and Gupta, 2004). In addition, it is hard to establish a definitive causal effect of household final demand on services growth using the data available at the all-India level. Hence, in the next chapter, we turn to a more detailed analysis of household survey data, which, because of the level of disaggregation, enables us to capture expenditure on services per se rather than on services and goods for a category of service expenditure.

FOUR

The Demand for Services in India

A Mirror Image of Engel's Law for Food?

4.1. Introduction

Chapters 1 and 3 referred to the literature on structural change, in which changing patterns of demand as an explanation for the increasing importance of the services sector have received special emphasis. Fisher (1935) refers to this transformation as a 'hierarchy of needs', where the growth of the services sector is defined by saturation of demand for manufactured goods and high-income elasticity of demand for services. This is based on the notion that while goods fulfil the need of basic necessities, services fulfil the desire for luxuries. However, such generalizations do not provide unambiguous conclusions about shifts in the relative importance of services and goods in consumer expenditure because, as incomes rise, consumers may substitute a service they previously hired for a good to satisfy the same want (Kravis et al., 1982). For example, as incomes rise, individuals may substitute the use of bus or auto-rickshaw[1] services with a motorcycle or car they buy in the market. Similarly, as incomes rise, individuals may substitute the services of a *dhobi* (laundry services) with a washing machine. In this context, most consumer durables are a case in point as they provide a flow of services over the duration of their life. According to Kravis et al. (1982), because goods and services are often close substitutes in satisfying the same wants, technology and relative prices (in addition to the income elasticity of demand) also play an important role in determining their relative expansion paths.

Chapter 3 showed that data at the macroeconomic level suggest that the high-income elasticity argument appears to be important in explaining the rapid growth of the services sector in India. However, these macroeconomic

---

[1] A rickshaw powered by an engine.

data, derived from India's National Accounts Statistics, do not allow a precise disaggregation of private final consumption expenditure into a goods and services component (Gordon and Gupta, 2004). Hence, to establish the significance of private final demand as an explanation for the increasing importance of the services sector, it is necessary to analyse patterns of expenditure at the level of the household. Given the preceding discussion, the objective of this chapter is to estimate demand-side relationships for different consumer services using household survey data from India. In doing so, it estimates Engel curve-type relationships for six categories of services and for these services in the aggregate.

It is important to emphasize the fact that such an exercise has not been attempted in the literature on India. There are a few studies which estimate Engel curves for expenditure on education and medicines in India while analyzing the presence of gender bias in household expenditure patterns (Kingdon, 2005; Lancaster, et al., 2008). However, their definition of education includes expenditure on both goods and services, whereas medicines are simply a good. There are similar studies in the literature on the subject for other countries and regions. They estimate Engel curve-type relationships for expenditure on education and health (goods and services) as a part of larger exercise which also includes analysis for food items and manufactured goods such as clothing and footwear. For services alone, there is one cross-country study by Falvey and Gemmell (1996) that uses data at the level of countries to analyse the income elasticity of demand for different service categories. There is no systematic analysis establishing Engel-curve type relationships for different services at the level of the household.

The scope of the chapter is limited to an analysis of household survey data from India for two points in time: 1993–94 and 2004–05. The choice of years is determined by the fact that the period from 1990–91 saw the most dramatic increase in the output share of the services sector, whereas 2004–05 is the latest year for which data are available. The structure of the chapter is as follows. Section 4.2 provides an overview on the concept of an Engel curve. Section 4.3 discusses the data under consideration. Section 4.4 presents the econometric methodology used for estimating Engel curves – the choice of functional form, the choice of estimation technique and other estimation issues. Section 4.5 discusses results of the estimation. Section 4.6 provides robustness checks for the empirical estimation. Section 4.7 augments our estimation of Engel curves by analyzing changes over time. Section 4.8 presents conclusions. It is worth noting that this chapter, unlike the previous one, does not attempt to ascertain the importance of private final demand in domestic households in the growth of the services sector, relative to other potential explanations.

4.2. Engel Curves

In a seminal article, using cross-section data from household surveys of working-class families in Belgium, Ernst Engel (1857) found that the proportion of expenditure spent on food decreases with income. This relationship, known as Engel's law, has since been found to hold in most economies and time periods. Given that Engel's Law relates to cross-section analysis, it assumes that all households face the same commodity prices at one point in time. In general, an Engel curve may be defined as a function that describes the relationship between a consumer's expenditure on some particular good or service and the consumer's total resources,[2] holding prices fixed. The goods are typically aggregate commodities such as food or transportation, consumed over some weeks or months, rather than discrete purchases.

Engel curves (Engel, 1857) are most often specified as the relationship between the budget share allocated to a particular good or service and total income or expenditure. Under this specification, luxuries are goods that take up a larger share of the budget for better-off households, whereas necessities are goods that take up a smaller share of the budget for better-off households. The literature also distinguishes between luxury and necessity goods using income or expenditure elasticities of demand[3] (Hicks, 1939). Goods with income or expenditure elasticities of demand below zero, between zero and one and above one are called 'inferior goods', 'necessities' and 'luxury goods', respectively. Of course, elasticities can themselves vary with income – a good that is a necessity for the rich can be a luxury for the poor (Lewbel, 2008).

The level of aggregation across goods may affect Engel-curve estimates. For instance, food in the aggregate is a necessity, but it could include inferior goods like cabbage and luxuries like caviar. Other empirical Engel-curve complications include unobserved variations in the quality and price of goods purchased, which may be correlated with total income or expenditure.

---

[2] Total expenditure is often used to measure total resources. This serves to separate the problem of allocating total consumption to various goods from the decision of how much to save out of current income.

[3] The expenditure elasticity of demand for a commodity is defined as the ratio of the proportionate change in the expenditure on a particular good or service to the proportionate change in total expenditure.

For example, the wealthy may systematically favour higher-quality goods or the poor may face higher prices than other consumers because they cannot afford to buy in bulk or travel to discount stores (Lewbel, 2008).

4.3. Data

4.3.1. Sample: Source and Size

To analyse patterns of expenditure for different consumer services at the level of the household in India, a necessary condition is the availability of consumption data at the level of the household. Surveys on consumer expenditure, conducted regularly by India's National Sample Survey Organisation (NSSO), collect such micro-level data, thereby providing the opportunity to carry out empirical research hitherto not done.

The first comprehensive survey on consumer expenditure was carried out during the period from September 1972 to October 1973, corresponding to the twenty-seventh round of NSSO. After that round, seven comprehensive quinquennial (once in five years) surveys on consumer expenditure in India have been carried out by the NSSO. These were carried out during the thirty-second (July 1977 to June 1978), thirty-eighth (January 1983 to December 1983), forty-third (July 1987 to June 1988), fiftieth (July 1993 to June 1994) fifty-fifth (July 1999 to June 2000), sixty-first (July 2004 to June 2005) and sixty-sixth (July 2009 to June 2010) rounds. These surveys do not track the same individuals over time. Moreover, the data for the sixty-sixth round is not yet available.

For the present exercise, the data are taken from two of the seven comprehensive quinquennial surveys on consumer expenditure conducted in independent India by the National Sample Survey: the fiftieth round (1993–94) and the sixty-first round (2004–05). The choice of surveys analysed is explained in the introduction. Spread over 6,951 villages and 4,650 urban blocks, the former has a sample size of 115,354 households. Similarly, spread over 7,999 villages and 4,602 urban blocks, the latter has a sample size of 124,644 households (Table 4.1). Moreover, in both surveys, 60 per cent of the households in the sample are located in rural areas and 40 per cent of the households are located in urban areas. Importantly, these large sample sizes are a strength of the econometric analysis to follow. In terms of geographical coverage, both surveys cover the whole of India except certain districts of Jammu and Kashmir and certain interior areas of Nagaland and of the Andaman and Nicobar Islands.

Table 4.1. *Sample size*

	1993–94 (50th Round)	2004–05 (61st Round)
Number of Villages Surveyed	6,951	7,999
Number of Urban Blocks Surveyed	4,650	4,602
Number of Households Surveyed (Total)	115,354	124,644
Number of Households Surveyed (Rural areas)	69,206	79,298
Number of Households Surveyed (Urban areas)	46,148	45,346

Source: Surveys on Employment, National Sample Survey Organisation.

4.3.2. Sample Design

For both 1993–94 and 2004–05, the survey periods were divided into four sub-rounds, each with a duration of three months. For 1993–94, the first sub-round period ranges from July to September 1993, the second sub-round from October to December 1993, the third sub-round from January to March 1994, and the fourth sub-round from April to June 1994. The round for 2004–05 follows the same pattern. Furthermore, in both years, an equal number of sample villages or blocks were allotted for survey in each of these four sub-rounds (NSSO, 1996b; NSSO, 2006b).

The sample design adopted in these surveys was a stratified two-stage design for both rural and urban areas (NSSO, 1996b; NSSO, 2006b). The first-stage units (FSUs) were villages for rural areas and the NSSO Urban Frame Survey (UFS) blocks for urban areas. The second-stage units (SSUs) were households for both rural and urban areas. The method of selection of the first-stage and second-stage units was as follows. At an all-India level, for rural areas, the list of the most recent census villages constituted the sampling frame for selection of sample FSUs.[4] Similarly, at an all-India level, for urban areas, the latest lists of UFS blocks constituted the sampling frame for selection of sample FSUs. Villages and urban blocks with populations above a certain threshold level were divided into a suitable number of sub-groups with equal population count. These groups were called hamlet-groups and sub-blocks for rural areas and urban areas respectively. The total number of first-stage units in the survey was allocated to the different states in proportion to population as per census data. This, in turn, was then allocated

[4] For the rural areas of Kerala, however, the list of *panchayat* wards was used as the sampling frame for selection of FSUs.

between rural and urban sectors also in proportion to population as per census data. In other words, within each district of a state, two separate basic strata were formed for rural areas and urban areas. All rural areas of the district comprised the rural stratum and all the urban areas of the district comprised the urban stratum (NSSO, 1996b; NSSO, 2006b).

After the selection of the first-stage units (villages and urban blocks), second-stage units – which are households – were selected. In rural areas, for selected villages, certain relatively affluent households were identified and considered as second-stage stratum 1 and the rest as stratum 2. In fact, a total of ten households were surveyed from the selected village groups, two from the first category and eight from the second. In urban areas, households with a monthly per capita expenditure above a certain threshold were considered as second stage stratum 1 and the rest as stratum 2. Once again, a total of ten households were surveyed from the selected urban blocks: four households from second-stage stratum 1 and six households from second-stage stratum 2 for the relatively affluent classes, and two households from second-stage stratum 1 and eight from second-stage stratum 2 for the other strata or classes. It is worth noting that within each stratum, for both rural and urban areas, the surveys used the interview method of data collection on a sample of randomly selected households (NSSO, 1996b; NSSO, 2006b).

4.3.3. Types of Services

A household's consumer expenditure comprises the total monetary value of consumption of all goods and services. To facilitate meaningful analysis, we aggregate different items covered in the survey questionnaire to form six distinct categories of services: education, health, entertainment, personal, communication and transport services. Usually, this total consumer expenditure is expressed on a thirty-day basis. For education and institutional health care, however, we use information on expenditure in the "last 365 days"[5] (scaled down to a per month basis) (NSSO, 1996b; NSSO, 2006b). Our choice of services is determined by the limitations of the dataset under consideration.

Table 4.2 shows that the services under consideration constituted about 28 per cent of India's GDP and about half of India's services GDP in

---

[5]   For clothing, footwear, education, institutional health care and durable goods, there are two estimates for household consumption: expenditure in the 'last 30 days' and expenditure in the 'last 365 days' (NSSO, 1996b; NSSO, 2006b).

Table 4.2. *Sub-sectors of services in GDP*

Sub-sector	Share in GDP (2004–05)	Rate of growth between 1993–94 and 2004–05 (per cent per annum)
Wholesale and retail trade	14.6	7.5
Hotels and restaurants	1.1	9.4
Transport	5.7	6.4
Storage	0.0005	1.1
Communication	4.9	19.0
Banking and insurance	6.9	8.4
Real estate, renting and business services	6.1	6.1
Public administration and defence	5.6	6.6
Education and health services	9.2	8.7
Entertainment and personal services	3.9	5.2

Source: Author's estimates based on Central Statistical Organisation, National Accounts Statistics.

2004–05. Of the service categories covered in our household survey data, communications, hotels and restaurants and community (education and health) services were characterised by high annual average rates of growth between 1993–94 and 2004–05 at 19.0, 9.4 and 8.7 per cent, respectively. This conforms to the findings of Gordon and Gupta (2004), which show that among the different sub-sectors of services, business, communication, financial, hotels and restaurants and community services experienced an acceleration in their rates of growth during the 1990s relative to the previous decade. Table 4.2 also shows that transport and personal and entertainment services, the other categories under our consideration, grew at an average annual rate of 6.4 and 5.2 per cent, respectively, between 1993–94 and 2004–05. This validates the findings of Bosworth et al. (2007) who find that even though communication, business and financial services stand out, the acceleration of the services sector during recent years has been broad-based.

4.3.4. Survey Questions: Distinguishing Services from Goods

The survey questions cover household expenditure in highly disaggregated categories, thereby enabling us to capture expenditure on services per se rather than on services and goods for a category of service expenditure (see discussion under each category). This marks a considerable improvement from National Accounts Statistics which cannot distinguish precisely between goods and services in its estimates of private consumption expenditure.

Education services primarily consist of expenditure on tuition fees, boarding costs and other compulsory payments[6] at schools, colleges and training institutes. Donations to schools made voluntarily are not included because they are regarded as transfer payments. Education services also comprise expenses incurred in hiring private tutors, joining coaching centres, library charges and securing Internet connectivity for the purposes of education. This category, however, does not include expenditure on goods purchased for the purpose of education, such as uniforms, books, journals, newspapers and stationery. Transport costs such as expenditure on school buses are also not included.

Health services consist of two categories: institutional and non-institutional, where institutions include private as well as government hospitals and nursing homes. The former comprise expenditure on doctor's fees, hospital or nursing home charges and medical tests such as X-rays, ECG and pathological tests. The latter comprise expenditure on all of the above except hospital or nursing home charges – as an in-patient of a medical institution. It also includes expenditure on family planning. Health insurance premiums are not included as they are not covered in the questionnaire. Importantly, this category does not include expenditure incurred by individuals on purchasing medicine.

Entertainment services include expenditure on cinema, theatre, fairs, picnics and processing of photographic film. This category also consists of charges paid for hiring video cassette recorders (VCRs), video cassettes and DVDs. Membership fees for clubs offering facilities for sports and recreational activities are also included here. Expenditure on sports goods and other goods for recreation, however, is not included.

Personal services entail expenditure on domestic servants, cooks, individuals who repair non-durables, tailors, laundry and ironing services, sweepers, barbers and beauticians. It also includes expenditure on services rendered by priests (religious services) and other consumer services such as those provided by hotels and restaurants. Expenditure on legal services is not included in our analysis as it has negligible non-zero entries.

Communication services consist of expenditure on postage, telephone charges and Internet connectivity charges. Expenditure on computers is not included here, but falls under the category of consumer durables.

---

[6] Even if termed 'donations' by institutions collecting them.

Transport services primarily consist of expenditure on trips undertaken and transportation of goods made by any of the following means of conveyance: airlines, the railways, buses, trams, taxis, auto-rickshaws, cycle rickshaws, steamers, boats and horse carts. Transport services also consist of porter charges. The cost of fuel for owner-used conveyance is not included.

It is important to note that the items covered to estimate household expenditure under each of the six service categories are the same for both 1993–94 and 2004–05. The one exception is expenses incurred on subscription to cable television facilities, a category which did not exist in the survey questions during 1993–94. Hence, this has been excluded from our estimates of household expenditure on entertainment services.

4.4. Estimation of Engel Curves: Econometric Analysis

4.4.1. Choice of Functional Form

We estimate Engel curve-type relationships for six categories of services and for these services in the aggregate using the following linear budget share specification. All the following regression equations are estimated at the all-India level, for rural areas, and for urban areas, both in 1993–94 and 2004–05.

$$SERVICESPROP_i = \alpha_i + \beta \log(TOTALEXP_i) + \gamma X + \varepsilon_i \tag{4.1}$$

$$EDUPROP_i = \alpha_i + \beta \log(TOTALEXP_i) + \gamma X + \varepsilon_i \tag{4.2}$$

$$HEALTHPROP_i = \alpha_i + \beta \log(TOTALEXP_i) + \gamma X + \varepsilon_i \tag{4.3}$$

$$ENTPROP_i = \alpha_i + \beta \log(TOTALEXP_i) + \gamma X + \varepsilon_i \tag{4.4}$$

$$PERSONALPROP_i = \alpha_i + \beta \log(TOTALEXP_i) + \gamma X + \varepsilon_i \tag{4.5}$$

$$COMMPROP_i = \alpha_i + \beta \log(TOTALEXP_i) + \gamma X + \varepsilon_i \tag{4.6}$$

$$TRANSPROP_i = \alpha_i + \beta \log(TOTALEXP_i) + \gamma X + \varepsilon \tag{4.7}$$

Table 4.3 explains the notation used for different variables that are used in the equations above and in those to follow.

First proposed by Working (1943), the above specification is known as the Working-Leser model as Leser (1963) found that this functional form fits better than the alternatives. The use of total household expenditure as

Table 4.3. *Notation and description of variables*

Variable notation	Variable description
TOTALEXP	Total expenditure of a household
	Proportion of total household expenditure on:
SERVICESPROP	The six following services in the aggregate
EDUPROP	Education services
HEALTHPROP	Health services
ENTPROP	Entertainment services
PERSONALPROP	Personal services
COMMPROP	Communication services
TRANSPROP	Transport services
X	Vector of control variables, which includes household size, household social group, household religion, age-sex categories that capture household composition and age, gender and level of education of household head

a proxy for total household income is a consistent feature of the literature on Engel-curve analysis. In addition, following the literature, we control for other variables which may help to explain cross-section variation in demand. For example, Engel's (1857) original work highlighted the relevance of household size. More recent studies include other covariates such as age, gender, location, race and ethnicity (Banks, et al., 1997; Lewbel, 2008).

To capture any non-linear impact of total expenditure on the household budget share allocated to different services, we augment the above equations by adding the square of the total household expenditure variable. The literature shows that whereas Engel curves are close to linear for some goods, they are highly non-linear for others. Engel (1857, 1895) found that budget share devoted to food was close to linear in the logarithm of total expenditure or income. More recent work, however, highlights considerable non-linearity in Engel curves, especially for several manufactured goods (Banks, et al., 1997; Bierens and Pott-Buter, 1990; Hardle and Jerison, 1991; Hausman, et al., 1995; Lewbel, 1991).

4.4.2. Choice of Estimation Technique

In many household expenditure surveys, respondents report zero expenditure on certain goods and services either because those are purchased

Table 4.4. *Households in the sample with zero expenditure on different services*

	Number (2004–05)	Number (1993–94)	Percentage (2004–05)	Percentage (1993–94)	Percentage difference (1993–94 to 2004–05)
Education services	56,841	63,281	45	55	−10
Health services	85,828	86,467	68	75	−7
Entertainment services	80,042	85,676	64	74	−10
Personal services	7,740	33,040	6	29	−23
Communication services	68,528	88,641	55	77	−22
Transport services	33,780	45,925	27	40	−13

Total Number of Households in the Sample (2004–05): 124,644
Total Number of Households in the Sample (1993–94): 115,354

Source: National Sample Survey Organisation, Surveys on Consumer Expenditure.

infrequently or never at all (Beatty, 2006).[7] Importantly, if a large number of households report zero expenditure – a general rule of thumb prescribes more than 10 per cent of the sample under consideration – the estimation of a model by OLS results in biased and inconsistent parameter estimates (Wooldridge, 2002). Table 4.4 shows that in both the surveys under consideration, the percentage of households that report zero expenditure on the different services is greater than ten for each of the six categories of services.[8] For education and health services, a large number of zero expenditure entries may be attributable to government subsidies that waive tuition fees at school and cover doctors' fees and other hospital charges. Moreover, it can be seen that the percentage of households that report zero expenditure in each of the six categories of services is lower in 2004–05 relative to 1993–94. This may reflect a rise in living standards for lower-income groups during this period.

Given these findings, we follow the literature in estimating Engel curve-type relationships by using the standard censored Tobit model (Tobin, 1956), which is most appropriate to analyse variables which take the value of zero with positive probability but are a continuous random variables over strictly positive values. It is a well-established solution to the problem of zero expenditure, because values of the relevant variable

---

[7] Non-consumption represents a utility-maximizing solution to an expenditure choice problem. Infrequency of purchase occurs when the survey period is not long enough to capture expenditures on goods.

[8] The one exception is personal services for the survey of 2004–05.

are truncated at zero and only positive values are assumed (Wooldridge, 2002). Deaton and Irish (1984) were amongst the first to use the Tobit model to analyse the demand for commodities. Tobit models, however, do not give consistent parameter estimates if the error term is heteroscedastic or non-normally distributed (Wooldridge, 2002). Given this, an alternative method used by the literature to overcome the zero expenditures problem is censored quantile regressions. To ensure the robustness of our estimates, we use this estimator as well. Quantile regressions – where quantiles of the conditional distribution of the response variable are expressed in terms of observed covariates – in themselves avoid the problem of zero expenditure in household consumption data only at the higher quantiles. At the lower quantiles, the process of censoring follows Tobit (Gustavsen, et al., 2008; Gustavsen and Rickertsen, 2004; Muller, 1999). Quantile regressions, more generally, are also well suited to the analysis of household survey data for the reason that they are robust to outliers (Deaton, 1997).

4.4.3. Other Estimation Issues

The vector of control variables, X, comprises household size, social group, religion, age-sex categories that capture household composition and age, gender and level of education of household head. Its inclusion is an important robustness check as many of its constituent variables are likely to be correlated both with the level of total household expenditure and the proportion of household expenditure allocated to a particular service category. Furthermore, it may be argued that the within the cross section, households living in different neighbourhoods may face different prices for the same service category or may have non-uniform access to different services due to location-specific availability. This is likely to affect both the dependent variable and total household expenditure, thereby resulting in an omitted variable bias. Taking this under consideration, we also include district dummy variables. For the all-India sample, each of the district dummy variables is interacted with a dummy variable for urban areas as well.

4.5. Results

4.5.1. Coefficients and Marginal Effects

In our specification, where the dependent variable is household budget shares, the service under consideration may be classified as a luxury good

Table 4.5. *Engel curve for services: Tobit*

Dependent Variable: Proportion of Household Expenditure on Services

Explanatory Variables ↓	All-India (2004–05)	Rural (2004–05)	Urban (2004–05)	All-India (1993–94)	Rural (1993–94)	Urban (1993–94)
Log of Household Expenditure	0.071*** [0.0007]	0.059*** [0.0009]	0.082*** [0.0013]	0.036*** [0.0004]	0.031*** [0.0004]	0.038*** [0.0008]
Constant	−0.459*** [0.0083]	−0.384*** [0.011]	−0.540*** [0.014]	−0.197*** [0.0053]	−0.157*** [0.0074]	−0.207*** [0.0090]
Vector of Control Variables	Yes	Yes	Yes	Yes	Yes	Yes
District Dummy Variables	Yes	Yes	Yes	Yes	Yes	Yes
Observations	124,640	79,295	45,345	115,192	69,119	46,073

Note: Standard errors in brackets; ***p<0.01, **p<0.05, *p<0.1.
A dummy variable for urban areas is interacted with the district dummy variable in the all-India sample.
Source: Regression estimates based on primary data from National Sample Survey Organisation.

if $\hat{\beta} > 0$. This is equivalent to the elasticity of expenditure on services with respect to total household expenditure being greater than 1 in a specification where the dependent variable is in absolute levels (see Appendix D). The model is estimated for both 1993–94 and 2004–05. The use of cross-section data circumvents the statistical difficulties associated with adjusting for price change in the context of services output.

Table 4.5 shows that in 2004–05, the estimated $\hat{\beta}s$ for the service categories under consideration in the aggregate are 0.071, 0.059 and 0.082 for the all-India sample, rural areas and urban areas respectively, each being significant at the 1 per cent level. In 1993–94, the corresponding $\hat{\beta}s$ are 0.036, 0.031 and 0.038, respectively, each again significant at the 1 per cent level.[9] Similarly, both for 2004–05 and 1993–94, the estimated $\hat{\beta}s$ for each of the six service categories are positive and significant at the 1 per cent level of significance. This holds true for the all-India sample,

[9] The vector of control variables is reported in Appendix Table B.1.

rural areas and urban areas (see Appendix Tables B.2 to B.7). However, because the Tobit model involves a non-linear transformation of the dependent variable, the magnitude of the coefficients cannot be viewed as the true estimates of the marginal effect of an explanatory variable on the dependent variable (Wooldridge, 2002). Hence, a $\hat{\beta}$ that is close to zero may actually result in a marginal effect which is less than zero. This could alter the classification of a service category from being a luxury to being a necessity.[10]

In light of the above, we compute marginal effects which represent the true effect of total expenditure or income of the household on the budget share allocated to each type of service.[11] We consider two estimates of marginal effect. First, there is the expected value of the dependent variable, conditional on it being censored at a lower bound zero. Second, there is the unconditional expected value of the dependent variable, which equals its expected value when it is greater than zero multiplied by the probability of it being greater than zero. Hence, the second marginal effect takes into account people who initially spend nothing on a particular service as well those are initially spending something on that service.

Tables 4.6 and 4.7 show that the marginal effect of total household expenditure on the budget share allocated to services under consideration, in the aggregate, is positive for the samples of both 2004–05 and 1993–94.[12] The result holds true for the all-India sample, rural areas and urban areas. Moreover, the marginal effects (both conditional and unconditional) are positive for each service category as well (see Appendix Tables B.8 to B.13). Hence, we can conclude that for each category of services under consideration and for them in the aggregate, we find upward-sloping Engel curves, indicating that these services represent luxury or superior goods. This is in contrast to the findings of Falvey and Gemmell (1996) who, using macroeconomic data in a cross-country study, reject the hypothesis that the demand for services (and transport and education individually) is income-elastic. At the same time, it reinforces their findings that the income elasticity of demand for health, communication and recreation services is greater than unity.

---

[10] The marginal effect is always smaller than the coefficient as the former is obtained by multiplying the latter by an adjustment factor which lies strictly between zero and one (Wooldridge, 2002).

[11] They represent elasticities as routinely obtained from statistical packages such as STATA – i.e. $\dfrac{dSERVICESPROP}{dTOTALEXP} * \dfrac{TOTALEXP}{SERVICESPROP}$

[12] The marginal effects are calculated at the means of the independent variables.

Table 4.6. *Marginal effects from the Tobit regression for services (2004–05)*

Dependent Variable: Proportion of Household Expenditure on Services

Explanatory Variable ↓	All-India conditional expectation	Rural conditional expectation	Urban conditional expectation	All-India unconditional expectation	Rural unconditional expectation	Urban unconditional expectation
Log of Household Expenditure	0.048	0.039	0.057	0.064	0.053	0.075

Source: Regression estimates based on primary data from National Sample Survey Organisation.

Table 4.7. *Marginal effects from the Tobit regression for services (1993–94)*

Dependent Variable: Proportion of Household Expenditure on Services

Explanatory Variable ↓	All-India conditional expectation	Rural conditional expectation	Urban conditional expectation	All-India unconditional expectation	Rural unconditional expectation	Urban unconditional expectation
Log of Household Expenditure	0.021	0.018	0.022	0.030	0.026	0.031

Source: Regression estimates based on primary data from National Sample Survey Organisation.

The results also show that for each service category, the marginal effect of an increase in total expenditure on the household budget share allocated to a particular service is higher for urban areas relative to rural areas. This may be attributable to the fact that households in urban areas may have a stronger preference for buying or better access to several services. Moreover, within the three samples (all-India, rural and urban), marginal effects of an increase in total household expenditure on the budget share allocated to personal services and entertainment services are small. Once again, this may be attributable to preferences whereby as incomes increase, households begin to purchase certain consumer durables that substitute for services they purchased in the market earlier. For example, washing machines may reduce demand for laundry services, whereas ready-made garments may reduce demand for tailors.

4.5.2. Non-Linearities

Table 4.8 shows that the coefficient on the log of total expenditure-squared term is greater than zero in the Engel curve for the service categories under

Table 4.8. *Engel curve for services: Tobit (non-linearities)*

Dependent Variable: Proportion of Household Expenditure on Services

Explanatory Variables ↓	All-India (2004–05)	Rural (2004–05)	Urban (2004–05)	All-India (1993–94)	Rural (1993–94)	Urban (1993–94)
Log of Household Expenditure	0.002 [0.0065]	0.037*** [0.0080]	−0.006 [0.011]	−0.010 [0.0039]	0.0042 [0.0040]	−0.033 [0.0074]
Log of Household Expenditure Squared	0.004*** [0.0004]	0.001*** [0.0005]	0.005*** [0.0007]	0.003*** [0.0003]	0.002*** [0.0002]	0.005*** [0.0004]
Constant	−0.189*** [0.026]	−0.302*** [0.032]	−0.193*** [0.047]	−0.0304** [0.015]	−0.0624*** [0.016]	0.0519* [0.028]
Vector of Control Variables	Yes	Yes	Yes	Yes	Yes	Yes
District Dummy Variables	Yes	Yes	Yes	Yes	Yes	Yes
Observations	124640	79295	45345	115192	69119	46073

Note: Standard errors in brackets; ***p<0.01, **p<0.05, *p<0.1
A dummy variable for urban areas is interacted with the district dummy variable in the all-India sample.
Source: Regression estimates based on primary data from National Sample Survey Organisation.

consideration in the aggregate. This holds true for the all-India sample, rural areas and urban areas, both in 2004–05 and in 1993–94. The result implies that the Engel curve is convex going upwards. Hence, there is a consistent increase in the household budget share allocated to these services as the total income or expenditure increases, which implies that these services in the aggregate are a luxury good at all levels of income.

Using the previously described quadratic specification, we derive non-linear Engel curves for each of the six different categories of services as well (see Appendix Tables B.14 to B.19). The results show that Engel curves for transport and personal services are convex going upwards whereas that for communication services approximates a linear trajectory.[13] This implies that

---

[13] For the survey of 1993–94, the Engel curve for communication services is convex going upwards for the sample of urban areas only.

these two categories of services are luxury goods at all levels of income. In contrast, Engel curves for education, health and entertainment services are concave going upwards. This suggests that after a certain threshold level of expenditure, the household budget share devoted to education and health starts declining. Importantly, however, we find that the concave shape of these Engel curves is being driven by outliers – there are a negligible number of households beyond the threshold level of expenditure after which the household budget share devoted to education and health services begins to decline. In particular, the peak fitted value of the household budget share allocated to education, health and entertainment services is 0.07, 0.04 and 0.02, respectively. This corresponds to the logarithm of total expenditure that equals 10.8, 9.5 and 11.2, respectively. In a sample of 124,644 households, only 0.2 per cent (286 households) – those with extremely high levels of total expenditure – have a higher level of the logarithm of total household expenditure. Hence, in these cases, linear Engel curves are a good approximation of the true relationship.

4.6. Robustness Checks

4.6.1. Instrumental Variable Estimation

The results of two repeated cross sections (one for 2004–04 and one for 1993–94) reinforce each other. But within each sample, despite the inclusion of a large number of control variables, the possibility of bias induced by unobservables (Wooldridge, 2002) that may affect both the level of total household expenditure and the budget share allocated to a particular service remains. This could, for instance, include household tastes, such as preference for quality, or area-specific availability of services. Hence, we re-estimate the equation for the six service categories in the aggregate using instrumental variable estimation. Given that total household expenditure is the potentially endogenous variable, a valid instrumental variable is one that is significantly correlated with household expenditure, but one that is not correlated with omitted variables that affect the budget share allocated to a particular service.

Hence, we use average household expenditure in a state as an instrument for household expenditure. The two are likely to be highly correlated, and this is validated by the test for instrument relevance (see Table 4.9 for the first-stage F-statistic). It may be argued that average household expenditure in a state is correlated with overall income in the state, which, in turn, is an important determinant of the availability of services in different

The Demand for Services in India

Table 4.9. *Engel curve for services: Instrumental variable Tobit estimation*

Dependent Variable: Proportion of Household Expenditure on Services

Explanatory Variables ↓	All-India (2004–05)	Rural (2004–05)	Urban (2004–05)	All-India (1993–94)	Rural (1993–94)	Urban (1993–94)
Log of Household Expenditure	0.119*** [0.005]	0.122*** [0.003]	0.126*** [0.006]	0.070*** [0.002]	0.071*** [0.003]	0.069*** [0.006]
Constant	−0.69*** [0.018]	−0.73*** [0.025]	−0.72*** [0.047]	−0.401*** [0.013]	−0.42*** [0.016]	−0.40*** [0.044]
Vector of Control Variables	Yes	Yes	Yes	Yes	Yes	Yes
District Dummy Variables	Yes	Yes	Yes	Yes	Yes	Yes
Observations	124640	79295	45345	115192	69119	46073
First-Stage F-statistic	104.89 [0.000]	92.95 [0.000]	45.28 [0.000]	82.41 [0.000]	48.51 [0.000]	29.28 [0.000]

Note: Standard errors in brackets; ***p<0.01, **p<0.05, *p<0.1.
A dummy variable for urban areas is interacted with the district dummy variable in the all-India sample.
Source: Author's estimates based on primary data from National Sample Survey Organisation.

areas. Given that availability is likely to influence household budget share allocated to a service, this suggests that our instrument will not meet the instrument exogeneity criteria. However, it must be noted that because district dummy variables are included, any state-specific variation in availability of services is already controlled for. We cannot conduct a test of over-identifying restrictions because of the lack of another suitable instrumental variable.

Table 4.9 shows that both in 1993–94 and 2004–05, the Engel curve estimated for the service categories under consideration – in the aggregate – using the instrumental variable method does not make any difference to the sign or statistical significance of the coefficient on the level of total household expenditure. In fact, a comparison of Tables 4.5 and 4.9 shows that the size of the coefficients (and hence marginal effects, which are not reported for reasons of space) on the level of total household expenditure are higher in the IV specification. This implies that measurement error in the endogenous variable outweighs any potential upward bias caused by unobservables.

4.6.2. Censored Quantile Regressions

Next, given the possible limitations of the Tobit model outlined earlier, we estimate Engel curves for the six categories of services and for these services in the aggregate using censored quantile regressions (see Appendix Tables B.20 to B.26 for the survey of 2004–05 and Appendix Tables B.27 to B.33 for the sample of 1993–94).[14] In addition, censored quantile regressions permit an analysis of the differential impact of a rise in total income or expenditure on the budget share allocated to a particular good or service across high-consumption and low-consumption (conditional on household size, social group, religion, age-sex composition and age, gender and level of education of household head) households.

Figures 4.1 and 4.2 depict three fitted regression lines which correspond to the 35th, 50th, and 85th percentiles of the distribution of the budget share allocated to services, conditional on the logarithm of household expenditure and a set of control variables[15] for the all-India sample. We use the 35th percentile as opposed to the 25th percentile because the 25th percentile of the distribution of the budget share allocated to most service categories is zero.[16] Moreover, we use the 85th percentile rather than the 75th percentile as the former is further away from the median and hence highlights the differences between high-consumption and low-consumption (conditional on the set of control variables) households (referred to as high and low conditional consumption households from here on).[17]

It is evident from Figures 4.1 and 4.2 that Engel curves for each percentile of the distribution of the budget share allocated to these services in the aggregate is upward sloping, thereby implying that they are luxury goods. Importantly, the results are similar for each of the six service categories individually. This validates the results from our Tobit estimation. In addition, these figures show that the Engel curve for a higher quantile lies above that for a lower quantile. This implies that the household budget share allocated to services increases more for high conditional consumption households relative to low conditional consumption households, as total household expenditure increases. Given that household size, age-sex

---

[14] Given the results of the previous section, we do not include an expenditure-squared term in these regressions.

[15] Same as in the Tobit model.

[16] For some service categories, we do not get fitted lines for even the 50th and 75th percentiles because of the large number of zero-expenditure entries.

[17] The corresponding curves for rural and urban areas are broadly similar, but not reported for reasons of space.

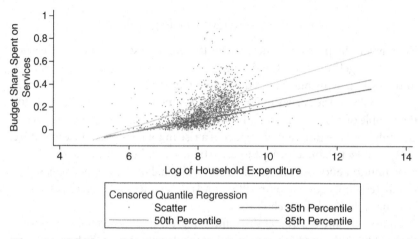

Figure 4.1. Engel curve for aggregate services: Censored quantile regressions (2004–05).
Source: Primary data from National Sample Survey Organisation, India.

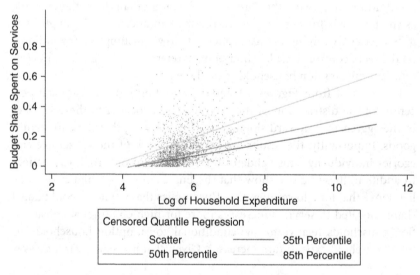

Figure 4.2. Engel curve for aggregate services: Censored quantile regressions (1993–94)
Source: Primary data from National Sample Survey Organisation, India.

composition of households, social group and religion, age of the household head, gender of the household head, the level of education of the household head and district dummy variables are controlled for, this greater increase for high-consuming household is explained by the residual term which may represent tastes or preferences of households. In fact, estimating Engel curves on datasets from a range of countries, several empirical studies that followed Engel (1895) interpret large errors in these models to be indicative of considerable heterogeneity in tastes across consumers (Allen and Bowley, 1935; Ogburn, 1919). For example, it may be the case that households with high conditional consumption of education and health services value quality and hence pay significantly larger amounts for it. Similarly, households which have high conditional consumption of transport services may care more about their mode of transport, which determines comfort and convenience. Hence, with an increase in total income, bus journeys may be replaced by more expensive train journeys and train journeys may be replaced by more expensive flights. Within rail and air travel, it may be the case that people move up from standard to premier class.

4.7. Changes over Time

In estimating Engel curve-type relationships for services in India, we analysed a cross section of households at two points in time: 1993–94 and 2004–05. The analysis suggested that at a given point in time, richer households spend a higher proportion of their budget on services. For this to imply that households spend a larger proportion of their budget on services as they get richer over time, we assume that richer households provide a good prediction for how poor households will spend their money when their income rises. This is a plausible assumption followed in most studies estimating Engel curves. It may be argued, however, that this does not necessarily hold as tastes across households may vary. Unfortunately, we cannot carry out panel data analysis at the level of the household, as the two surveys do not cover the same households.

Table 4.10 shows that during the period from 1993–94 to 2004–05, both mean household expenditure per capita and mean percentage of household expenditure spent on services has increased. This supports the results of our cross-sectional econometric analysis. To substantiate this finding, we carry out a Blinder-Oaxaca decomposition exercise using our results of the two repeated cross sections at the household level and even undertake panel data analysis at the level of 'regions'.

Table 4.10. *Some time-series evidence*

	Mean (1993–94)	Mean (2004–05)
Percentage of Household Expenditure Spent on Aggregate Services	10.5 %	12.7 %
Total Household Expenditure per Capita (nominal terms) (Rupees per month)	432	852
Total Household Expenditure per Capita (real terms) (Rupees per month)	384	455

Source: Author's estimates based on primary data from National Sample Survey Organisation.

4.7.1. Blinder-Oaxaca Decomposition

On the basis of our results from the econometric analysis of two repeated cross sections (instrumental variable specification of the Tobit model), we undertake a Blinder-Oaxaca decomposition exercise to decompose the change in household budget share allocated to the service categories under consideration in the aggregate between 1993–94 and 2004–05 into a part that is 'explained' by changes in a vector of explanatory variables and a part that cannot be 'explained' by these changes. The vector of explanatory variables includes total household expenditure, household size, age, sex and education level of the household head, proportion of household members in different age-sex categories, dummy variables for household caste and religion and district dummy variables interacted with a dummy variable for urban areas. The decomposition exercise is carried out for the all-India sample.

Over the eleven-year period from 1993–94 to 2004–05, mean proportion of household expenditure on the service categories under consideration in the aggregate increased from 10.5 per cent to 12.7 per cent. Table 4.11 presents a decomposition of this growth in the proportion of household expenditure on services using two alternative decomposition formulae. When the coefficients of either 1993–94 or 2004–05 are used, the effect of a change in mean characteristics of households accounts for about 77 per cent of the increase in budget share allocated to services. This constitutes the 'explained' part of the decomposition. In fact, it is the difference in mean real[18] household

---

[18] Deflated using the Consumer Price Index for Agricultural Labourers for rural areas and the Consumer Price Index for Urban Non-Manual Employees for Urban areas.

Table 4.11. *Decomposition of an increase in household budget
share allocated to services: 1993–94 to 2004–05*

Percentage change due to:	Based on means of 2004–05 and coefficients of 1993–94	Based on means of 1993–94 and coefficients of 2004–05
Mean Characteristics:	77.0	76.0
Total Household Expenditure	67.0	67.0
Coefficients	23.0	24.0

Source: Derived from regression estimates based on primary data from National Sample Survey Organisation.

expenditure that accounts for about 67 per cent of the increase in household budget share allocated to services. This implies that income effects are paramount. The 'unexplained' part of the decomposition (changes in the coefficients of mean characteristics and the intercept), which accounts for only 23 per cent of the increase in budget share allocated to services, may reflect relative price changes. This is because along with changes in total household expenditure, changes in relative prices may affect the quantity demanded of a particular service, which, in turn, may affect the household budget share allocated to that particular good or service.

4.7.2. Panel Data Analysis at the Level of Regions

Even though the surveys on household expenditure conducted by India's NSSO do not cover the same households over time, estimates are comparable at the 'below-state' level. In particular, they are representative at the level of 'regions', which are collections of several districts grouped together on the basis of similar agro-climatic conditions. They are not administrative units. The NSSO has delineated a total of seventy-eight regions in the country.

Given the above, we estimate Engel curves for the six service categories under consideration in the aggregate, and for each individually, at the level of 'regions' over time. In doing so, we use a fixed-effects model. The estimation is carried out only for the all-India sample.

$$SERVICESPROP_{jt} = \alpha + \beta \log(TOTALEXP)_{jt} + \gamma X_{jt} + \eta_j + \varepsilon_{jt} \qquad (4.8)$$

$$EDUPROP_{jt} = \alpha + \beta \log(TOTALEXP)_{jt} + \gamma X_{jt} + \eta_j + \varepsilon_{jt} \qquad (4.9)$$

$$HEALTHPROP_{jt} = \alpha + \beta \log(TOTALEXP)_{jt} + \gamma X_{jt} + \eta_j + \varepsilon_{jt} \qquad (4.10)$$

$$ENTPROP_{jt} = \alpha + \beta \log(TOTALEXP)_{jt} + \gamma X_{jt} + \eta_j + \varepsilon_{jt} \qquad (4.11)$$

$$PERSONALPROP_{jt} = \alpha + \beta \log(TOTALEXP)_{jt} + \gamma X_{jt} + \eta_j + \varepsilon_{jt} \qquad (4.12)$$

$$COMMPROP_{jt} = \alpha + \beta \log(TOTALEXP)_{jt} + \gamma X_{jt} + \eta_j + \varepsilon_{jt} \qquad (4.13)$$

$$TRANSPROP_{jt} = \alpha + \beta \log(TOTALEXP)_{jt} + \gamma X_{jt} + \eta_j + \varepsilon_{jt} \qquad (4.14)$$

The above equations describe how the proportion of household expenditure allocated to a service, averaged for the region, is affected by average real household expenditure in a region,[19] controlling for a number of other factors. The vector of control variables is reformulated for regions as the unit of analysis[20] and in this case also includes 'region' fixed effects and state domestic product. Yet, there may be unobservables which affect both the level of average household expenditure and the average household budget share allocated to a particular service. As before, this could include household tastes, such as preference for quality. In an analysis over time, this may also include changes in relative prices[21] or in the availability of different services.

To address the potential endogeneity bias from unobservables, we use average household expenditure in a state as an instrument for average household expenditure in a region. The two are likely to be highly correlated, and this is validated by the test for instrument relevance (see Table 4.12 for the first-stage F-statistic). It may be argued that changes in average household expenditure in a state are correlated with changes in overall income in the state, which, in turn, are an important determinant of changes in the availability of services in different areas. Given that changing availability is likely to influence household budget share allocated to a service, this suggests that our instrument will not meet the instrument exogeneity criteria. However, because state domestic product is included, any state-specific variation in

[19] Deflated using the Consumer Price Index for Agricultural Labourers for rural areas and the Consumer Price Index for Urban Non-Manual Employees for Urban areas.

[20] It includes average household size, proportion of households classified as scheduled caste, scheduled tribe or other backward class, proportion of household classified as *Hindus*, average proportion of household members in different age-sex categories, proportion of households with male heads, proportion of households in each of the three education levels for household heads, the average age of household heads and the proportion of households located in urban areas.

[21] Chapter 3 showed that during the period from 1993–94 to 2004–05, the price of services did not increase notably, relative to the price of non-services.

Table 4.12. *Engel curve for services: 'Region' fixed-effects model*

Dependent Variable: Average Proportion of Household Expenditure on Services

Explanatory Variable ↓	All-India (OLS)	All-India (IV)
Log of Average Household Expenditure	0.096***	0.091***
	[0.017]	[0.029]
Constant	0.211	–0.331***
	[0.597]	[0.581]
Vector of Control Variables	Yes	Yes
First-Stage F-Statistic	–	14.03
Observations	152	152

Note: Standard errors in brackets; ***p<0.01, **p<0.05, *p<0.1
Source: Regression estimates based on primary data from National Sample Survey Organisation.

availability of services is already controlled for. We cannot conduct a test of over-identifying restrictions because we could not find a second suitable instrumental variable.

Table 4.12 shows that at the level of 'regions', as average total household expenditure increases, the (average) household budget share allocated to the six service categories under consideration, in the aggregate, increases. This reinforces the results of the cross-sectional analysis. It also holds true for each of the six categories individually.[22]

4.8. Conclusion

The rapid growth of the services sector in India, which constituted 57 per cent of the country's GDP in 2010, is now well documented. Chapter 3 included an analysis of macroeconomic data, which suggested that high-income elasticity of household final demand may be an important explanation for the growth of India's services sector. However, these data, based on National Accounts, do not permit a precise split of private final consumption expenditure into a goods and a services component. Hence, to explore the importance of high-income elasticity of demand for services as an explanation for the increasing share of the services sector in total output, we used household survey data for a sample of over 120,000 households at two points in time – 1993–94 and 2004–05 – to estimate Engel curve-type

---

[22] Estimates are available with the author.

relationships for six types of services: education, health, entertainment, personal, communication and transport. These services accounted for about half of India's services GDP in 2005 and many of them were characterised by high rates of growth between 1993–94 and 2004–05. Importantly, the survey data used cover household expenditure in highly disaggregated categories, thereby enabling us to capture expenditure on services per se rather than on services and goods for a category of service expenditure. Such an exercise has not been attempted in the literature on India, or indeed elsewhere.

Following the literature, we estimated these relationships using a Tobit model because the problem of zero expenditure in consumption data renders OLS estimates inconsistent. Our results revealed that each services category under consideration can be classified as a luxury good – a mirror image of Engel's Law for food – both in 1993–94 and 2004–05. This implies that as total household income or expenditure increases, education, health, entertainment, personal, communication and transport services – both individually and in the aggregate – take up a larger share of household budgets. Non-linearities in the Engel curves were not found to be robust, being driven by outliers – few very rich households. This indicates that there is a consistent increase in the household budget share allocated to these services as total expenditure increases, thereby implying that they are luxury goods at all levels of income. To ensure the robustness of our results, we estimated the Tobit model in an instrumental variable specification and even used an alternative estimator – censored quantile regressions. These specifications also revealed upward-sloping Engel curves for all categories of services, thereby reinforcing our earlier results. The results from the censored quantile regressions also showed that as total household expenditure increases, the increase in the household budget share allocated to a particular service increases more for high-consumption (conditional on household size, social group, religion, age-sex composition and age, gender and level of education of household head) than for low-consumption (conditional on the same set of variables) households. This is likely to represent tastes or preferences of households.

The aforementioned analysis was cross-sectional, and not panel data, as the surveys under consideration do not cover the same households over time. Hence, it suggests that at a given point in time, richer households spend a higher proportion of their budget on services. For this to imply that households spend a larger proportion of their budget on services as they get richer over time, we assumed that richer households provide a good prediction for how poor households will spend their money when their income rises. This is a plausible assumption. But we also analysed changes over time in two ways. First, using the results of the two cross-section models, we carried out a Blinder-Oaxaca decomposition exercise, which suggested that increases in mean household expenditure are paramount in explaining increases in the mean household budget share allocated to services during the period from 1993–94 to 2004–05. Second, we carried out panel data analysis at the level of 'regions'. This showed that as average household expenditure of a 'region' increases, so does the average household budget share allocated to the six categories of services under consideration.

In sum, Engel curve-type relationships established for six types of services and for these services in the aggregate using household consumption data reveal that services take up a larger share of household budgets as incomes or expenditures increase. Given that these services account for almost half of India's services GDP, this rigorous micro-econometric analysis lends credence to the view that high expenditure or income elasticies of demand for services are an important explanation for the increasing importance of the services sector in India. The explanation of high-income elasticity of demand for services in India – unusual for a country of its level of development – may lie in increasing inequality of incomes and household preferences that have led to the introduction of a host of consumer services which households can spend on (Rakshit, 2007). For education and health services, it may reflect peoples' perception – even at lower levels of income – about the quality of private versus public provision. For example, as total household income increases, individuals may shift their child from a government-subsidised municipal school to a private one. It is worth noting that the results of this research do not preclude the importance of other possible explanations for the growth of India's services sector, as identified in Chapter 3.

FIVE

The Services Sector in India

Inside the Black Box

5.1. Introduction

Chapter 2 highlighted the fact that most service-sector activities produce non-tangible, non-storable, non-physical products, as opposed to the tangible, storable and physical products of the agricultural and industrial sectors. Chapter 4 showed that the different categories of services are similar if not homogenous inasmuch as they are all 'luxury goods'. But it is also clear that the services sector in India, like elsewhere, covers a wide range of economic activities which may differ from each other in several ways. In the literature on the subject so far, however, economists have treated the services sector as a black box in much the same way as they treated technology for a long time.[1] Often, services are seen as a residual. Sometimes, services are seen as a composite category that is diverse, yet homogenous enough for the purpose of economic analysis. Importantly, aggregates may conceal more than they reveal. Therefore, any meaningful analysis of the role of the services sector in the process of development needs to be carried out at a disaggregated level. As a result, the object of this chapter is to look inside the black box of the services sector. Such an exercise has not been attempted in the literature, either for India or elsewhere.

The chapter seeks to disaggregate the service sector in India with reference to a set of ten attributes to provide an analysis of its characteristics, which may differ significantly across sub-sectors. The choice of attributes is determined by their relevance in analysing certain characteristics of development, as suggested by economic theory. These attributes are divided into five broad categories: structural characteristics, employment characteristics, factor-use

---

[1] See Rosenberg (1982). The title of the book, *Inside the Black Box: Technology and Economics*, is most appropriate.

characteristics, productivity-enhancing technology characteristics and international trade characteristics. Let us analyse each category briefly, in turn.

First, we use three structural characteristics in our analysis: the distinction between organized and unorganized economic activity, the distinction between public provision and private provision and the distinction between intermediate and final demand. These structural characteristics provide a description of the basic nature of economic activity in different service sectors. They are also useful in analyzing the nature of different services in the context of the other sets of characteristics that we consider.

Second, we consider one employment characteristic: educational barriers to entry for job seekers. It reflects the ease or difficulty of securing employment for a predominantly unskilled labour force. An analysis of this characteristic is important, because growth accounting exercises show us that, in part, economic growth may be explained by factor accumulation (at given levels of productivity). Hence, employment creation in a sector may be associated with growth as long as that expansion of employment does not involve a corresponding contraction of employment in other sectors. Furthermore, the inclusiveness of economic growth is a function of the employment it creates for ordinary people. In fact, an analysis of this characteristic becomes especially important given trends which show that the services sector has not been generating employment commensurate to its output growth (discussed in Chapter 1).

Third, the productivity-enhancing technology characteristics we analyse comprise economies of scale, contribution to technological progress and the incorporation of technological advance. An analysis of these characteristics is necessary to explain why the services sector could be driving productivity growth and hence economic growth in India. In a way, it also lends perspective to a seminal paper by Baumol (1967) in which he argues that, unlike manufacturing, services, because of their relatively labour-intensive nature, permit only sporadic increases in productivity.

Fourth, we analyse the trade of different services in international markets. For many years, services were essentially considered to be non-traded or non-tradable. In recent years, however, rapid technological progress in transport and communications has made several services tradable. Analyzing the trade of different services in world markets is a useful exercise because international trade is associated with economic growth. Importantly, an analysis of factors such as economies of scale, contribution to technological progress, the incorporation of technological advance, international trade and employment creation lends perspective to the sustainability of services-led growth in India.

Fifth, we analyse two characteristics which are indicative of the nature of factor use: capital intensity and skill intensity. These characteristics reveal the importance of physical capital and human capital, relative to unskilled labour, in the organization of production. This is relevant as the relative importance of different factors of production is likely to reflect the nature of growth in a particular sector, which in turn may have implications for poverty and inequality.

The structure of the chapter is as follows. Section 5.2 provides a brief discussion of the economic activities carried out in different service sectors, as specified by India's National Accounts Statistics. Section 5.3 explains the methodology used to develop a taxonomy for the services sector in India. Section 5.4 develops a taxonomy which disaggregates the services sector in order to assess the relative importance of the chosen set of attributes in each of the sub-sectors. Section 5.5 draws implications from the taxonomy. Section 5.6 presents conclusions.

5.2. A Brief Description of the Different Services Sectors

The following is a brief description of the economic activities included in different services sectors. The choice of the level of disaggregation is determined by two factors. First, to a large extent, it classifies the services sector into categories that are appropriate to facilitate meaningful economic analysis. Second, much of the data on the selected variables are not available beyond this level of aggregation. The following section may be somewhat mundane and descriptive, but it is imperative in providing us with an understanding of the nature of activities performed in the services sector. The description of activities included in the different sub-sectors of services is based on information provided in India's National Accounts Statistics (CSO, 2007a).

5.2.1. Wholesale and Retail Trade

Wholesale and retail trade involves the sale and purchase of commodities between individuals or enterprises. Wholesale trade consists of enterprises which sell goods to retailers, industries, commercial establishments, institutional users or to other wholesalers. Retail trade consists of enterprises which sell goods for personal or household consumption. In addition, the sector also includes services rendered by purchase and selling agents, brokers and auctioneers.

5.2.2. Hotels and Restaurants

The nature of economic activity in this sector is self-explanatory. It includes services rendered by hotels and other lodging places, restaurants, cafes and other eating or drinking places.

5.2.3. Railways

The railways are a state monopoly, which provide both passenger and freight services. The manufacture of coaches and wagons and the construction of tracks are excluded from output estimates of the railways sector.[2]

5.2.4. Transport by Other Means

Transport by other means consists of three major segments: air transport, road transport (mechanized and non-mechanized) and water transport. The air transport segment is characterized by an oligopolistic market structure (dominated by a few large publicly owned and privately owned corporations), where passenger services are more important, relative to cargo services. Moreover, like the railways, it is characterized by homogeneity in forms of transportation.

Road transport services are a heterogeneous mix that range from passenger services provided by buses, metro rail systems (or equivalents), taxis and rickshaws to freight services provided by trucks. Similarly, the water transport segment consists of passenger and freight services provided by large ships, boats, canoes and rafts. Unlike the railways and air transport, road transport and water transport are characterized by heterogeneity in modes of transportation. The sector also includes services incidental to transport. Examples of such services are economic activities of the Airport Authority of India and supporting services to water transport.

5.2.5. Storage

This sector consists of the provision of warehousing facilities for storing all types of goods. There is a public-sector component, which consists of

---

[2] Railway manufacturing establishments such as Chittaranjan Locomotive Works, Integral Coach Factory, Diesel Locomotive Works, and Wheel & Axle Plant are included under 'manufacturing' activities. Moreover, construction activity of the Railways is included in the 'construction' sector.

the Central Warehousing Corporation and various state warehousing corporations, and a private-sector component, which consists primarily of
warehousing facilities for cold storage.

5.2.6. Communications

The communications sector comprises two major segments: postal services
which include the delivery of letters, telegrams and parcels and telecommunication services which consist of the provision of landline telephone
connections, public call office booths, cellular telephone connections
and Internet services. For much of the time since independence, both
segments of this sector were public-sector monopolies. In fact, until the
mid-1980s, these services were provided by an integrated Department of
Post and Telecom. Subsequently, the department was divided into different companies whereby postal services were delivered by INDIA POST,
and telecommunication services were delivered by MTNL (Mahanagar
Telephone Nigam Limited) and VSNL (Videsh Sanchar Nigam Limited).
In recent years, however, a private-sector component has emerged. While
several courier service companies rival INDIA POST in providing postal
services, large corporations such as the Tatas, Reliance and Airtel are now
major players in the provision of both telephone (cellular and landline) and
Internet services.

5.2.7. Finance (Banking and Insurance)

This sector consists of two types of institutions: banking and non-banking
financial intermediaries. Banking intermediaries comprise services provided by commercial banks, post-office savings banks and cooperative
credit societies. For many years, these services were dominated by the public sector. Non-banking financial institutions consist of companies that
provide insurance services, long-term lending, institutional lending and
mutual fund services. Over the years, these services have also been characterized by a large public-sector component.[3]

The banking and insurance sector in India is in the process of change. Its
dynamism is reflected in the fact that financial-sector reforms have liberalized the sector, which has resulted in the entry of both domestic private

[3] Life insurance provided by the Life Insurance Corporation (LIC), postal life insurance
(PLI), Employees State Insurance (ESI), and Employees Provident Fund Organisation
(EPFO).

corporations and foreign participants into the sector. This greater private participation has dismantled the dividing line between banking and non-banking financial institutions. For instance, there are now several large corporations providing banking services and other financial services such as mutual fund management, equity management and long-term lending.

5.2.8. Real Estate and Renting Services

Real estate consists of services provided by operators, developers and agents connected with real estate. It includes buying, selling, renting and operating of owned or leased real estate such as apartment buildings, dwellings and non-residential buildings. It also includes ownership of dwellings, which consists of residential houses acquired on rent and the imputed value of owner-occupied dwellings. Renting services consist of individuals involved in renting out transport equipment, machinery and other equipment as well as personal and household goods to consumers.

5.2.9. Business Services

Broadly speaking, this sector may be divided into two segments: information-technology-enabled services and conventional business services. The former consists of computers-related activities including software consultancy and supply, hardware consultancy, business process outsourcing, call centres and data processing. These services relate to the 'knowledge economy' or 'new economy' where information flows more easily and the importance of location is diminished. The latter segment comprises the more conventional business services such as accounting activities, auditing and tax consultancy services, legal services, management consultancy, market research, advertising, architectural, engineering and other technical activities. Until recently, several of these conventional business services were provided in-house by manufacturing establishments.

5.2.10. Public Administration and Defence

This sector represents the governmental arm of the economy, which guides the socio-economic policy of the country. It comprises government departments and other administrative entities at different levels of government: central, provincial and local. The activities covered under these administrative departments relate to organs of state dealing with defence services, law and justice, external affairs, general administrative services like the police and fiscal services such as collection of taxes and servicing of debt. What is more, governments provide public goods for citizens. These often relate to services which cannot otherwise be conveniently and economically provided by private agents.

5.2.11. Community Services

This sector primarily consists of education and health services.[4] Education services include services provided by schools and colleges in the public and private sector (recognized by the government), unorganized educational institutions, coaching centres and individuals providing private tutoring. Health services consist of medical services provided by government hospitals, privately owned hospitals, nursing homes, clinics and mobile clinics. The sector also includes activities of membership organizations, international organizations and other extraterritorial bodies.

5.2.12. Personal, Recreational and Entertainment Services

Analytically, it may be useful to divide this sector into two broad segments. First, there is a personal-services segment that consists of domestic services provided by maids and servants, sanitary services, hairdressing, beauty treatment, custom tailoring, laundry services, hawkers, building caretakers, home security guards, car park attendants and so on. Second, there is a miscellaneous segment which comprises entertainment services as well as cultural, sporting and other recreational activities.

5.3. Methodology for Developing a Taxonomy of the Services Sector in India

It is important to reiterate that the object of the chapter is to look inside the black box of the services sector. In doing so, each service sub-sector is analysed in the context of ten economic attributes.

5.3.1. An Illustrative Example

Consider the distinction between public and private provision in economic activity, an attribute used in our taxonomy that follows. Table 5.1 presents data on the share of the public sector in the GDP of different services sectors for the period from 1993–94 to 2008–09.

---

[4]   Health services include both human health and veterinary services.

Table 5.1. *Share of the public sector in the GDP*
of a services sector: 1993–94 to 2008–09

Sector	Public-Sector Component as a Percentage of the Gross Domestic Product of the Sector
Wholesale and Retail Trade	3.8
Hotels and Restaurants	2.1
Railways	100
Transport by Other Means	26.2
Storage	30.4
Communication	56.9
Banking and Insurance	55.9
Real Estate, Renting and Business Services	0.5
Public Administration and Defence	100
Other Community, Social and Personal services	34.0

Note: The figures are rounded off to the first decimal.
Source: Central Statistical Organisation, National Accounts Statistics.

The numbers presented in Table 5.1 are simple averages computed using annual data for the period under consideration. For the taxonomy in general, our analysis covers the period from 1980–81 to 2008–09. There are two reasons for this choice of the time period. First, there are constraints imposed by the availability of data. Whereas data on variables taken from National Accounts Statistics are available from 1950–1951 onwards, this is not true for data on other selected attributes. Second, the period from 1980–81 to 2008–09 saw a dramatic increase in the share of the services sector in GDP, while the share of the industrial sector in GDP remained largely constant (Chapter 1). Furthermore, 1980–81 is considered a turning point in India's growth process as it represented a marked acceleration in India's economic growth following independence (Rodrik and Subramanian, 2005).

The use of simple averages is attributable to the fact that a single number enables us to define unique threshold points for the variable in question. At the same time, it may be argued that over a long period of time, variables could display distinct trends. This would imply that the threshold points might differ from year to year. However, most of the variables in the subsequent analysis are characterized by fluctuations around a constant value as opposed to a discernible trend. For example, the division between public-sector and private-sector activity during the period from 1980–81 to 2008–09 would entail a discernible trend, because the process

Table 5.2. *Share of the public sector in total output for
different services sectors: Z-scores*

Sector	Z-scores
Wholesale and Retail Trade	−0.95
Hotels and Restaurants	−1.00
Railways	1.90
Transport by Other Means	−0.29
Storage	−0.16
Communication	0.62
Banking and Insurance	0.59
Real Estate, Renting Services and Business Services	−1.00
Public Administration and Defence	1.90
Other Social, Community and Personal Services	−0.06

Note: Z-score = (Value − Mean) / Standard Deviation.
Source: author's estimates.

of deregulation and privatization began in the early 1990s. Hence, for this variable, we consider the time period from 1993–94 to 2008–09.

Table 5.2 presents the corresponding Z-scores for the numbers used in our illustrative example. The data appear to be normally distributed, given that we find an approximately linear normal probability plot[5] and the fact that 95 per cent of the observations lie within two standard deviations of the mean. The z-scores shown in Table 5.2 indicate the number of standard deviations away from the mean a particular value is. Hence, a z-score of −0.95 implies that for wholesale and retail trade, the share of the public sector in total output is 0.95 standard deviations below the mean. In contrast, a z-score of 1.90 implies that for public administration and defence services, the share of the public sector in total output is 1.90 standard deviations above the mean. Given that the data are normally distributed, around 50 per cent of all observations fall within 0.67 standard deviations above or below the mean. All observations with values within this range are classified into the 'part public, part private' category. As a corollary, observations which are more than 0.67 standard deviations above the mean are classified into the 'largely public' category whereas those that are more than 0.67 standard deviations below the mean are classified into the 'largely private' category. Using this formal statistical technique as a means of classification, we classify the different sectors in to the following categories.

[5] Not reported for reasons of space.

LARGELY PUBLIC: Railways, Public Administration and Defence
LARGELY PRIVATE: Wholesale and Retail Trade, Hotels and Restaurants, Real Estate, Renting and Business Services
PART PUBLIC, PART PRIVATE: Transport, Storage, Communication, Banking and Insurance, Other Community, Social and Personal Services

In this way, the aforementioned statistical technique divides each chosen attribute in the taxonomy into three broad categories. Subsequently, for each attribute, each service sector is placed into one of the three categories. While the use of this formal statistical technique involves a subjective judgement in deciding the thresholds which classify a characteristic into categories of 'high', 'medium' and 'low', it introduces a degree of objectivity into the classification criteria. Unfortunately, for certain attributes, the data only allow us to compute the relevant threshold points for certain sectors at a level of aggregation that may not facilitate meaningful economic analysis. Two groupings of individual service activities – real estate, renting and business services and other social, community and business services – are a case in point. These two groupings are characterized by considerable internal diversity which, in the context of different attributes, may result in a mischaracterization of individual services by virtue of them being clubbed together. Hence, to disaggregate these groupings for the purpose of classification, we use other available information. This enables us to arrive at qualified, but reasonable, conclusions.

In the case of a few characteristics for which the data series are not close to being normally distributed, using normal deviations above and below the mean value results in a classification of sectors which appears somewhat counter-intuitive. Median-based formal statistical techniques, such as an analysis of percentiles, also result in similar problems. Hence, for these characteristics, we draw thresholds based on an intuitive judgement and patterns in the data. For instance, in our illustrative example, using the data presented in Table 5.1, we may adopt the following classification criteria:

1. If the public-sector component is more than 80 per cent of the GDP of the sector, we classify the sector as 'largely public'.
2. If the public-sector component is less than 20 per cent of the GDP of the sector, we classify the sector as 'largely private'.
3. Sectors which do not satisfy either of the previous two criteria, and are somewhere between the two thresholds, are classified as 'part public, part private'.

Hence, two thresholds are drawn using data on the share of the public sector in the GDP of different sub-sectors of services: the public sector component equal to 80 per cent of total output of a sector and the public sector component equal to 20 per cent of total output of a sector. This divides the attribute into three categories: largely public, largely private, and part public, part private. Consequently, each sector is placed into one of the three categories. According to the criteria presented above, we classify the different sectors into the following categories.

LARGELY PUBLIC: Railways, Public Administration and Defence
LARGELY PRIVATE: Wholesale and Retail Trade, Hotels and Restaurants, Real Estate, Renting and Business Services
PART PUBLIC, PART PRIVATE: Transport, Storage, Communication, Banking and Insurance, Other Community, Social and Personal Services

This classification is identical to the previous one where we used a formal statistical technique based on normal deviates above and below the mean. Hence, even though thresholds derived in this way may appear somewhat arbitrary, it leads to sensible cut-off points. This is especially true in the case of skewed data which exhibit distinct patterns. Given these findings, in the context of the few characteristics for which the data are not close to being normally distributed, we rely on our intuitive judgement looking at patterns in the data to draw thresholds for the purpose of classification. In fact, these thresholds – drawn on the basis of our intuitive judgement – are fairly robust in that minor alterations to the thresholds in either direction do not change the classifications for different sectors.

5.4. The Taxonomy

The following is a set of attributes which enable a disaggregation of the services sector in India in a way that facilitates meaningful economic analysis: (1) organized versus unorganized economic activity; (2) public provision versus private provision; (3) intermediate versus final consumption; (4) educational barriers to entry for job seekers; (5) capital intensity; (6) skill intensity; (7) economies of scale; (8) trade in international markets; (9) contribution to technological progress; and (10) incorporation of technological advance. Chapter 2 highlighted statistical difficulties associated with National Accounts Statistics that impose constraints on an analysis of the services sector. In particular, this relates to the problem of defining services output and using unreliable constant price estimates of services output to make comparisons with other sectors of the economy. Importantly, the data for many attributes in our taxonomy are based on sample survey data for households and firms. Moreover, for attributes which are analysed using

National Accounts data, the problems associated with its use are reduced because the focus of our taxonomy is the services sector alone.

5.4.1. Organized versus Unorganized Economic Activity

In general, the informal or unorganized sector is larger and hence relatively more important for developing countries (Gerxhani, 2004). This is attributable to weak legal frameworks, property rights and contract enforcement mechanisms (Pratap and Quintin, 2006). India is no different (NSSO, 2001). The unorganized sector (defined in the context of India's National Accounts Statistics in Chapter 2) assumes importance as it creates employment opportunities for unskilled workers. At the same time, the absence of contracts, the non-applicability of labour laws and the lack of employment benefits may render the quality of such employment questionable. The relative importance of organized and unorganized segments within a service sector can be measured in terms of their share in output or employment. We choose to use output data because they are more complete. This is attributable to the fact that data on employment are based on sample surveys that are conducted only every five years, whereas national accounts statistics provide data on output every year. Table 5.3 presents data on the share of the organized segment in the net domestic product (NDP)[6] of different services sectors for the period from 1993–94 to 2007–08. The choice of time period is determined by the availability of data on output, disaggregated into organized and unorganized economic activity.

Using these data, on the basis of normal deviations above and below the mean, we classify the different sub-sectors into the following categories. Furthermore, to disaggregate two large groupings – real estate, renting and business services and other social, community and personal services – we use other available information to make common-sense inferences.

LARGELY ORGANIZED: Communication, Banking and Insurance, Public Administration and Defence, Business Services, Railways, Community Services
LARGELY UNORGANIZED: Wholesale and Retail Trade, Real Estate and Renting Services, Personal, Recreational and Entertainment Services
PART ORGANIZED, PART UNORGANIZED: Hotels and Restaurants, Storage, Transport by Other Means

---

[6] We take shares of organized and unorganized segments in the Net Domestic Product of different sectors instead of the Gross Domestic Product of different sectors because national accounts statistics provide data on only the former.

Table 5.3. *Share of organized segment in the net domestic product of a services sector: 1993–94 to 2007–08*

Sector	Organized segment as a percentage of the net domestic product of the sector	Z-scores
Wholesale and Retail Trade	17.6	−1.37
Hotels and Restaurants	40.6	−0.63
Railways	100	1.26
Transport by Other Means	40.2	−0.64
Storage	49.4	−0.35
Communication	81.9	0.69
Banking and Insurance	90.2	0.95
Real Estate and Renting and Business Services	20.8	−1.26
Public Administration and Defence	100	1.26
Other Community, Social and Personal services	63.3	0.09

Note: The numbers are simple averages of annual data for the period from 1993–94 to 2007–08. The figures are rounded off to the first decimal.
Source: Central Statistical Organisation, National Accounts Statistics.

In recent years, there has been a sharp increase in the share of the organized sector in the combined NDP of real estate, renting and business services – from about 6 per cent in 1993–94 to 39 per cent in 2007–08. At the same time, there has been a comparable increase in the share of business services in this combined NDP – from about 13 per cent in 1993–94 to about 57 per cent in 2007–08. This suggests that the business services sector is 'largely organized'. Moreover, given that the organized sector accounts for about 20 per cent of the combined NDP of real estate and renting services and business services, it is likely to constitute less than 20 per cent of the NDP of the former, thereby placing it in the 'largely unorganized' category.

A study by India's National Commission for Enterprises in the Unorganized Sector, using an average for two points in time – 1999–2000 and 2004–05 – estimates that the organized sector constituted about 81.3 per cent of the GDP of education and health services. What is more, services provided by membership organizations – the third component of community services – are likely to be entirely organized. Hence, it is reasonable to classify community services as being are 'largely organized'. Finally, whereas radio and TV broadcasting and other recreational and entertainment services are likely to be organized economic activity, the unorganized sector is likely to be dominant in the delivery of personal services such as domestic services, laundry services, tailoring and barber shops. But data show that during the period from 1993–94 to 2007–08, the share of personal services constituted more than 75 per cent of the GDP of this grouping. Hence, we classify personal, recreational and entertainment services as being 'largely unorganized'.

Let us now consider whether the previously outlined classifications, resulting from our analysis of the data, conform to economic intuition.

5.4.1.1. Largely Organized

Public administration and defence services represent the governmental arm of the economy. By definition, these services lie exclusively within the domain of the public sector. The same holds true for the railways. Hence, it is only logical that these sectors are classified as 'largely organized'. Similarly, the classification of communication and financial services as sectors that are 'largely organized' is only to be expected, as both these sectors were public-sector monopolies for much of the time after independence (Panagariya, 2002). Moreover, in recent years, although private participation has emerged, it is limited to large corporations which, in the case of telecommunication and insurance, coexist in oligopolistic market structures (Jain, 2004). The classification of business services as being 'largely organized' should also come as no surprise given that software, accountancy, business process outsourcing and consulting services are provided by large, medium and small firms that submit regular accounts of their economic activities. For community services, although the unorganized sector has a presence in education and health – through coaching centres and medical service providers that are not regulated under legal provisions – this presence is likely to be negligible relative to government providers and large privately run schools, colleges and hospitals. In addition, activities of membership organizations and international organizations are likely to be entirely organized.

5.4.1.2. Largely Unorganized

The classification of the wholesale and retail trade sector as 'largely unorganized' is robust in terms of economic intuition given that small, petty traders are dominant in the provision of these services. This is especially true for the retail trade segment (Joseph et al., 2008). The same holds true for personal services (domestic services, laundry services, hairdressing) which are provided primarily by individuals or small groups of individuals. The classification of the real estate and renting services sector as 'largely unorganized' should also come as no surprise given that it may consist of a large number of small firms that may not submit regular accounts of their economic activities (Nijman, 2000).

5.4.1.3. Part Organized, Part Unorganized

Hotels and restaurants and storage services are two sectors characterized as 'part organized, part unorganized'. This classification is intuitively plausible for the hotels and restaurants sector which is a combination of large hotel chains on the one hand and small catering and lodging service providers on the other. Similarly, this classification is only to be expected for the storage sector that is a combination of large public warehousing corporations and small private warehousing facilities. Finally, transport by other means is classified as 'part organized, part unorganized' because this middle category represents a mix of air transport services – 'largely organized' as they are dominated by a small number of large public and private firms – and road transport and water transport services – 'largely unorganized' given that they are dominated by small firms and even individuals.

5.4.2. Public versus Private Provision

The public sector in India consists of the following segments: administrative departments, departmental enterprises, non-departmental enterprises, subsidiaries of government companies and statutory corporations set up under special enactments of parliament or state legislatures (see Chapter 2 for a description). In the literature, privately provided services may be referred to as market services whereas publicly provided services may be referred to as non-market services (Caplan, 1998). This differentiates between services paid for directly by a consumer (industry or private household) and those paid for indirectly through taxes. However, it is important to note that some publicly provided services such as postal and railway services (departmental enterprises) may be paid for directly by consumers. Hence, not all publicly provided services are non-market services. Table 5.4 presents data on the share of the public sector in the GDP of different services sectors for the period from 1993–94 to 2008–09.

Using these data, on the basis of normal deviations above and below the mean, we classify the different sub-sectors into the following categories.

LARGELY PUBLIC: Public Administration and Defence, Railways
LARGELY PRIVATE: Wholesale and Retail Trade, Hotels and Restaurants, Real Estate and Renting Services, Business Services, Personal, Recreational and Entertainment Services

Table 5.4. *Share of the public sector in the GDP
of the services sector: 1993–94 to 2008–09*

Sector	Public-sector component as a percentage of the gross domestic product of the sector	Z-scores
Wholesale and Retail Trade	3.8	−0.95
Hotels and Restaurants	2.1	−1.00
Railways	100	1.90
Transport by Other Means	26.2	−0.29
Storage	30.4	−0.16
Communication	56.9	0.62
Banking and Insurance	55.9	0.59
Real Estate, Renting and Business Services	0.5	−1.00
Public Administration and Defence	100.0	1.90
Other Community, Social and Personal services	34.0	−0.06

Note: The numbers are simple averages of annual data for the period from 1993–94 to 2008–09. The figures are rounded off to the first decimal.

Source: Central Statistical Organization, National Accounts Statistics.

PART PUBLIC, PART PRIVATE: Transport by Other Means, Communication, Storage, Banking and Insurance, Community Services

The number measuring the size of the public sector in the combined GDP of real estate, renting and business services is used to classify each of its two components – real estate and renting services and business services – as 'largely private' because it is intuitively robust. For other social, community and personal services, we use other available information to make common-sense inferences. With the exception of radio and TV broadcasting and sanitary services, personal, recreational and entertainment services are likely to be entirely privately provided. Data show that during the period from 1993–94 to 2008–09, radio and TV broadcasting and sanitary services accounted for only about 17 per cent of the grouping's GDP. Furthermore, of this 17 per cent, only a certain fraction is publicly provided. Hence, we classify personal, recreational and entertainment services as being 'largely private'. In light of this, we make the simplifying assumption that the aforementioned grouping is entirely private, and compute the share of the public sector in the community services segment of other social, community and personal services to be 44.3 per cent over the period from 1993–94 to 2008–09. Hence, we classify community services as being 'part public, part private'.

Let us now analyse whether the previously described classifications, resulting from the data, conform to economic intuition.

5.4.2.1. Largely Public

It should come as no surprise that the public administration and defence is classified as 'largely public' because *the* sector represents the governmental arm of the economy. The same holds true for the railways, which are entirely publicly owned.

5.4.2.2. Largely Private

Wholesale and retail trade, hotels and restaurants,[7] real estate and renting services, business services, and personal, recreational and entertainment services are classified as 'largely private' as the government has traditionally had little or no involvement in these sectors.

5.4.2.3. Part Public, Part Private

There are some sectors in which both the public-sector and private-sector components are significant. We refer to them as 'part public, part private'. Storage, banking and insurance, communication and community services are four such sectors. The storage sector is a combination of public warehouses on the one hand and private warehousing facilities for cold storage on the other. Similarly, the banking and insurance sector consists of large national banks and other financial corporations owned by the government on the one hand and a number of large private corporations and small-scale moneylenders on the other (CSO, 2007a). Private-sector participation in the form of banking and insurance companies has grown rapidly over the last fifteen years (Prasad and Ghosh, 2007). Similarly, whereas postal and telecommunication services were state monopolies until the mid-1990s (Panagariya, 2002), private telephone service providers, Internet service providers and courier service firms entered the sector thereafter. Hence, while public-sector companies continue to remain important, they now coexist with widespread private participation. Finally, in the community services sector, while public service providers in education and health services are likely to be important in developing countries (Jimenez, 1994), private sector participation has increased in

---

[7] The government in India does own five-star hotels and other lodging places.

recent years, in the form of both large institutions and smaller coaching centres and clinics.

In contrast, the classification of transport by other means as 'part public, part private' may appear counter-intuitive. This result may be driven by the fact that despite the increased private-sector participation, public provision of air transport services continues to be important.

5.4.3. Intermediate Consumption versus Final Consumption

In considering sources of demand for services' output, it is useful to distinguish between final and intermediate demand. Final demand is based on the end-use customer. It refers to purchases of services by their ultimate users and it includes household consumption of services, government final consumption expenditure, and exports of services. Intermediate demand relates to the use of services as inputs. It refers to services sold to other firms and agencies for further production. In the literature, services predominantly serving intermediate demand are referred to as producer services, whereas those predominantly serving final demand are referred as consumer services (Illeris and Phillipe, 1993).

In an ideal world, we would measure the division between intermediate and final demand for a sector's output by analyzing data on final consumption expenditure, both private and government. Importantly, although this data is available from India's National Accounts Statistics, it is at a level of disaggregation that is different from what is used in the rest of our study. Hence, we identify the extent to which different services serve intermediate demand by analyzing input-output data from the input flow (absorption) matrix given in India's National Account Statistics. In doing so, we compute the share of a service sub-sector's output that is consumed as inputs by the different sectors of the economy. For example, in the case of wholesale and retail trade, we divide the flows of intermediate transactions from wholesale and retail trade to the entire economy by the sector's total output. Table 5.5 presents data on the share of output of different services sectors that satisfies intermediate demand in the economy from 1993–94 to 2006–07 – the first and last year for which these data are available.

Using these data, on the basis of normal deviations above and below the mean, we classify the different sub-sectors into the following categories.

RELATIVELY MORE INTERMEDIATE: Storage, Banking and Insurance
RELATIVELY MORE FINAL: Hotels and Restaurants, Public Administration and Defence, Real Estate and Renting Services, Community Services, Personal, Cultural and Recreational Services

Table 5.5. *Share of the GDP of a services sector that satisfies
intermediate demand: 1993–94 to 2006–07*

Sector	Percentage of a sector's output used as an input into further production	Z-scores
Wholesale and Retail Trade	50.1	0.39
Hotels and Restaurants	14.2	−0.69
Railways	58.6	0.64
Transport by Other Means	45.4	0.25
Storage	98.8	1.85
Communications	58.4	0.64
Banking and Insurance	78.6	1.24
Real Estate and Renting Services	1.7	−1.06
Business Services	34.6	−0.07
Public Administration and Defence	0.0	−1.11
Community Services	1.5	−1.07
Personal, Recreational and Entertainment Services	3.1	−1.02

Note: The numbers are simple averages for four points in time: 1993–94, 1998–99, 2003–04 and 2006–07. The figures are rounded off to the first decimal. For real estate, renting services and ownership of dwellings, business services, social and community services and personal, recreational and entertainment services, we take the average for 2003–04 and 2006–07 because relevant disaggregated data is not available for the two earlier years.
Source: Central Statistical Organisation, National Accounts Statistics.

PART INTERMEDIATE, PART FINAL: Wholesale and Retail Trade, Railways, Transport by Other Means, Communication, Business Services

Let us now analyse whether these classifications, based on our analysis of the data, conform to economic intuition.

5.4.3.1. Relatively More Intermediate

The classification of the storage services as 'relatively more intermediate' is intuitively robust as warehouse facilities are likely to be used heavily by producers in the agricultural and industrial sectors to store their goods for further use in future production. Similarly, the classification of financial services as 'relatively more intermediate' should come as no surprise for they serve as important inputs for agricultural, industrial and services output by facilitating the flow of resources necessary to establish production units.

5.4.3.2. Relatively More Final

The classification of hotels and restaurants, public administration and defence, real estate and renting services, community services and personal, recreational and entertainment services as 'relatively more final' is only to be expected, owing to the nature of activities of the sector, which are oriented towards consumption rather than use in further production. Hotels and restaurants provide lodging and catering services to consumers. Public administration and defence provides the country's citizens with defence services, law and justice, general administrative services like the police and fiscal services such as collection of taxes. It can be argued that some of these services are important in providing a secure environment for investors and entrepreneurs to carry out production. While this may be the case, the value of such inputs would not be reflected in input-output data as these services are not explicitly charged for. Real estate services include the services of agents who facilitate the sale and lease of property to citizens, and renting services include the services of people who rent out machinery, equipment and personal goods to consumers. Finally, community services – education and health – and personal, recreational and entertainment services are naturally relevant only for final consumption.

5.4.3.3. Part Final, Part Intermediate

The classification of wholesale and retail trade, railways and transport by other means as 'part final, part intermediate' is robust in terms of economic intuition. This is because while these industries serve final consumers – as buyers of goods and passengers – they also are important conduits for the distribution and sale of agricultural and industrial output. The same holds true for communication and business services. Communication services – post and telecommunications such as landline and mobile telephone connections – and business services such as accounting and legal services serve final demand. At the same time, telecommunication services and business services such as software, hardware and engineering services have become increasingly important inputs for manufacturing production. The use of software services has also become crucial in the delivery of several services such as banking, education and health.

5.4.4. Educational Barriers to Entry for Job Seekers

We identify the extent of educational barriers to entry for job seekers in a sector by analyzing education intensities – that is, the percentage of people in the sectoral labour force in two end-point 'education classes': illiterates and graduates. This is a plausible measure for barriers to entry for job seekers, guided by theories of 'human capital' (Becker, 1964; Schultz, 1961) and 'labour market signalling' (Arrow, 1973; Spence, 1976). Of course, there

Table 5.6. *Illiterates and graduates (and above) as a percentage of the labour force of different services sectors: 1983 to 2004–05*

Sector	Illiterates as a percentage of total labour force	Z-scores	Graduates (and above) as a percentage of total labour force	Z-scores
Wholesale and Retail Trade	23.8	0.70	10.0	−0.77
Hotels and Restaurants	25.1	0.81	4.2	−1.08
Railways	10.9	−0.38	16.2	−0.43
Transport by Other Means	24.9	0.79	3.5	−1.12
Storage	23.5	0.68	8.6	−0.84
Communication	1.8	−1.14	25.1	0.05
Banking and Insurance	1.2	−1.19	49.6	1.38
Real Estate and Renting Services	9.3	−0.51	17.9	−0.34
Business Services	1.8	−1.14	53.3	1.58
Public Administration and Defence	6.6	−0.74	27.4	0.17
Community Services	4.4	−0.92	46.3	1.20
Personal, Recreational and Entertainment Services	36.4	1.75	3.6	−1.11

Note: The numbers are simple averages for four points in time: 1983, 1987–88, 1993–94, 1999–2000 and 2004–05. The figures are rounded off to the nearest first decimal place. It is important to note that the rows do not add up to 100 as the labour force is divided into six education classes, four of which are not reported here.*Source*: National Sample Survey Organization, Surveys on Employment and Unemployment

may be several other factors such as access to capital and hiring policies of employers that also represent barriers to entry. For this variable, figures at an aggregate level have been tabulated using primary data. It is important to note that the data consists of seven education classes: not literate, literate without primary schooling, literate and up to primary schooling, primary school, middle school, secondary school and graduate and above. However, we choose to use data on only the end-point 'education classes', for two reasons. First, it provides a better distinction between sectors, which, in turn, facilitates more meaningful comparisons. Second, the inclusion of too many 'education classes' would make it difficult to draw thresholds. Table 5.6 presents data on illiterates and graduates as a percentage of the labour force for different services sectors for the period from 1983 to 2004–05.

Using these data, on the basis of normal deviations above and below the mean, we classify the different sectors into the following categories. For sectors to be classified as 'low' or 'high', the z-scores for both parameters (illiterates and graduates) must lie outside ±0.67 standard deviations of the mean.

LOW: Wholesale and Retail Trade, Hotels and Restaurants, Transport by Other Means, Storage, Personal, Recreational and Entertainment Services
MEDIUM: Railways, Communication, Real Estate and Renting Services, Public Administration
HIGH: Banking and Insurance, Business Services, Community Services

Let us now analyse whether these classifications, based on our analysis of the data, conform to economic intuition. It is worth reiterating that there may be some barriers to entry that have nothing to do with levels of education. Hence, for some sectors, basic education may be a necessary but not sufficient condition for gaining employment.

5.4.4.1. Low Educational Barriers to Entry for Job Seekers

Given the nature of activities involved, the possibility of securing a job in wholesale and retail trade or storage services is likely to be independent of education. This is especially so for the wholesale and retail trade sector, which is classified as 'largely unorganized'. The classification of personal, recreational and entertainment services as a sector with low barriers to entry should also come as no surprise. Personal services such as domestic services, sanitary services, laundry services and beauty treatment are unlikely to have educational requirements. Custom tailoring and hairdressing may require a certain element of specialized skill, but it relates more to innate ability or skills that can be learnt on the job in a short span of time. Similarly, cultural and sports activities require skills and training that can only be acquired over a long period of time.

For hotels and restaurants, educational barriers to entry are likely to be a function of the nature of different occupations in the sector. Entering the sector as a potential entrepreneur may require a basic level of education. Securing employment as managerial staff in large hotels and more upmarket restaurants would also require some basic level of education. Importantly, however, the number of people entering the sector as entrepreneurs or managers may be small relative to non-professional service providers such as gatekeepers, bellboys, cleaners, drivers in large hotels, waiters, kitchen staff and cleaners. These occupations are unlikely to entail any educational requirements, thereby making this sector largely free-entry.

The classification of transport by other means as having low barriers to entry requires careful analysis given that education intensities are likely to vary significantly across its different segments – air, water and road trans-port. Employment as a professional in the air transport segment is associ-ated with high educational barriers to entry. For instance, being a pilot or an engineer requires a relatively high level of education. Similarly, being part of the non-technical flight crew also requires a basic level of education and good English-language skills. At the same time, however, there is non-professional staff doing small chores in airline offices, at airports, providing cleaning services, and so forth. For these occupations, education require-ments are likely to be negligible. Furthermore, in the maritime industry, people employed in the shipping segment may require some basic educa-tion, but those employed in providing inland water transport services may not have an education requirement. Similarly, for road transport services, potential job seekers are unlikely to have any educational requirement. They may need to acquire a skill, which they can do in a short time frame at little or no cost – driving a taxi or bus, for example. Hence, an overall classifica-tion of low barriers to entry in the transport by other means sector may be because a larger number of people are employed in segments with few education requirements relative to those which are likely to have significant education requirements.

5.4.4.2. Medium Educational Barriers to Entry for Job Seekers

Real estate services comprise individuals performing tasks such as buying, selling, renting and operating owned or leased real estate. It is logical that these activities require individuals to have a basic level of education, which serves to constrain entry in this sector moderately. For the other sectors in this category, the 'medium' classification is attributable to the combination of 'high' and 'low' in different occupations.

The classification of the railways as a sector with medium educational barriers to entry is likely to be attributable to the combination of profes-sional staff – whether technical or administrative – which requires a rela-tively high level of education and non-professional staff doing clerical jobs in offices, small chores at railways stations and on trains, providing clean-ing services and so forth. Similarly, whereas administrative and manage-rial workers in the communications may require relatively high levels of education, a large majority of individuals employed for delivering letters, installing phone lines, operating public call office booths and providing cable television services are likely to require only a moderate level of edu-cation. In the public administration and defence sector, a high standard of education is a prerequisite for professional staff that gain employment through competitive public examinations. But for non-professional staff, which constitutes a large proportion of the numbers employed in the government sector, there is little or no education or skill requirement. Hence, its classification as a sector with medium barriers to entry should come as no surprise.

5.4.4.3. High Barriers to Entry for Job Seekers

Given the nature of activities included in banking and insurance services, a reasonably high standard of education is a prerequisite (typically an undergraduate degree for most professional staff) for gaining employment in the sector. Most business services including all information technology related activities, management consultancies, accountancy services and other technical services require high levels of education and specialized knowledge as well. The same holds true for community services – education and health. The education services sector, after all, consists of those who impart knowledge. In the health services segment, high levels of education are required not only for doctors, but also for nurses and other support staff.

5.4.5. Capital Intensity

We identify the capital intensity of a sector by analyzing the ratio of net capital stock to the total number of people employed. The capital-labour ratio is a standard measure of capital intensity used in the economics literature (Lim, 1976). Net capital stock[8] in India's National Accounts Statistics covers three types of assets: construction, machinery and equipment and software. Table 5.7 presents data on the ratio of net capital stock to the number of persons employed for different services sectors for the period from 1980–81 to 2004–05.

Using these data, on the basis of normal deviations above and below the mean, we classify the different sectors into the following categories. In doing so, we exclude the number for real estate, renting and business services because it is an outlier.

LOW: Wholesale and Retail Trade, Hotels and Restaurants, Community Services, Personal, Recreational and Entertainment Services
MEDIUM: Transport by Other Means, Banking and Insurance, Public Administration and Defence, Business Services
HIGH: Railways, Storage, Communication, Real Estate and Renting Services

---

[8] Data on gross capital stock is computed in the National Accounts Statistics using the expenditure method.

Table 5.7. *Ratio of net capital stock to the number of persons employed in different services sectors: 1980–81 to 2004–05*

Sector	Constant 2004–05 Rupees per Person (000's)	Z-scores
Wholesale and Retail Trade	80	−1.12
Hotels and Restaurants	110	−1.03
Railways	704	0.87
Transport by Other Means	230	−0.64
Storage	659	0.72
Communication	921	1.56
Banking and Insurance	248	−0.59
Real Estate, Renting and Business Services	4,799	Excluded from the distribution
Public Administration and Defence	445	0.04
Other Social, Community and Personal Services	59	−1.19

Note: The numbers are simple averages of annual data for the period from 1980–81 to 2004–05. The numbers, being rupees (in 000's), are rounded off to the nearest rupee (in 000's).
Source: Central Statistical Organisation, National Accounts Statistics and National Sample Survey Organisation.

The grouping of real estate, renting and business services has a combined capital stock per labour input ratio which is more than five times that of the sub-sector with the next-highest ratio. Data suggest that during the period from 1980–81 to 2004–05, the combined capital intensity of the grouping declined by about 70 per cent. At the same time, data also show that the share of business services in the combined GDP of the grouping increased by about 35 per cent during the same period. It suggests that the 'high' capital intensity for grouping is being driven by the real estate and renting segment. This is not surprising given that the real estate and renting services sector has a very large capital stock consisting of (largely self-occupied) dwellings which give rise to output, in the form of actual or imputed rental income, for which virtually no employment is required. In fact, the data show that the increase in output of the real estate and renting services sector was four times larger than the increase in employment it created between 1980–81 and 2004–05. In contrast, the increase in output of business services sector was about twice the increase in employment it created during the same period. In light of this information, we classify real estate and renting services as a sector with high capital intensity and the business services sector as one with medium capital intensity.

Similarly, the data only allow us to compute the combined magnitude of capital intensity for other social, community and personal services. In this case, we use the overall figure of the latter to classify both its components – community services and personal, recreational and entertainment services – as having low capital intensity because it is intuitively robust.

Let us now analyse whether these classifications, resulting from our analysis of the data, conform to economic intuition.

5.4.5.1. Low Capital Intensity

The classification of wholesale and retail trade as a low capital intensity sector is intuitively robust as these are services intensive in the use of labour, but not in the use of machinery, software or construction activity. On the other hand, the classification of hotels and restaurants as a low capital intensity sector may seem counter-intuitive as one would expect large hotels to incur significant outlays on construction and equipment. However, it is likely that the classification is being driven by small restaurants and lodging places which have a very low capital requirement. Community services such as education, and personal services, recreational and cultural activities naturally have a low capital requirement, relative to labour. Hence, its classification as a low capital intensity sectors is appropriate. Health services are an exception, as outlays on construction of hospitals, equipment and software are likely to be high.

5.4.5.2. Medium Capital Intensity

The classification of banking and insurance, business services and public administration and defence[9] as medium capital intensity sectors is intuitively plausible. This is because although they do not require machinery, outlays on construction and software related inputs are likely to be high. In contrast, the classification of transport by other means as a sector with medium capital intensity represents a mix of high capital intensity and low capital intensity in its different segments. Whereas air transport services are likely to be very intensive in the use of machinery, equipment and software, road and water transport services are not (CSO, 2007a).

---

[9] Capital outlays of defence enterprise on ordinance and clothing factories are included in the estimation of gross capital formation, but construction for military purposes and defence equipment is excluded.

5.4.5.3. High Capital Intensity

It should come as no surprise that the railways sector is classified as a high capital intensity sector. This is attributable to large-scale construction (primarily of tracks) activity it entails as well as the intensive use of machinery and equipment. The same holds true for the storage sector where outlays on construction are likely to be extremely high given that the basic function of the sector is to provide warehousing facilities. It is also likely to be intensive in the use of machinery and equipment given that storage facilities include refrigerated warehouses and farm products storage. In real estate and renting services, there are likely to be large outlays on construction activity as well. Given that postal and courier services are largely labour-intensive, the classification of the communications sector as a high capital intensity sector is attributable to the telecommunications segment, which is likely to be highly intensive in its use of machinery, equipment and software.

5.4.6. Skill Intensity

We identify the skill intensity of a sector by analyzing the distribution of its workforce between two occupation categories. In particular, we analyse the percentage of professional and technical workers and administrative, executive and managerial workers in the labour force of each service sector. This includes scientists, engineers, architects, scientists, social scientists, doctors, teachers, accountants, legislative officials, government officials, directors and managers of companies. This is an intuitively plausible measure of skill intensity given that individuals employed in these occupations are likely to be well endowed with specialized skills and knowledge.

For this variable, tabulation has been carried out from the primary data in order to compute figures at an aggregate level for different services sectors. It is worth noting that the two occupational categories specified earlier follow from a National Classification of Occupations (NCO) issued by the Directorate General of Employment and Training, Ministry of Labour, Government of India. In fact, this classification of occupations also consists of five other categories: clerical and related workers, sales workers, service workers, farmers and related workers and production and related workers. Table 5.8 presents data on the percentage of professional, technical, administrative, executive and managerial workers as a percentage of the labour force for different services sectors for the period from 1993–94 to 2004–05.

Table 5.8. *Professional, technical and related workers and administrative,
executive and managerial workers as a percentage of the labour force
for different services sectors: 1993–94 to 2004–05*

Sector	Total number of professional, technical, executive and managerial workers as a % of the labour force	Z-scores
Wholesale and Retail Trade	8.6	−0.75
Hotels and Restaurants	17.6	−0.30
Railways	4.2	−0.97
Transport by Other Means	9.0	−0.73
Storage	8.9	−0.74
Communication	19.7	−0.19
Banking and Insurance	25.9	0.12
Real Estate and Renting Services	27.0	0.17
Business Services	37.6	0.71
Public Administration and Defence	15.5	−0.40
Community Services	76.6	2.67
Personal, Recreational and Entertainment Services	8.3	−0.76

Note: The numbers are simple averages for three points in time: 1993–94, 1999–2000 and 2004–05. The figures are rounded off to the first decimal.
Source: National Sample Survey Organisation, Surveys on Employment and Unemployment.

Using these data, on the basis of normal deviations above and below the mean, we classify the different sectors into the following categories.

LOW: Wholesale and Retail Trade, Railways, Transport by Other Means, Storage, Personal, Recreational and Entertainment Services
MEDIUM: Hotels and Restaurants, Communications, Banking and Insurance, Real Estate and Renting Services, Public Administration and Defence
HIGH: Business Services, Community Services

Let us now analyse whether these classifications, based on a study of the data, conform to economic intuition.

5.4.6.1. Low Skill Intensity

The classification of the wholesale and retail trade and storage as low skill intensity sectors is logical. Given that the former simply involves the sale and purchase of goods between individuals and the latter entails the operation of warehousing facilities, the number of white-collar workers engaged in technical, executive or managerial tasks is likely to be negligible. In the personal, recreational and entertainment services sector, even though cultural and sports activities are likely to employ professional workers such as poets, authors, journalists, painters, photographers and performing artists, it is dominated by personal services such as hairdressing, domestic services, laundry services and sanitary services that do not employ any professional workers.

The classification of the railways sector as one with low skill intensity may appear somewhat counter-intuitive, as one would expect there be a large number of individuals employed in technical, administrative, executive and managerial occupations. These would include engine drivers, engineers, technicians and managers. However, people employed in such occupations may be small in number compared to the large clerical staff and other non-professional staff doing small chores in offices, railway stations, on trains, providing cleaning services and so forth.

Similarly, in the transport by other means sector, one would expect the air transport segment to have large numbers of individuals employed in technical, administrative, executive and managerial occupations. These would include pilots, engineers and managers in company offices. However, people employed in such occupations may be small in number compared to non-professional staff doing small chores in offices, at airports, providing cleaning services and so forth. In addition, in the water and road transport segments, the majority of individuals providing inland water transport, bus and truck services are unlikely to be highly skilled professional, executive or managerial staff.

5.4.6.2. Medium Skill Intensity

The classification of hotels and restaurants as a medium skill intensity sector is appropriate. On the one hand, large upmarket hotels may employ large numbers of administrative, executive and managerial workers. These workers are well educated and are proficient in speaking English. At the same time, this sector is also likely to employ non-professional, non-technical service providers such as gatekeepers, bellboys, drivers, kitchen staff and cleaners in both large hotels and smaller restaurants. Similarly, the classification of banking and insurance and real estate and renting services as medium capital intensity sectors should come as no surprise. Firms in both sectors are likely to employ large numbers of administrative, executive and managerial workers, but they are equally likely to employ large numbers of clerical, sales and service workers. The same holds true for the communications sector. Whereas mail delivery and landlines and mobile telephone connections are unlikely to be provided by highly trained professional workers, firms providing these services are likely to employ large numbers of individuals in administrative and managerial jobs as well.

The classification of public administration and defence as a medium skill intensity sector may appear counter-intuitive. Given that the sector represents the governmental arm of the economy, it naturally consists of a large number of technical, administrative and executive workers. These include civil servants, engineers, technicians, social scientists, teachers, health officers and so forth. Hence, one may expect this sector to be classified as a high skill intensity sector. However, the medium classification may be the result of large numbers of clerical and subordinate staff employed in this sector.[10]

5.4.6.3. High Skill Intensity

The classification of business services as a high skill intensity sector should come as no surprise. First, given the nature of activities of the sector, it is likely to employ a large number of professional and technical workers such as scientists, engineers, architects, economists, social scientists and accountants. Second, it is also likely to employ a large number of executive and managerial workers who work in software firms, accounting firms, management consultancies, engineering firms and similar outfits. The same holds true for community services where the delivery of education is dominated by technical workers such as teachers, scientists, engineers and social scientists, whereas that of health care is dominated by technical workers such as physicians, surgeons and nurses.

5.4.7. Scope for Economies of Scale

In economic theory, economies of scale refer to the advantages of large-scale production that result in lower unit costs. We identify a sector's potential to achieve economies of scale by analyzing the number of workers employed by units or firms. Of course, this is one of several measures that can be used for capturing the scale of operations. Others include capital employed,

---

[10] Professional, technical and related workers and administrative, executive and managerial workers accounted for 15 per cent of the workforce of the government sector; clerical and other subordinate staff accounted for 36 per cent.

Table 5.9. *The proportion of enterprises with more than 20 workers:*
1999–2000 to 2004–05

Sector	Proportion of enterprises with greater than 20 workers	Z-scores
Wholesale and Retail Trade	3.4	−0.86
Hotels and Restaurants	5.3	−0.79
Railways	100	2.57
Transport by other means	12.0	−0.55
Storage	24.8	−0.10
Communication	29.1	0.05
Banking and Insurance	33.9	0.22
Real Estate and Renting Services	2.5	−0.89
Business Services	48.7	0.75
Public Administration and Defence	47.4	0.70
Community Services	22.1	−0.20
Personal, Recreational and Entertainment Services	2.4	−0.89

Note: The numbers are simple averages for two points in time: 1999–2000 and 2004–05. The figures are rounded off to the first decimal.
Source: National Sample Survey Organisation, Surveys on Employment and Unemployment.

turnover and profits. Table 5.9 presents data on the number of enterprises with greater than twenty workers as a percentage of the total number of enterprises in different services sectors for the period from 1999–2000 to 2004–05. Surveys on employment and unemployment conducted by the National Sample Survey Organisation (NSSO) divide enterprises in a sector into four categories according to the number of workers employed: fewer than six, between six and ten, between ten and twenty, greater than twenty. For our analysis, we use the last category as it provides a clearer distinction between smaller and larger operations by defining a unique cut-off point.

Using these data, on the basis of normal deviations above and below the mean, we classify the different sectors into the following categories.

SMALL: Wholesale and Retail Trade, Hotels and Restaurants, Real Estate and Renting Services, Personal, Recreational and Entertainment Services
MEDIUM: Communications, Storage, Community Services, Transport by Other Means, Banking and Insurance
LARGE: Business Services, Railways, Public Administration and Defence

Let us now analyse whether these classifications, resulting from the data, conform to economic intuition.

5.4.7.1. Small Scope for Economies of Scale

For wholesale and retail trade, this classification may appear somewhat counter-intuitive given that there is a trend towards exploiting economies of scale in all parts of the distribution chain the world over (Ofer, 2005). Key trends reflecting this may include mergers or close collaborations between companies, the formation of voluntary chains and centrally run franchises. In India, some large manufacturers have established their brand names and developed massive distribution networks, reaching more than a million retail outlets altogether. This has resulted in potential economies of scale to wholesalers. The number of wholesale traders exploiting these potential economies of scale, however, may still be limited. On the other hand, a large number of small independent stores that are a part of the unorganized sector dominate the retail trade structure (Joseph et al., 2008). This is in sharp contrast to several industrialized countries where the retail sector is dominated by large supermarket chains. These small independent stores are unlikely to achieve economies of scale in their operations. The situation may be similar for the hotels and restaurant sector, which is dominated by a large unorganized segment comprising small restaurants and lodging places (Section 5.4.1)[11].

In theory, real estate companies are very capital intensive, and therefore, economies of scale in capital costs are probably most crucial for efficiency gains[12] in this sector. However, the real estate sector is likely to be dominated by small companies that may have not expanded through mergers and acquisitions. Finally, personal services such as domestic services, tailoring, hairdressing and sanitary services, as well as recreational activities and sporting activities, are most often provided by individuals as opposed to groups. Given this, the potential opportunity of achieving economies of scale in these services is negligible.

5.4.7.2. Medium Scope for Economies of Scale

Given the high fixed costs associated with storage facilities, there are likely to be economies of scale in operating large warehouses. In India, public-sector warehouses – which constitute a significant part of the industry – tend to

[11] These small-scale operations are unable to get discounts on bulk purchases, employ advanced technology, engage in advertising or enjoy market power.
[12] Efficiency gains from consolidation may take the form of a decline in general and administrative expenses, management fees, interest expenses and other operating expenses.

be large in size, but private warehouses do not (CSO, 2007a). Hence, this sector is likely to have experienced moderate economies of scale.

Community services such as education and health services may be subject to economies of scale. In theory, consolidation of schools in a district may result in moderate economies of scale by receiving benefits of negotiating bulk purchases of equipment and by providing better facilities such as computer labs at a lower average cost. In health services, economies of scale may be achieved at both the industry and firm level. At the industry level, economies of scale may be attributable to costs savings from lower prices for medical supplies and equipment associated with bulk purchases. At the level of the firm, economies of scale may result from 'chain ownership' as opposed to single establishments where a larger scale of operation leads to joint input-purchasing arrangements, sharing of professional specialists and capital savings from reduced interest expenditures on buildings and equipment. Despite the presence of a large number of large hospitals and schools in urban areas, community services in rural areas are still dominated by small local hospitals – public and private – mobile clinics, village schools and individuals providing private tuition. Given this, the classification of the sector as one with a medium scope for economies of scale seems appropriate.

In theory, mergers and acquisitions can develop integrated banking systems which, in turn, can facilitate scale economies. In India, the banking and insurance sector is dominated by the public sector (Section 5.4.2). Moreover, the private-sector component of the industry in the country has been characterized by some mergers and acquisitions (Prasad and Ghosh, 2007). Its classification as a sector with a medium scope of economies of scale may be attributable to the fact that it also comprises a large number of moneylenders in rural areas and group lending schemes – financial services provided by an individual or a small group of individuals.

For the communications and transport by other means sector, the medium classification represents a mix of a small scope of achievable economies of scale and a large scope of achievable economies of scale in different segments of the sector.

The communications sector consists of two broad segments: postal services and telecommunication services. In the postal services segment, economies of scale may result from merging smaller postal offices (operating in the same or adjacent service area), thereby integrating collecting, processing and distributing functions. However, given that the objective of a government in establishing a postal service is to reach even the remotest of areas, such mergers may not have taken place. Moreover, the rapidly growing private courier services segment is characterized by a large number of small companies that may not have achieved economies of scale. In contrast, the scope for achieving economies of scale in telecommunications – where the cost of connecting one more customer to the existing network is negligible – is high. There may also be economies of scale on the demand side. These are often referred to as 'network effects', whereby the addition of one more customer to the network increases the aggregate social value of the network beyond the private value gained by the additional customer (Grajek, 2007).

The classification of transport by other means as a sector with a medium scope to achieve economies of scale is appropriate. In India, greater density of passenger traffic using air transport in recent years (Planning Commission, 2002) is likely to have resulted in economies of scale. Furthermore, potential economies of scale may have possibly been exploited by an amalgamation of firms either through mergers or acquisitions (e.g. Jet Airways buying out Sahara Airlines).[13] In contrast, the maritime industry has experienced diseconomies of scale relating to the loading and unloading of cargo (Svendsen, 1981). Moreover, inland water transport services, which are dominated by country boats and small ferries catering to passenger traffic, are unlikely to achieve any significant economies of scale. Similarly, road transport services including bus, truck and taxi services are dominated by small private operators who are unlikely to achieve economies of scale. It is worth noting that our chosen measure of economies of scale assigns higher weights to segments with a larger number of small enterprises (water and road transport), and a much lower weight to segments such as air transport, which has a few enterprises, each employing a large number of workers. Hence, we must view this classification of the transport by other means sector as one with 'small' potential economies of scale with caution.

5.4.7.3. High Scope for Economies of Scale

The potential for economies of scale in the public administration and defence sector is high as government departments are highly centralised, employing large numbers of people. This may result in more streamlined managerial operations, bulk purchases of inputs, and consolidation of several interrelated activities. However, given poor flows of information between different government departments, an increase in the number of bureaucrats may also result in diseconomies of scale such as duplication of

[13] news.bbc.co.uk, 12 April 2007.

work, delays and red tape. The same holds true for the railways sector which consists of a single government enterprise that employs a large number of people to serve a growing passenger and freight market. Evidence suggests that in recent years, the Indian Railways has been able to exploit economies of scale (Raghuram, 2007).

Business services are classified as a sector with a high scope for economies of scale. This is intuitively robust given that most of the services in this sector – computer-related services, consultancy, advertising and accounting services – are provided primarily by medium-sized and large enterprises. Potential economies of scale – which may take the form of reduced costs resulting from more streamlined managerial operations and bulk purchases of inputs, and from reduced per-unit costs for advertising and promotional activities – in this sector can be exploited by an amalgamation of firms either through mergers or acquisitions.

5.4.8. Trade in International Markets

International trade in services is divided into four categories: those in which the producer moves to the consumer; those in which the consumer moves to the producer; those in which either the producer or the consumer moves to the other; and those in which neither the consumer nor the producer moves to each other (see Chapter 2). The standard variable used in the literature to measure trade of goods or services in international markets is the exports plus imports to GDP ratio (Dollar and Kraay, 2004). The Reserve Bank of India compiles data on exports and imports of services for different services sectors in the balance-of-payments statistics. Table 5.10 presents data on exports and imports of services as a percentage of GDP for different services sectors for the period from 1990–91 to 2008–09.

Given that the presented data are skewed – not close to being normally distributed – we cannot classify the different sectors on the basis of normal deviations above and below the mean value. Instead, we use our intuitive judgement to identify distinct patterns in the data to adopt the following classification criteria:

1. If exports plus imports of services in a sector are greater than 50 per cent of its GDP, we classify the sector as one with high trade in international markets.
2. If exports plus imports of services in a sector are less than 5 per cent of its GDP, we classify the sector as one with low trade in international markets.

Table 5.10. *Trade in services as a percentage of GDP for different services sectors: 1990–91 to 2008–09*

Sector	Exports plus imports of services as a % of GDP
Wholesale and Retail Trade	0.0
Hotels and Restaurants	–
Transport	22.8
Storage	0.0
Communication	15.0
Banking and Insurance	5.7
Real Estate, Renting Services and Ownership of Dwellings	0.0
Business Services	85.8
Public Administration and Defence	0.0
Social and Community Services	19.4
Personal, Recreational and Entertainment Services	1.1

Note: The numbers are simple averages of annual data for the period from 1990–91 to 2008–09. The numbers are rounded off to the first decimal.
Source: Reserve Bank of India, Monthly Bulletin, March 2010.

3. If exports plus imports of services in a sector lie between 5 and 50 per cent of its GDP, we classify the sector as one with medium trade in international markets.

On the basis of these criteria presented, we divide the different sectors into the following categories.

LOW: Wholesale and Retail Trade, Railways, Storage, Real Estate and Renting Services, Public Administration and Defence, Personal, Recreational and Entertainment Services

MEDIUM: Hotels and Restaurants, Transport by Other Means, Communication, Banking and Insurance, Community Services

HIGH: Business Services

Unfortunately, the data are not available at a level of disaggregation to include the services sub-sector of hotels and restaurants. But these data do show that 'travel services' accounted for almost 30 per cent of India's trade in services during the period from 1990–91 to 2008–09. Given that 'travel' is defined to include expenditure by foreign tourists in India (exports) and expenditure by Indian tourists abroad (imports), and that a large proportion of tourist expenditure is likely to be on hotels and restaurants, we classify the sector as one with 'medium' trade in international markets. Similarly, data are not available at a level of disaggregation that separates railways from transport by other means. Given that railways services are tradable in international markets only to a very small extent through 'consumption abroad' – use by foreigners who travel for either tourism or business purposes – we classify the sector as one with 'low' trade in international markets. In light of this, we make the simplifying assumption that railways are not traded at all in international markets. This implies that exports plus imports as a percentage of GDP amounts to 22.8 per cent for the transport by other means sector. This results in its classification as a sector with 'medium' trade in international markets.

Let us now analyse whether these classifications, based on our reading of the data, conform to economic intuition.

5.4.8.1. Low Tradeability of Output

Public administration and defence, wholesale and retail trade, storage, real estate and renting services, railways and personal (hairdressing, domestic services, laundry services) and recreational activities[14] are essentially non-traded services. Hence, it should come as no surprise that these sectors are classified as sectors with 'low' trade in international markets.

5.4.8.2. Medium Tradeability of Output

The classification of banking and insurance services as a sector with 'medium' trade in international markets may be attributable to the fact that whereas India's imports of financial services are high (moderated to an extent by ceilings on FDI), exports – through cross-border supply or establishing a commercial presence abroad – are relatively low. This is not surprising given that India's financial service providers may not be as competitive as their counterparts in advanced countries in the context of meeting international prudential norms (Chanda, 2005). At the same time, India may have been successful in exporting financial services to a moderate extent through 'consumption abroad', namely services rendered to non-resident Indians and foreign nationals residing in India (Banga, 2005).

International trade in telecommunication services can occur through three channels: establishing a commercial presence abroad (through the establishment of foreign subsidiaries); consumption abroad (which includes

---

[14] Custom tailoring and beauty treatment (ayurvedic and herbal) may be exported to a very small extent by means of 'consumption abroad' (foreigners availing of these services while in India). The same may hold true for entertainment services which may be traded by the cross-border movement of people such as artists, musicians and actors.

activities such as mobile roaming services) and cross-border movement of staff (which often refers to telecommunication consulting services). At present, in India, the export of telecommunication (and even postal) services is largely attributable to consumption abroad and cross-border movement of staff (Banga, 2005). At the same time, imports of telecommunication services occur through the establishment of subsidiaries in India, but are constrained by limitations on foreign equity participation. In light of this, it is only logical that communication services are classified as a sector with 'medium' trade in international markets.

Community services – education and health – are likely to be moderately traded in international markets. For India, health services have high export potential and may be exported in four ways: cross-border exports through telemedicine, inflows of foreign patients for treatment in India from both developed and developing countries (medical tourism), securing a commercial presence abroad via overseas health consultancy establishments (providing laboratory-pathology services, for instance) and the movement of health personnel abroad (Chanda, 2001). In contrast, India imports education services via cross-border supply (distance education) or consumption abroad. At present, exports of education services are likely to be negligible because of the lack of international curricula and world-class infrastructure (Agarwal, 2006). However, India may export education services through establishing branch campuses abroad in certain areas of education such as engineering, *ayurvedic* medicine, yoga and Sanskrit. The cross-border movement of a large number of well-educated, world-class researchers, teachers and trainers would also constitute exports to the extent that remittances flow back into the country.

The classification of hotels and restaurant services as a sector with 'medium' trade in international markets may appear somewhat counter-intuitive given that these services were generally considered non-traded. However, a rapid increase in tourism is likely to have strengthened the tradeability of hotels and restaurant services in international markets. For India, exports from this sector can be achieved either by consumption abroad (hotels and restaurants used by foreign tourists) or through establishing a commercial presence abroad, via franchises, for example. In the case of hotels, exports of their services may have been further strengthened through developments in communication technology, as producers and consumers may often use the Internet to advertise and make reservations, respectively.

The classification of transport by other means as a sector with 'medium' trade in international markets should come as no surprise. This is because

transportation of freight and passengers by air or sea are generally considered to be traded services. On the other hand, road transport services are
not similarly tradeable in international markets. They may be exported
to a small extent through 'consumption abroad' (used by foreigners who
come to India for both tourism and business purposes). In fact, in recent
times, the advent of advanced communication technology has enabled
Internet bookings, which are likely to have increased exports of all transport services.

5.4.8.3. High Tradeability of Output

It should come as no surprise that business services are classified as a sector with 'high' trade in international markets. This is primarily attributable
to software services which constituted almost half of India's total services
exports in 2009 (Chapter 3). Software services may be exported in two
ways. First, software and processed data can be transmitted abroad via the
Internet or satellite. Second, much like goods, software that can be stored on
disks and transmitted abroad (Balasubramanyam and Balasubramanyam,
1997). India's comparative advantage in software services lies in its endowment of skilled but low-cost labour resources (Rakshit, 2007). At the same
time, there has been a dramatic increase in exports of other information-
technology-enabled professional services, especially business process outsourcing and call centres for which Bangalore has been the world hub in
recent years (Kumar and Joseph, 2005). Business process outsourcing refers
to the establishment of back-office operations by several multinational
corporations in India. These back-offices provide relatively low-skill services such as data entry, accounting and information technology support.
Similarly, call centres refer to the offshore outsourcing of customer services
by several large multinational corporations where India's success is largely
attributable to its endowment of a large English-speaking workforce.

5.4.9. Contribution to Technological Progress

We measure a sector's contribution to technological progress by analyzing research and development (R&D) expenditure as a percentage of gross
value added for a sample of 4,000 firms in that sector. Intuitively, this is an
appropriate measure given that R&D expenditure is the basic input variable that captures technological development. We use data at the level of
firms to make inferences for sectors in the aggregate because data at the
macroeconomic level are not available at a level of disaggregation that is

Table 5.11. *Research and development expenditure as a proportion of gross value added for different services sectors: 1990–91 to 2005–06*

Sector	R&D Expenditure as a Proportion of Gross Value Added (per cent)
Wholesale and Retail Trade	0.1
Hotels and Restaurants	0.1
Transport	0.0
Storage	0.0
Communication	0.1
Banking and Insurance	2.6
Real Estate and Renting Services	0.0
Business Services	18.7
Public Administration and Defence	–
Other Social, Community and Personal Services	0.3

Note: The numbers are simple averages of annual data for the period from 1990–91 to 2005–06. The numbers are rounded off to the first decimal.
Source: Centre for Monitoring the Indian Economy, PROWESS Database.

consistent with National Accounts Statistics. In doing this, we recognize that corporate firms account for a part of the provision of most services. In fact, in some service sub-sectors, they may constitute only a small fraction of total output, whereas in others they may be entirely absent. But because R&D is an activity intensive in the use of sophisticated technology and highly skilled individuals, it is most likely to be carried out in large corporate firms. Table 5.11 presents data on R&D expenditure as a percentage of gross value added for a sample of 4,000 firms for different services sectors for the period from 1990–91 to 2005–06.

Given that the presented data are skewed – not close to being normally distributed – we cannot classify the different sectors on the basis of normal deviations above and below the mean value. Instead, we use our intuitive judgement to identify distinct patterns in the data to adopt the following classification criteria:

1. If R&D expenditure is less that 1 per cent of gross value added, we classify the sector's contribution to technological progress as low.
2. If R&D expenditure lies between 1 per cent and 10 per cent of gross value added, we classify the sector's contribution to technological progress as medium.
3. If R&D expenditure is more than 10 per cent of gross value added, we classify the sector's contribution to technological progress as high.

On the basis of these criteria, we classify the different sectors into the following categories.

LOW: Wholesale and Retail Trade, Hotels and Restaurants, Railways, Transport by Other Means, Storage, Communications, Real Estate and Renting Services, Personal, Recreational and Entertainment Services, Public Administration and Defence
MEDIUM: Banking and Insurance, Community Services
HIGH: Business Services

Given that we are using a firm-level database, it includes no information on the public administration sector. Similarly, much of the community and personal services sectors are not covered in the data as the public sector and non-corporate private individuals are dominant providers in the former and latter, respectively. Given that R&D activity is unlikely to occur in the public administration sector, the focus of which is to provide its citizens with basic goods and services, we classify it as one with a low contribution to technological progress. We do the same for personal, cultural and recreational services. In contrast, R&D expenditure in certain parts of the community services is likely to be high; higher education and large research hospitals are a case in point. Hence, we classify the sector as one with a medium contribution to the technological progress.

Let us now analyse whether these classifications, resulting from our analysis of the data, conform to economic intuition.

5.4.9.1. Low Contribution to Technological Progress

It is only to be expected that wholesale and retail trade, hotels and restaurants, railways, transport by other means, storage, communications, real estate and renting and personal, recreational and entertainment services make a low contribution to technological progress. This is attributable to the fact that the nature of activities in these sectors does not provide an incentive for firms to invest in R&D. Instead, firms in these sectors are likely to invest in advertising, which would provide them with greater returns.

5.4.9.2. Medium Contribution to Technological Progress

The classification of banking and insurance services as a sector with a medium contribution to technological progress is intuitively plausible. This is because many financial firms operate on a very large scale and may comprise in-house research divisions. The same holds true for community services because certain parts of the sector – higher education and large research hospitals – are likely to be centres of R&D activity.

5.4.9.3. High Contribution to Technological Progress

Business services are the only sector with a high contribution to technological progress. This is logical given that firms engaged in software services are working on cutting-edge issues, developing sophisticated technology. Some other professional service providers such as management and technology consultancy establishments may also contribute to technological progress through their research units.

5.4.10. Incorporation of Technological Advance

We identify the incorporation of technological advance in a sector by analyzing the trend rate of growth of output per worker over a period of time. This is a fair measure given that economic theory predicts that technological improvements are a principal driver of productivity increase (Basu et al., 2001). For example, the increasing use of information technology is likely to result in productivity increases for several sectors of the economy (Griliches and Siegel, 1992). Of course, the trend rate of growth of output per worker is not a perfect measure of the incorporation of technological advance in a sector. This is attributable to the fact that there may be other factors such as structural change within a sector, which influence the former as well. Data on output (constant price estimates at 2004–05 prices) and employment are used to compute an output per worker variable. Subsequently, trend rates of growth of output per worker over a given period of time are computed by running Ordinary Least Squares regressions of the natural logarithm of output per worker on a time trend. Table 5.12 presents data on the trend rate of growth of output per worker for different services sectors for the period from 1980–81 to 2004–05.

Using these data, on the basis of normal deviations above and below the mean, we classify the different sectors into the following categories.

LOW: Storage, Real Estate and Renting Services, Personal, Recreational and Entertainment Services

MEDIUM: Wholesale and Retail Trade, Railways, Transport by Other Means, Public Administration and Defence, Hotels and Restaurants, Community Services

HIGH: Banking and Insurance, Communications, Business Services

Table 5.12. *Trend rate of growth of output per worker in different*
services sectors: 1980–81 to 2004–05

Sector	Per cent per annum	Z-scores
Wholesale and Retail Trade	1.1	−0.34
Hotels and Restaurants	1.8	0.10
Railways	1.9	0.16
Transport by Other Means	1.2	−0.27
Storage	−2.0	−2.28
Communications	3.4	1.10
Banking and Insurance	2.9	0.79
Real Estate and Renting Services	−0.3	−1.21
Business Services	3.5	1.16
Public Administration and Defence	2.1	0.29
Community Services	2.3	0.41
Personal, Recreational and Entertainment Services	0.2	−0.90

Note: The numbers are rounded off to the nearest first decimal place
Source: Author's estimates based on Central Statistical Organisation, Nationals Accounts Statistics
and National Sample Survey Organisation, Surveys on Employment and Unemployment.

Let us now analyse whether these classifications, based on our analysis of
the data, conform to economic intuition.

5.4.10.1. Low Incorporation of Technological Advance

Storage and warehousing facilities may have some scope for adopting technological innovations to increase productivity, especially in the cold-storage
segment. However, it may be the case that firms in this sector have been
unable to incorporate such technological advance, for a number of reasons.
First, given that more than 50 per cent of this sector is unorganized (Section
5.4.1), several small enterprises may face capital constraints to finance the
adoption of new technology. Second, more than 50 per cent of the organized-sector component is publicly provided. This presence of a significant
public-sector component may hinder the adoption of new technologies
because of the attitudes of senior public-sector officials in developing countries (Heeks, 2000). Real estate and renting services may not require the use
of high-level technology as productivity in these services is more likely to
be a function of individual enterprise, education and skill. Finally, personal,
recreational and entertainment services[15] are unlikely to be intensive in the
use of sophisticated equipment or technological know-how.

---

[15] The incorporation of up-to-date technology may have resulted in significant productivity
improvements for those involved in film and television production.

5.4.10.2. Medium Incorporation of Technological Advance

Employing technological improvements in rail tracks, wagons and coaches, electric multiple units and locomotives can yield considerable productivity improvements. However, for national account purposes, railway manufacturing and construction activity is not included in the railways sector. At the same time, the sector may experience productivity increases because of innovations in information and communication technologies. For instance, greater use of information technology in the Indian Railways is already bringing about productivity improvements in both the passenger and freight segments. In the former, it has increased efficiency in collecting information and for the reservation of tickets. In the latter, it has resulted in better utilization of existing infrastructure, rolling stock and manpower (Raghuram, 2007). Hence, the classification of the sector as one with 'medium' incorporation of technological advance seems appropriate.

For the other sectors in this category, the 'medium' classification represents a mix of 'high' incorporation of technological advance and 'low' incorporation of technological advance in their different segments.

In the hotels and restaurants sector, which primarily consists of labour-intensive services, the scope for incorporating technological advances is likely to relate to developments in information and communication technologies. Whereas five-star hotels, luxury resorts and upmarket restaurants are likely to have incorporated such technological advance, cheap restaurants, inexpensive guesthouses and roadside *dhabas*[16] are unlikely to have done so owing to capital constraints.

In wholesale and retail trade, this classification is likely to be a result of the existence of two diverse sub-segments: petty traders and large-scale retailers and wholesalers. In the former sub-segment, operations on a small scale and low profit margins may hinder the adoption of sophisticated technology, which is likely to entail a significant fixed cost. In the latter sub-segment, large-scale operations and higher profit margins are likely to result in the adoption of sophisticated technology relatively easily.

In the public administration and defence sector, it is logical to assume that the former has some scope for incorporating advances in information and communication technologies. However, evidence shows that it has failed to do so in India owing to the negative attitudes of senior public-sector officials towards technology (Heeks, 2000). In the defence segment, however, incorporation of technological advance is vital owing to the importance of sophisticated arms, equipment and communication devices. It is

[16] Small roadside restaurants.

likely that for this reason, the defence sector has made use of such technological advances. Hence, the 'medium' classification for the sector seems
appropriate.

Within the transport by other means sector, an increase in technology is
naturally related to an increase in productivity in the air transport segment.
Hence, employing relevant technological innovations can yield productivity improvements in this segment. In the maritime industry, increased auto-
mation may have contributed to improved efficiency in the management of
port services (Planning Commission, 2002)[17]. But in the road transport segment, both passenger transport (buses) and freight transport (trucks) have
been characterized by technological stagnation (Planning Commission,
2001). Hence, the sector's overall classification as the one with 'medium'
incorporation of technological advance is appropriate.

Finally, in the community services sector, technological advances are
likely to have yielded significant productivity increases in the health service
segment. This is because the provision of health services in hospitals and
nursing homes requires highly sophisticated equipment. For education services, in contrast, productivity may be a function of the intellectual prowess, dedication of teachers, training of teachers, and quality of textbooks.
However, the productivity of those employed in this sector may have also
improved owing to the availability of better technology in the classroom,
such as computers and up-to-date software programmes, audio and visual
equipment which may enhance interactive discussion. Hence, the overall classification of this sector as 'medium' incorporation of technological
advance seems appropriate.

5.4.10.3. High Incorporation of Technological Advance

Advanced technological know-how and sophisticated equipment are an
important prerequisite for telecommunication services such as the provision of telephone lines (cellular and landline connections) and Internet
connectivity. Hence, the adoption of technological innovations is likely to
have yielded significant productivity improvements in this segment. Even
in the postal and courier services segment, innovations in information and
communication technologies may have resulted in considerable productivity improvements, such as tracking services for postal deliveries. Hence, the

---

[17] According to the tenth five-year plan, efforts to employ sophisticated technology in a
bid to increase productivity of water transport services will focus on three areas: use of
the Vessel Traffic Management System for navigation of ships; use of computers in cargo
operations; and use of e-commerce for trade-related document transactions.

overall classification of this sector as one with 'high' incorporation of technological advance is intuitively robust.

The same holds true for the financial services sector where the adoption of technological improvements in the field of information technology and communication devices is likely to have yielded significant productivity improvements. For example, the widespread incorporation of information and communication technology in the form of Internet and telephone banking reduces transaction and delivery costs (Nitsure, 2003; Uppal, 2007).

Finally, the classification of business services as a sector with 'high' incorporation of technological advance should come as no surprise. Software, hardware and engineering services require the use of high levels of technology, and hence, adoption of technological innovations is likely to have resulted in significant productivity improvements.

5.5. Implications

The taxonomy developed in this chapter disaggregated the service sector in order to assess the relative importance of the chosen attributes in each of the sub-sectors. The choice of attributes was determined by their relevance in analyzing characteristics of economic development, as guided by economic theory and analysis. They were divided into five broad categories: structural characteristics (the division between organized and unorganized economic activity, public and private provision and intermediate and final demand), employment (educational barriers to entry for job seekers), factor-use (capital and skill intensity), international trade and productivity-enhancing technology characteristics (potential to achieve economies of scale, contribution to technological progress and the incorporation of technological advance). An overview of the results from our taxonomy is provided in Table 5.13.

First and foremost, we found that services comprise highly heterogeneous economic activities. This is an important conclusion, relevant for advancing significant research questions. It suggests that economic analysis which considers services as a composite category may conceal more than it reveals. Furthermore, this heterogeneity is indicative of sub-sector-specific implications for economic growth, employment, balance of payments, the sustainability of services-led growth, poverty and inequality. These sub-sector-specific implications, in turn, help provide answers to certain questions raised and help qualify specific findings of a growing literature on India's services sector.

Table 5.13. *Exploring the heterogeneity of the services sector*

	Wholesale and retail trade	Hotels and restaurants	Railways	Transport by other means	Storage
Organized versus Unorganized	Largely Unorganized	Part Organized, Part Unorganized	Largely Organized	Part Organized, Part Unorganized	Part Organized, Part Unorganized
Public versus Private Provision	Largely Private	Largely Private	Largely Public	Part Public, Part Private	Part Public, Part Private
Intermediate versus Final Consumption	Part Final, Part Intermediate	Largely Final	Part Final, Part Intermediate	Part Final, Part Intermediate	Largely Intermediate
Barriers to Entry for Job Seekers	Low	Low	Medium	Low	Low
Capital Intensity	Low	Low	High	Medium	High
Skill Intensity	Low	Medium	Low	Low	Low
Economies of Scale	Small	Small	High	Medium	Medium
International Trade	Low	Medium	Low	Medium	Low
Contribution to Technological Progress	Low	Low	Low	Low	Low
Incorporation of Technological Advance	Medium	Medium	Medium	Medium	Low

Many attributes analysed in our taxonomy are related and interdependent. The discernible interdependence between some of the attributes is consistent with simple economic intuition. It is worth noting some examples. First, sectors that are largely organized have high educational barriers to entry for job seekers and high skill intensities; the opposite correlation also applies. Second, sectors that are largely public are also largely organized. Third, capital intensity, potential for economies of scale, incorporation of technological advance and contribution to technological progress tend to go hand in hand, albeit not perfectly. In contrast, trade in international markets and the distribution between final and intermediate demand appear to be somewhat independent of the other attributes under consideration. Given this interdependence, Table 5.14 identifies certain patterns across the four categories of characteristics – structural, employment, factor use and productivity-enhancing technology characteristics – in order to

Communications	Banking and insurance	Real estate and renting services	Business services	Public administration and defence	Community services	Personal, recreational and entertainment services
Largely Organized	Largely Organized	Largely Unorganized	Largely Organized	Largely Organized	Largely Organized	Largely Unorganized
Part Public, Part Private	Part Public, Part Private	Largely Private	Largely Private	Largely Public	Part Public, Part Private	Largely Private
Part Final, Part Intermediate	Largely Intermediate	Largely Final	Part Final, Part Intermediate	Largely Final	Largely Final	Largely Final
Medium	High	Medium	High	Medium	High	Low
High	Medium	High	Medium	Medium	Low	Low
Medium	Medium	Medium	High	Medium	High	Low
Medium	Large	Small	High	High	Medium	Small
Medium	Medium	Low	High	Low	Medium	Low
Low	Medium	Low	High	Not applicable	Medium	Low
High	High	Low	High	Medium	Medium	Low

define a smaller set of archetype sub-sectors of services for the purpose of analysis.

5.5.1. Economic Growth and Growth Accounting

A recent set of empirical studies show that the services sector has been the primary source of India's growth surge, consistently outperforming the industrial sector (Balakrishnan and Parameswaran, 2007; Bosworth et al., 2007; Rakshit, 2007). Importantly, while Bosworth and Maertens (2010) show that these gains in services output maybe explained both by increases in employment and increases in total factor productivity (TFP), Bosworth et al. (2007) argue that gains in services output are dominated by the latter. These empirical findings draw on growth accounting exercises, which show that economic growth can be decomposed into increases in factor accumulation (at given

Table 5.14. *Clusters across sectors and characteristics*

Sectors → Characteristics →	Wholesale and Retail Trade Hotels and Restaurants Transport by Other Means Storage Real Estate and Renting Personal, Recreational and Entertainment Services	Railways Public Administration and Defence Community Services	Communications Banking and Insurance Business Services
Structural characteristics			
organized-unorganized	largely unorganized to part organized, part unorganized	largely organized	largely organized
public-private	largely private to part public, part private	largely public	largely private to part public-part private
intermediate-final	Everything	Largely final to part final-part intermediate	Largely intermediate to part final-part intermediate
Barriers to Entry for job seekers	low to medium	medium	medium to high
Factor Use capital intensity skill intensity	low to medium	medium	medium to high
Technology economies of scale contribution to technological progress incorporation of technological advance	low to medium	medium	medium to high

levels of productivity) and increases in factor productivity. Of course, economic growth may also be increased by a transfer of resources, such as labour, from low-productivity to high-productivity sectors.

Analysis carried out at an aggregate level, however, ignores possible differences between different sub-sectors of services. The taxonomy shows that wholesale and retail trade, hotels and restaurants, transport by other means, storage, real estate and renting and personal, recreational and entertainment services are characterized by 'low to medium' barriers to entry for employment and 'low to medium' productivity-enhancing technology characteristics (Table 5.14). This implies that whereas these sectors are unlikely to be associated with economic growth via increases in factor productivity, they may be associated with growth through employment expansion, provided that it does not lead to a corresponding contraction of employment in other sectors of the economy.[18] It is worth noting that all of the aforementioned service sectors are classified as 'largely unorganized' or 'part organized, part unorganized'. This is intuitively robust given that unorganized sector, characterized by the absence of formal contracts and the non-applicability of labour laws, is likely to consist of a large number of small-scale enterprises providing employment to several unskilled workers. Storage services and real estate and renting services may also be associated with growth through increases in capital accumulation as they are 'high' capital intensity sectors.

In contrast, communication, financial and business services are characterized by 'medium to high' barriers to entry for employment and 'medium to high' productivity-enhancing technology characteristics (Table 5.14). Hence, these sectors are likely to be associated with economic growth primarily via increases in factor productivity. Moreover, to a small extent, communication and business services may also be associated with growth through the accumulation of capital and labour. Here it is worth noting that each of these three service sectors is classified as 'largely organized'. Furthermore, they are classified as either 'largely private' or 'part public, part private' and either 'largely intermediate' or 'part final, part intermediate'. This suggests that service sectors that are likely to contribute to economic growth via increases in factor productivity are located in the private organized sector which caters, at least in part, to intermediate demand.

The remaining sub-sectors – railways, public administration and defence and community services – are characterized by 'medium' barriers to entry for employment and 'medium' productivity-enhancing technology characteristics

---

[18] This qualification is applicable in subsequent paragraphs where the same argument is made.

(Table 5.14). These sectors maybe associated with economic growth either via increases in factor productivity or through employment expansion.

5.5.2. Sustainability of Services-Led Growth

Kaldor's (1966) structural theory of economic growth views manufacturing as the main engine of growth for an economy. Its three laws include a positive association between growth of manufacturing output and average GDP growth (explained via a transfer of labour from agriculture that is characterized by disguised unemployment), growth of manufacturing output and manufacturing productivity (attributable to static and dynamic economies of scale) and growth of manufacturing output and overall productivity of the economy (owing to spillover effects). Similarly, the seminal work of Baumol (1967) emphasizes the primacy of manufacturing over services in asserting that productivity in the latter cannot be readily increased through capital accumulation, innovation or economies of scale. The taxonomy, however, suggests that this traditionally assumed dichotomy between services and manufacturing may not necessarily hold because communication, business and financial services are characterized by 'medium to high' scope to achieve economies of scale, contribution to technological progress, and incorporation of technological advance (Table 5.14). This implies Kaldor's first and second laws may now be applicable to certain service sub-sectors as well. It also provides an indication as to which sub-sectors of services may be driving the results of Dasgupta and Singh (2005) who find, for a sample of Indian states, that Kaldor's first law is applicable to the services sector.

In the context of Kaldor's third law, on whether growth of the services sector can enhance the economy's overall productivity, the taxonomy suggests the following. First, it shows that business services, and financial services to some extent, have a 'high' contribution to technological progress. This is indicative of spillover effects in terms of technology enhancing overall productivity. Second, spillover effects may also be generated through inter-sectoral demand and supply linkages. For instance, Hansda (2001) shows that in 1993–94, the services sector in India had the largest expansionary effect on the rest of the economy in terms of backward and forward linkages.[19] Similarly, Banga and Goldar (2004) find that the growing use of services had a significant favourable effect on growth of output and productivity in Indian manufacturing during the 1990s, thereby implying that

---

[19] Singh (2006) shows that the result is much the same for 1998–99.

the services sector will be successful in creating its own demand – in other words, that it is possible for the services sector to sustain its growth. The taxonomy suggests that it is the sectors characterized as 'largely intermediate' – financial services and storage – or 'part final, par intermediate' – wholesale and retail trade, transport, communication and business services – which are likely to have these spillover effects.

Third, another way in which a sector can benefit the whole economy is through its effect on international trade. Given the increased tradeability of services in international markets, our analysis of international trade characteristics implies that business services and, to a lesser extent, transport by other means, hotels and restaurants, communication, financial and community services can facilitate growth by boosting the country's productivity through 'learning-by-exporting' effects, scale economies, transfer or technology and greater competition. However, like in the case of manufacturing, certain segments of the services sector may warrant some kind of 'infant services' protection if they generate positive externalities. Education, research and development, and telecommunications are sub-sectors of services that are likely to render such positive externalities on a significant scale (Rakshit, 2007).

In India's case, exports of business services – such as software, business process outsourcing, call centres, accountancy, law and engineering consulting – in particular may also serve to improve the country's balance of payments in a major way (see Chapter 3). This observation contradicts the argument highlighted by Bhattacharya and Mitra (1990) that services-led growth will not be sustainable as growth in services income would increase the demand for commodities (agriculture and goods) without an increase in their supply, thereby resulting either in inflation or an adverse balance of trade. The taxonomy shows that during the period from 1991 to 2009, business services were characterized by 'high' trade in international markets. In India's case, this is attributable to the exports of software services and business process outsourcing, thereby implying that imports of certain commodities may be financed by these export earnings.

In sum, given that certain sub-sectors of services are characterized by 'high' incorporation of technological advance, 'high' potential for achieving scale economies, 'high' contribution to technological progress, 'high' trade in world markets and considerable inter-sectoral linkages, the sustainability of services-led growth appears less unfeasible than before. At the same time, growth impulses from other sectors cannot be discounted. The sustainability of this growth process is also likely to be a function of the amount of employment the services sector generates.

5.5.3. Employment, Poverty and Inequality

The taxonomy shows that wholesale and retail trade, hotels and restaurants, transport by other means and personal, recreational and entertainment services are characterized by 'low to medium' capital and skill intensity (Table 5.14). This suggests that these services sub-sectors are likely to absorb a large unskilled workforce, and thereby reduce poverty directly. Joshi (2004) finds that with the exception of hotels and restaurants, the remaining three aforementioned services did not see a declining trend in employment elasticities during the period from 1994 to 2000.

On the other hand, the taxonomy shows that communication, financial and business services are characterized by 'medium to high' capital and skill intensity (Table 5.14). Joshi (2004) finds that none of these experienced a declining trend in employment elasticities during the period from 1994 to 2000. Employment expansion in these sectors, however, is likely to be biased in favour of individuals who are more educated and skilled and hence less relevant in terms of direct benefits to the relatively less well-off sections of society. At the same time, it may generate trickle-down effects. The remaining sub-sectors – storage, real estate and renting, railways, public administration and community services – are characterized by 'medium' capital and skill intensity when grouped together; in other words, high levels in some counterbalance low levels in others. It suggests that they may be somewhat biased in favour of the relatively more educated or capital-rich. Although the services sector has clearly not created employment commensurate with its increased share in output, its different sub-sectors do have the potential to create jobs, both for the skilled and unskilled. And as Joshi (2004) argues, given the sluggish growth of manufacturing employment and possible saturation in agriculture, the services sector needs to do more for employment creation and poverty alleviation.

Furthermore, the taxonomy shows that sectors that are classified with 'medium to high' productivity-enhancing technology characteristics – communication, financial and business services (Table 5.14) – are likely to create a small amount of employment opportunities and are likely to favour capital and skilled labour over unskilled labour. On the flipside, it also shows that sectors classified with 'low to medium' productivity-enhancing technology characteristics are likely to create a large amount of employment opportunities and are not likely to favour capital and skilled labour over unskilled labour. This dichotomy suggests that, for example in communication, financial and business services, skilled workers and owners of capital are likely to benefit from productivity increase. But a large amount of unskilled labour in other sub-sectors of services, such as wholesale and retail trade, hotels and restaurants, transport by other means and personal, recreational and entertainment services, may not benefit from such productivity increase. The resulting change in the relative earnings between different factor groups is likely to lead to higher income inequality. This validates the findings of Jha (2000) who argues that the rise in inequality in India during the post-reform period is attributable, in part, to the growth of financial and other services which increase the demand for skilled labour. In its classification of communication, business and financial services as 'largely organized' and 'medium-to-high' capital intensity (Table 5.14), the taxonomy also confirms the author's finding that the share of capital in total factor income tends to be higher in these 'organized' services.

5.6. Conclusion

Using statistical analysis of a set of ten economic characteristics, this taxonomy of India's services sector highlights its heterogeneous nature. This is an important conclusion in itself, relevant for advancing significant research questions. Moreover, classifications of sub-sectors resulting from the taxonomy reflect sub-sector-specific implications for economic growth, income distribution, poverty reduction and the sustainability of services-led growth. In doing so, these implications lend perspective to findings presented by a growing literature on India's services sector. Finally, the taxonomy also provides a stepping stone to construct a similar taxonomy for other developing countries. It would enable researchers to draw lessons, in a comparative country context, about the diverse nature of the services sector that constituted 70 per cent of world GDP in 2008.[20] This is especially relevant given that certain sub-sectors, such as financial and business services, may not have grown as much in certain other developing countries (Bosworth and Maertens, 2010).

It is important to reiterate that this characterization of different sub-sectors of services follows from their categorization in terms of the selected attributes developed in the taxonomy. This, in turn, is relevant for the analysis that follows in the subsequent chapters.

---

[20] World Bank, *World Development Indicators*, online database.

SIX

The Nature of Employment in India's Services Sector

Educational Requirements and Quality

6.1. Introduction

The literature on structural change suggests that once countries have industrialized and reached an advanced stage of economic development, the share of the manufacturing sector – in terms of both output and employment – declines whereas that of the service sector increases. This was highlighted in Chapter 1. Chapter 3 showed that this increasing importance of the services sector in India may be attributable to high-income elasticity of demand for services, increasing relative prices of services, policy liberalization, contracting out of services from firms in the manufacturing sector and increased international trade in services.

Importantly, the stylized facts presented in Chapter 1 showed that in the context of the literature on structural change, the case of India is unusual for two reasons. First, for a country of its level of development, the increase in the share of the services sector in GDP has been unusually substantial – so much so that it picked up more than 80 per cent of the decline in the share of the agricultural sector during the period from 1980–81 to 2009–10. Second, the increase in the share of the services sector in total employment during this period has not been commensurate with that in total output. The preceding discussion implies that during the last two and a half decades, the productivity of services has risen relative to industry. But does this mean that jobs in the service sector, on average, are characterized by relatively higher wages and better working conditions? Few empirical studies have investigated this question. There is a study on India by Ghose (1999) which analyses employment growth in four categories – regular wage employment in the organized sector, self-employment in the organized sector, regular wage employment in the unorganized sector and casual wage-employment – to show that the quality of employment was higher in services than in agriculture and industry during the period from 1977–78 to 1993–94.[1] Similarly, a study on the OECD economies reveals that, relative to the industrial sector, the services sector is characterized by higher average earnings, longer average job tenure and higher job satisfaction (OECD, 2001). More recently, Abraham (2007) concludes that wage inequality is widening between the service sector and other sectors in India.

These studies, however, do not base their results on rigorous econometric analysis and hence their results do not imply causality. In other words, it does not necessarily mean that if one shifts a particular worker from industry to the service sector, this worker would, on average, receive a higher wage. To establish such an effect, one would need to control for the selection of workers into different sectors of the economy by taking into account education, experience and other individual-specific factors (Bosworth and Maertens, 2008). Moreover, these studies view the services sector as a composite whole, which is not very meaningful given that services comprise a set of highly heterogeneous economic activities. For some observers, the dramatic increase in the productivity of the services sector reflects rapid strides made by educated professionals employed in software, financial and telecommunications services. But this dynamism is the visible dimension of India's services-sector growth. What about individuals employed as domestic servants, maids, cooks and drivers in the personal services sector? Or those working in retail trade, small restaurants and road transport services? Indeed, some observers see the growth of services sector as the expansion of the unorganized sector that provides employment to individuals because economic growth has not created sufficient employment opportunities elsewhere in the economy. This residual segment of the services sector, which employs a large number of unskilled workers, may not experience the same increase in productivity – and hence in wage and non-wage benefits – as the rest of the sector. It implies that the nature of employment generated in the service sector is likely to vary across its various segments. This heterogeneity, while not explicitly analysed, is emphasized in a recent study on India by Mazumdar and Sarkar (2008), which shows that the gap between low and high earners in the services sector has increased, relative to the industrial sector, during the period from 1983 to 1999–2000.

Given the above, the object of this chapter is to analyse, the nature of employment being created in the different sub-sectors of services. In doing

---

[1] Assuming that regular and casual wage employment offer, respectively, the highest and lowest quality of employment.

so, we define the nature of employment to include two broad attributes: educational requirements and quality of employment, where the latter is analysed using three measures that reflect quality of life: wages, job security and social protection. The scope of the chapter is limited to cross-sectional analysis of survey data for a sample of over 600,000 individuals in India at two points in time: 1993–94 and 2004–05. The choice of surveys analysed is determined by the following. First, the period from 1990–91 saw the most dramatic increase in the output share of the services sector. Second, while 2004–05 is the most recent survey for which data are available, those preceding 1993–94 are not as comprehensive in terms of the questions they ask and hence the variables they cover. It is important to emphasize the fact that such an exercise has not been attempted in the literature on India.

The structure of the chapter is as follows. Section 6.2 outlines the variables chosen to measure the nature of employment. Section 6.3 describes the data and highlights the potential opportunity that it provides for an unexplored research question. Section 6.4 presents descriptive statistics of the data under consideration. Section 6.5 specifies the notation used in the econometric analysis to follow. Section 6.6 differentiates between the various sub-sectors of services in terms of the importance of educational requirements in securing a job. Sections 6.7 and 6.8 present the econometric frameworks used and subsequently discuss results for the three chosen measures of employment quality. Section 6.9 discusses issues of endogeneity associated with the econometric analysis in Sections 6.7 and 6.8. Section 6.10 presents conclusions.

6.2. Nature of Employment: The Chosen Attributes

6.2.1. Educational Requirements

Education is a potentially important determinant of access to employment in any sector because it converts individuals into a different kind of labour. Developed most extensively by the Chicago school of economic thought, the 'human capital' theory is the most familiar theory of what education does (Becker, 1964; Schultz, 1961). Education imparts certain knowledge and skills which may be an important prerequisite for several jobs. Moreover, education may improve productivity and performance at work. In contrast, according to theories of signalling and screening, education does not raise individual productivity but simply conveys information to prospective employers about the innate ability of people (Arrow, 1973; Spence, 1976). In reality, education is likely to be of some value in most occupations, but the threshold value beyond which further education has no effect on productivity is unlikely to be uniform (Knight, 1979). Another view of the role of education in labour markets is that it is an instrument for job competition. If wages are sticky, access to jobs in a competitive market is determined by the cost of training those who get the job. In this context, the more educated have an advantage as education reduces training costs because it is a form of complementary human capital or because it serves as signal for higher innate ability (Thurow, 1976).

In sum, all the aforementioned theoretical frameworks imply that education can serve as a barrier that restricts access to employment. But given the diversity of economic activities included in the services sector, educational requirements are likely to vary considerably across its various segments. This suggests that access to employment may be greater in certain service sub-sectors. In turn, this may influence the quality of employment. For instance, the 'human capital' theory argues that education is rewarded with higher wages in the labour market. Moreover, better-educated people are largely employed in formal or organized segments of an economy in which they are likely to receive higher wage and non-wage benefits.

6.2.2. Quality of Employment

The quality of employment is a multidimensional and subjective concept, and hence difficult to define. We identify three parameters to analyse quality of employment: wages, the availability of written job contracts and the availability of social security benefits. These are objective measures that have implications for quality of life.

In the economics literature, the focus of the good-job-versus-bad-job debate is on wages or income. Wages earned in the labour market are naturally an important indicator of the quality of employment because they provide individuals with a source of livelihood. Income influences quality of life because it enables people to purchase goods and services and enjoy leisure. Economists also use wages to measure the quality of employment because it is the most systematically monitored characteristic of employment (Jackson and Kumar, 1998). In a neoclassical world with full employment and perfect competition, there should be no inter-sectoral wage differentials in equilibrium, after controlling for defining individual characteristics such as education and experience.[2] In the real world, however, there are several factors that cause labour market rigidities. The theory of

---

[2] They need to have identical tastes too.

segmented labour markets argues that labour markets consist of several distinct segments with different rules for wage determination (Doeringer and Piore, 1971), where the 'distinct segments' may be defined according to the industry of employment (Krueger and Summers, 1987), the nature of occupation (Dickens and Katz, 1987), organized and unorganized economic activity and the distinction between public and private ownership. For example, wages in the organized sector are institutionally determined, often kept above market clearing levels by profit sharing, labour unions, collective bargaining, the payment of efficiency wages and minimum wage laws (Krueger and Summers, 1988; Osburn, 2000). In contrast, unorganized-sector wages are lower, as it falls outside the labour regulation system. Even firm size may be a factor that explains inter-sectoral wage differentials (Gibson and Stillman, 2009; Oi and Idson, 1999a). This is because workers are more productive in larger firms and therefore demand higher wages (Oi and Idson, 1999b). In addition, large firms often enter into long-term relationships with their workers – by rewarding them better – because the complexity of management and technology gives rise to firm-specific skills (Black et al., 1999). Given the diversity of the services sector, there is likely to be considerable variation in the earnings or wages of similar workers across its different segments.

There is also a literature which highlights the importance of analyzing other job characteristics, which also influence quality of life (Ritter and Anker, 2002). For instance, it identifies jobs contracts and social protection[3] as important indicators of the quality of employment because they measure, respectively, job security[4] and insurance against risk (Dewan and Peek, 2007; Letourneux, 1998; Messier and Floro, 2008; Mishel et al., 2001). In this context, the distinction between the organized and unorganized sectors assumes importance. Enterprises located in the unorganized sector – defined by India's National Accounts Statistics to include economic activity not regulated under any legal provision – are likely to be characterized by the non-applicability of labour laws, absence of formal contracts and lack of social security benefits.[5] Given the heterogeneity of the services sector, the division of economic activity into organized and unorganized components varies considerably across its various segments (see Chapter 3). This, in turn, will result in significant inter-sector variation in the probability of receiving job contracts and social security benefits. Importantly,

---

[3] Health, retirement and disability insurance.
[4] For the self-employed, job security may refer to business failure or likelihood of losing independent work (Dewan and Peek, 2007).
[5] In India, these include pensions, gratuity, health care and maternity benefits.

the juxtaposition of an analysis of inter-sectoral differences in wages and non-wage benefits lends itself to an examination of the theory of compensating wage differentials, whereby one expects 'compensating variation' in the wage level for negative job traits such as poor job security and social protection (A. Smith, 1776).

It is worth noting that our choice of attributes does not imply that other measures indicative of the quality of employment – job satisfaction[6] and subjective well-being[7] (Clark and Oswald, 1996; Freeman, 1978; Layard, 1980) or intrinsic job characteristics such as job content, on-the-job training[8] and working conditions[9] (Beaston, 2000; Johri, 2005) – are less important. It reflects limitations of the dataset under consideration. It also keeps the task at hand to manageable proportions.

6.3. Data

6.3.1. Sample: Source and Size

To analyse the nature of employment in an economy, a necessary condition is the availability of data at the level of the individual. Surveys on employment, conducted regularly by India's National Sample Survey Organisation (NSSO), collect such micro-level data, thereby providing the opportunity for empirical analysis on the aforementioned research question.

The first comprehensive survey on employment was carried out during the period from September 1972 to October 1973, corresponding to the twenty-seventh round of the NSS. Thereafter, seven comprehensive quinquennial surveys on employment in India have been carried out by the NSSO. These were carried out during the thirty-second (July 1977 to June 1978), thirty-eighth (January 1983 to December 1983), forty-third (July 1987 to June 1988), fiftieth (July 1993 to June 1994), fifty-fifth (July 1999 to June 2000), sixty-first (July 2004 to June 2005) and sixty-sixth (July 2009

---

[6] Captures a worker's personal values, circumstances and expectations from his or her job (Freeman, 1978; Ritter and Anker, 2002).

[7] Relates well-being or happiness to how each individual perceives his or her level of income in relation to that of others, past experiences and expectations of the future, i.e. relative rather than absolute.

[8] Continuous training of individuals is important for career development as it influences their ability to retain a high-quality job or move to an even better one (OECD, 2001).

[9] This includes people being exposed to conditions with hazardous health risks as well as irregular work hours, limited work-time flexibility and limited work autonomy (OECD, 2001).

Table 6.1. *Sample size*

	1993–94 (50th round)	2004–05 (61st round)
Number of Villages Surveyed	6,983	7,999
Number of Urban Blocks Surveyed	4,670	4,602
Number of Individuals Surveyed (Total)	564,740	602,833
Number of Individuals Surveyed (Rural areas)	356,351	398,025
Number of Individuals Surveyed (Urban areas)	208,389	204,808

Source: Surveys on Employment, National Sample Survey Organisation.

to June 2010) rounds. These surveys do not track the same individuals over time. Furthermore, data from the sixty-sixth round are not yet available.

For the present exercise, the data are taken from two of the seven comprehensive quinquennial surveys on employment and unemployment conducted by the National Sample Survey: the fiftieth round (July 1993 to June 1994) and the sixty-first round (July 2004 to June 2005). The choice of surveys analysed is explained in the introduction. Spread over 6,983 villages and 4,670 urban blocks, the former has a sample size of 564,740 individuals. Similarly, spread over 7,999 villages and 4,602 urban blocks, the latter has a sample size of 602,833 individuals (Table 6.1). These large sample sizes are a real strength of the econometric analysis to follow. The geographical coverage and sample design is identical to that used in the surveys on consumer expenditure, also carried out by the NSSO (see Chapter 4).

6.3.2. Employment: Definitions and Categories

Individuals employed in different economic activities are classified into the following categories: self-employed, regular wage employees and labour employed on casual wage basis (daily or periodic work contract). The surveys also classify a working individual according to his or her industry of employment as well as occupation. Of course, there are unemployed people who are seeking or are available for work, and there are others who are out of the labour force. These particulars of working individuals as well as the division between the employed and the unemployed are based on three reference periods: one year, one week and each day of the week. They are referred to as 'usual status', 'current weekly status' and 'current daily status', respectively (NSSO, 1996a; NSSO, 2006a).

In the usual-status approach, the 'principal usual status' activity of an individual is defined as the activity on which he or she spent the longest time in the 365 days preceding the start date of survey. Accordingly, an individual is considered 'employed' if he or she was employed in an economic activity for a longer period than being unemployed or engaged in non-economic activities.[10] On the other hand, an individual is considered as 'seeking or available' for work or 'unemployed' if he or she was not working but was either seeking or available for work for a longer period than being employed or engaged in non-economic activities during the past year. Similarly, an individual is considered to be out of the labour force if he or she was engaged in non-economic activities for the majority part of the year preceding the survey.

In the current-weekly-status approach, individuals are assigned a unique activity status with reference to a period of seven days preceding the start date of the survey. For individuals pursuing more than one activity, the status of working gets priority over the status of not working but available for work, which, in turn, gets priority over the status of not working and not available for work. Within the broad categories of working and not working, the activity category is assigned by the 'majority time spent' criterion. In this approach, a person is considered employed if he or she was engaged in an economic activity for at least one hour on any day of the previous week. Similarly, an individual is considered as 'seeking or available' for work if he or she had been seeking or had been available for work at any time for at least one hour during the reference week. Others were considered out of the labour force.

6.4. Descriptive Statistics

Of the 564,740 individuals covered in the survey of 1993–94 and 602,833 in 2004–05, the total number employed was 202,000 and 221,309, respectively. Of these, the total number of people employed in the services sector was 59,992 and 75,827, respectively. This suggests that, in both samples, the services sector accounted for about one-third of total employment. Within the services sector, we consider eleven sub-sectors: wholesale and retail trade, hotels and restaurants, transport, communication, finance, real estate and renting, business, public administration and defence, education, health and other social, community and personal services.

Table 6.2 shows that among these, wholesale and retail trade is undoubtedly the largest employer, accounting, respectively, for about 35 per cent

---

[10] Includes individuals attending educational institutions, those performing domestic duties only, pensioners, beggars and infants.

Table 6.2. *Individuals in the sample employed in different sub-sectors of services: All-India (principal usual status activity)*

Sector	Number of Individuals		As a % of the total number of individuals employed in the services sector	
	1993–94	2004–05	1993–94	2004–05
Wholesale and Retail Trade	20,948	27,965	35.0	37.0
Hotels and Restaurants	2,262	3,980	3.8	5.0
Transport Services	6,836	9,899	11.4	13.0
Communication Services	509	1,258	0.8	2.0
Financial Services	1,782	1,698	3.0	2.0
Real Estate and Renting Services	260	554	0.4	0.5
Business Services	891	1,732	1.5	2.0
Public Administration and Defence	9,960	8,653	17.0	11.0
Education Services	5,717	9,194	9.5	11.0
Health Services	2,104	2,470	3.0	3.0
Other Social, Community and Personal Services	8,421	8,424	14.0	11.0
Services Sector (Aggregate)	59,992	75,827	100.0	100.0

Source: National Sample Survey Organisation, Surveys on Employment, 2004–05 and 1993–94.

and 37 per cent of total services employment in the sample of 1993–94 and 2004–05. Other sub-sectors that constitute a sizable proportion of total services employment include transport, other social, community and personal services, public administration and defence and education services. For the first two, this is not entirely surprising given that they are labour-intensive sectors with little or no educational requirements. On the other hand, while public administration and defence and education services require individuals to be well educated and skilled, the creation of a large number of jobs may be attributable to a dominant public sector. Finally, hotels and restaurants, communication, financial, business, real estate and renting and health services each account for a very small proportion of total employment in services. This is only to be expected given that, with the exception of hotels and restaurants, these sub-sectors are likely to require individuals to be well educated and skilled. The set of results described above holds true for both samples.

Table 6.2 also shows that during the period from 1993–94 to 2004–05, public administration and defence, financial services and other social,

Table 6.3. *Number of people in the sample employed in different sub-sectors of services: Rural-urban division*

Sector	Rural areas as a percentage of the total		Urban areas as a percentage of the total	
	1993–94	2004–05	1993–94	2004–05
Wholesale and Retail Trade	31	44	69	56
Hotels and Restaurants	27	37	73	63
Transport Services	31	48	69	52
Communication Services	31	43	69	57
Financial Services	19	31	81	69
Real Estate and Renting Services	22	37	78	63
Business Services	14	22	86	78
Public Administration and Defence	30	42	70	58
Education Services	46	59	54	41
Health Services	30	45	70	55
Other Social, Community and Personal Services	38	44	62	56
Services Sector (Aggregate)	33	45	67	55

Source: National Sample Survey Organization, Surveys on Employment, 2004–05 and 1993–94.

community and personal services saw a decline in their relative share of total services employment. For public administration and defence, this reflects government policy to reduce overstaffing. This result appears to be counterintuitive for financial services, but it may be indicative of the emergence of a more efficient private-sector component as well as policy to reduce overstaffing in the public-sector component. Finally, for other social, community and personal services, the decline may be a result of the heterogeneity of economic activity within the sector. An analysis of data that are further disaggregated shows that whereas employment has increased significantly in the domestic, refuse disposal, sanitation and other personal-services segment, it has contracted in activities of membership organizations and recreational, cultural and sports activities.[11]

Table 6.3 presents the distribution of individuals in the different subsectors of services across rural and urban areas. For the sample of 1993–94, of the total number of people employed in the services sector, 33 per cent are located in rural areas and 67 per cent are located in urban areas. For the sample of 2004–05, the corresponding figures are 45 per cent and

[11] Estimates available with the author.

55 per cent. This suggests that the period from 1993–94 to 2004–05 has seen the relative growth of a rural non-farm sector which consists of service activities. Moreover, within each sample, the distribution of people employed between rural and urban areas for most sub-sectors of services shows a broadly similar trend. Across both samples, the exceptions are business and financial services, in which about three-fourths (or more) of the individuals employed are located in urban areas. This should come as no surprise given that these services are associated with sophisticated technology and highly skilled individuals.

The industrial classification of an individual's place of work defines the precise sector of the economy in which he or she is employed. However, individuals employed in the same industry or sector may be employed in different occupations, where occupation refers to the nature of tasks performed. According to India's National Classification of Occupations (NCO), individuals may be employed in the following occupations at the one-digit level of classification: (1) professional, technical and related workers; (2) administrative, executive and managerial workers; (3) clerical and related workers; (4) sales workers; (5) service workers; (6) famers, fishermen, hunters, loggers and related workers; and (7) production and related workers, transport equipment operators and labourers.

Table 6.4 presents the distribution of individuals across occupations in the different sub-sectors of services. For the sample of 2004–05, it shows that communication, financial, real estate, business, public administration, education and health services are dominated by professional and technical workers, administrative and managerial workers or clerical workers. This suggests that individuals in these sub-sectors of services are likely to be well educated and skilled, on average. In contrast, wholesale and retail trade consists primarily of sales workers, whereas hotels and restaurants and other social, community and personal services are dominated by service workers. This implies that, on average, individuals in these sub-sectors of services are likely to have little to no specialized skills. In transport services, there is no single dominant occupation category. For 1993–94, the results are broadly similar, with one interesting difference. The number of clerical workers appears to be notably higher for communication, financial and business services in 1993–94 than in 2004–05. This decline may be indicative of government policy to reduce overstaffing in the public sector as well as increased privatization in the economy during this period.

The set of previously described summary statistics follows the 'principal usual status' reference period. Although not reported for reasons of space,

Table 6.4. *Employment in different sub-sectors of services by occupation in the sample*

Sector	Professional and technical workers (%)		Administrative, executive and managerial workers (%)		Clerical workers (%)		Sales workers (%)		Service workers (%)	
	1993–94	2004–05	1993–94	2004–05	1993–94	2004–05	1993–94	2004–05	1993–94	2004–05
Wholesale and Retail Trade	0.8	0.3	4.8	9.1	2.4	1.1	86.2	76.1	0.8	0.6
Hotels and Restaurants	0.2	0.1	14.9	20.0	3.2	1.4	14.1	7.6	60.0	65.8
Transport Services	1.4	0.6	5.6	9.9	12.4	8.2	0.8	0.6	3.0	1.5
Communication Services	6.5	3.6	1.9	21.0	69.0	54.4	1.8	6.7	2.1	2.4
Financial Services	4.1	2.8	21.8	19.1	60.1	45.5	10.0	26.4	2.4	4.6
Real Estate and Renting Services	2.3	2.3	27.4	40.3	7.2	4.0	48.8	29.6	2.7	5.9
Business Services	48.6	42.5	8.0	12.5	25.6	18.4	6.0	8.3	3.2	8.4
Public Administration and Defence	15.6	12.8	4.6	4.8	43.0	44.3	0.6	0.45	22.6	24.7
Education Services	79.7	85.6	1.6	1.5	12.4	7.8	0.1	0.1	4.6	3.9
Health Services	71.0	71.8	0.1	1.1	10.3	9.7	1.0	0.3	15.1	14.4
Other Social, Community and Personal Services	15.9	14.2	3.3	2.7	1.2	1.4	0.9	0.6	52.8	67.5

Source: National Sample Survey Organisation, Surveys on Employment, 2004–05 and 1993–94.

the use of the 'current weekly status' reference period does not alter the results in any notable way.

6.5. Notation and Description of Variables

Table 6.5 explains the notation for different variables used in the equations specified in the sections that follow. The table also provides a brief description of these variables.

6.6. Educational Requirements

6.6.1. Econometric Model I

To analyse the importance of education for securing employment in a sub-sector of services, we estimate Equation (6.1):

$$SECTOR_i = \lambda + \alpha_1 AGE_i + \alpha_2 AGESQ_i + \alpha_3 LAND_i$$
$$+ \alpha_4 MALEDUM_i + \alpha_5 EDUDUM2_i$$
$$+ \alpha_6 EDUDUM3_i + \beta SECTORDUMMIES_i$$
$$+ DISTRICTDUMMIES_i + \varepsilon_i$$

In the above equation, we define *SECTOR* as a binary dependent variable that takes the value of 1 when an individual is employed in a particular service sub-sector and zero if an individual is not employed in that sub-sector. The above regression equation is estimated separately for each sub-sector of services using a Logit model. Our variables of interest are the two dummy variables for education levels: one represents individuals who have completed secondary education, and the other represents those who have completed tertiary education. The omitted category is individuals who are illiterate or who have completed only primary education. We also control for personal characteristics such as age, gender and the amount of land owned. Each of the eleven equations (Equation 6.1) is estimated in three specifications: all-India, rural areas and urban areas. District dummy variables are also included to control for any district-specific unobservable heterogeneity.

6.6.2. Results

The marginal effects of the education dummy variables are indicative of the importance of higher levels of education for securing employment in a particular sub-sector of services (see Appendix Tables C.1 to C.11).

Table 6.5. *Notation and description of variables*

Notation	Description
SECTOR	Dummy variable that takes the value of one if an individual is employed in a particular sub-sector of services and zero if an individual is not employed in that sub-sector
SECTOR *(Used in the Multinomial Logit Model)*	Variable that consists of thirteen discrete outcomes where each outcome refers to an individual being employed in agriculture, industry or one of the eleven sub-sectors of the economy
EARNINGS	Weekly earnings of an individual (does not include the self-employed)
CONTRACT	Dummy variable that takes the value of one if an individual receives a written job contract and zero if an individual does not receive a written job contract
SOCIALSEC	Dummy variable that takes the value of one if an individual receives any social security benefits and zero if an individual receives no social security benefits
AGE	Age of an individual
AGESQ	Square of the age of an individual
LAND	Land owned by an individual measured in terms of hectares
MALEDUM	Dummy variable that equals one for those individuals who are male
EDUDUM2	Dummy variable that equals one for individuals who have completed medium, secondary or senior secondary school
EDUDUM3	Dummy variable that equals one for individuals who have completed an undergraduate degree, postgraduate degree or a diploma/certificate course
SECTORDUMMIES	Vector of dummy variables referring to the sector that individuals are employed in
OCCDUMMIES	Vector of dummy variables referring to the occupation of an individual at the one-digit level
SELFEMPDUM	Dummy variable that equals one if the individual is self-employed
PUBLICDUM	Dummy variable that equals one for enterprises characterized by public ownership
UNIONDUM	Dummy variable that equals one for enterprises which have an active labour union
SCALEDUM	Dummy variable that equals one for enterprises that have ten or more workers

For communication, financial, real estate and renting, business, public administration and defence, education and health services, the marginal effects of both education dummy variables are positive and significant at the 1 per cent level. This holds true for both 1993–94 and 2004–05. It is only to be expected as a majority of individuals employed in these sub-sectors of services are professional, managerial or clerical workers. In contrast, the marginal effect of both education dummy variables is negative and significant at the 1 per cent level for wholesale and retail trade, hotels and restaurants, transport, and other social, community and personal services. Once again, this holds true for both 1993–94 and 2004–05. This too should come as no surprise because a majority of individuals employed in these sub-sectors of services are non-professional, non-managerial workers. The results holds true for the all-India sample, rural areas and urban areas.

6.6.3. Econometric Model II

The set of regressions presented earlier outline the importance of education for getting a job in each different sub-sector of services, in absolute terms. To analyse the importance of education for securing employment in a sub-sector of services relative to the industrial sector, we estimate Equation (6.2).

$$SECTOR_i = \lambda + \alpha_1 AGE_i + \alpha_2 AGESQ_i + \alpha_3 LAND_i$$
$$+ \alpha_4 MALEDUM_i + \alpha_5 EDUDUM2_i$$
$$+ \alpha_6 EDUDUM3_i + \beta SECTORDUMMIES_i$$
$$+ DISTRICTDUMMIES_i + \varepsilon_i$$

In contrast to the previous model, this defines SECTOR as a dependent variable that has more than two discrete outcomes. In fact, it consists of thirteen discrete outcomes, each outcome referring to an individual being employed in agriculture, industry or one of the eleven sub-sectors of services. Moreover, these outcomes cannot be ordered in any meaningful way. Hence, we estimate the above regression equation using a Multinomial Logit model. Each outcome of the dependent variables refers to an individual being employed in industry, agriculture, or one of the eleven sub-sectors of services described above. Being employed in the industrial sector is taken as the base outcome. Hence, coefficients on the sector dummy variables may be interpreted as the impact of certain variable on the probability of being employed in a particular sector, relative to the industrial sector.

6.6.4. Results

For the all-India sample, we find that relative to the industrial sector, the marginal effects of both education dummy variables are positive and statistically significant at the 1 per cent level for communication, financial, real estate and renting, business, public administration and defence, education and health services. In contrast, relative to the industrial sector, the marginal effects of both education dummy variables are negative and statistically significant at the 1 per cent level for other social, community and personal services. Finally, relative to the industrial sector, we find that the marginal effect of both education dummy variables are statistically insignificant for wholesale and retail trade, hotels and restaurants and transport services. This set of results holds true for both 1993–94 and 2004–05 (see Appendix C, Tables C.12 to C.15).

6.6.5. Endogeneity Bias

It may be argued that the two dummy variables for levels of education suffer from endogeneity bias – in other words, unobservable variables such as ability, dedication and family background of individuals are likely to influence both the level of education attained and the probability of being employed in a particular sub-sector of services. Hence, the coefficients on these dummy variables are also likely to reflect the effects of these unobservables on the probability of getting a job in different sectors. However, given that the object of our analysis is not related to estimating the true returns to education, this endogeneity bias is not a cause for concern. We can simply redefine barriers to entry to include, along with education, the importance of the associated ability, dedication and family background in securing a job. Table 6.6 provides the summary of our conclusions from both sets of analysis.

The 'human capital' theory of education argues that human capital is rewarded with higher wages. Given that job quality is often defined in terms of wage benefits, heterogeneity of job quality according to the level of education of individuals is a possible implication of the theory. Moreover, more educated individuals are largely employed as white-collar workers in the formal or organized sector where employers are likely to reward their employees with relatively higher non-wage benefits. The latter may include dimensions of job quality such as relatively high job security and social protection. Hence, because more educated people are likely to receive higher wage and non-wage benefits, access to employment in terms of educational

Table 6.6. *Educational requirements*

High	Low	Largely free-entry
Communication Services	Wholesale and Retail	Other Social,
Financial Services	Trade	Community and
Real Estate and Renting Services	Hotels and Restaurants	Personal Services
Business Services	Transport Services	
Public Administration and Defence		
Education Services		
Health Services		

Note: Educational requirements may also reflect the importance of ability, dedication and family background.

requirements is likely to be an important indicator of the quality of employment opportunities in a sector. This is explored in the sections that follow.

6.7. Wages or Earnings

6.7.1. Econometric Model

Much of the empirical literature on earnings functions is concerned with estimating returns to education. It goes back to the seminal work of Mincer (1974) who expressed the natural logarithm of earnings as a function of education, years of experience and years of experience-squared. Usually, it is estimated by applying ordinary least squares (OLS) or instrumental variable (IV) analysis to the model described above or to an augmented version[12] of it (Knight and Sabot, 1987; Psacharopoulos, 1994; Schutz, 1988). To analyse whether the earnings of individuals employed in different sub-sectors of services are significantly different from those of individuals employed in other sectors of the economy, we estimate the following earnings function by OLS (Equation [6.3]).

$$\ln(EARNINGS)_i = \lambda + \alpha_1 AGE_i + \alpha_2 AGESQ_i + \alpha_3 LAND_i$$
$$+ \alpha_4 MALEDUM_i + \alpha_5 EDUDUM2_i + \alpha_6 EDUDUM3_i$$
$$+ \alpha_7 CASTEDUM_i + \alpha_8 RELIGIONDUM_i$$
$$+ \alpha_9 HRSWORKED_i + \beta SECTORDUMMIES_i$$
$$+ DISTRICTDUMMIES_i + \varepsilon_i$$

---

[12] Controlling for other variables that may affect earnings.

Our variables of interest are the different sector dummy variables. Their inclusion in an earnings function is fairly common in the empirical literature analyzing inter-sectoral wage differentials (Lucifora, 1993; Osberg et al., 1987). We include dummy variables for all sub-sectors of services and for the agricultural sector, keeping industry as the residual category. Hence, the coefficients on these variables are interpreted as the effect on earnings of being employed in a particular sub-sector of services relative to industry. Given that individual income is also a function of several personal characteristics, we control for age, sex, education, land owned, caste, religion and hours worked. District dummy variables are also included. The regression equation is estimated at the all-India level, rural areas and urban areas for two points in time: 1993–94 and 2004–05. It may be argued that the sector dummy variables are picking up the effect of an individual's occupation or a characteristic of his or her workplace. Hence, as a robustness check, we control for occupation, firm size, union activity and public ownership in Equation (6.4).[13]

$$
\begin{aligned}
\ln(EARNINGS)_i ={} & \lambda + \alpha_1 AGE_i + \alpha_2 AGESQ_i + \alpha_3 LAND_i \\
& + \alpha_4 MALEDUM_i + \alpha_5 EDUDUM2_i + \alpha_6 EDUDUM3_i \\
& + \alpha_7 CASTEDUM_i + \alpha_8 RELIGIONDUM_i \\
& + \alpha_9 HRSWORKED_i + \beta SECTORDUMMIES_i \\
& + DISTRICTDUMMIES_i + \gamma_1 OCCDUMMIES_i \\
& + \mu_1 PUBLICDUM_i + \mu_2 UNIONDUM_i \\
& + \mu_3 SCALEDUM_i + \varepsilon_i
\end{aligned}
$$

6.7.2. Results

The detailed set of results is provided in Appendix Table C.16. Figure 6.1 reports coefficients of the sector dummy variables and their statistical significance for the all-India sample in 2004–05.

For the all-India sample in 2004–05, coefficients of the dummy variables for communication, financial, business and public administration and defence services are positive and statistically significant – at the least at the 5 per cent level. This should come as no surprise because these sub-sectors of services are dominated by organized sector activity. Moreover, most

---

[13] For the sample of 1993–94, there are no data available on the different enterprise characteristics.

	All-India	Urban Areas	Rural Areas
0.3			
0.2	Finance* Business* Public administration*	Business* Finance* Transport*	Finance* Public administration*
0.1	Communication* Transport, Real estate	Public administration* Communication*	Real estate Communication* Transport
Industry 0	Hotels and restaurants	Real estate Hotels and restaurants*	Education, Business Hotels and restaurants*
−0.1	Trade* Education*,Other* Health*	Trade* Education* Health*	Trade*, Health* Other*
−0.2		Other*	
−0.3			

Figure 6.1. Variation in service sub-sector dummy variable coefficients for wage regression (2004–05).

individuals in these sectors are employed in professional, managerial, and clerical jobs, all of which require a reasonably high quality (not just level) of skill. In addition, communication, financial and business services may consist of a large number of highly profitable firms that generate profit-sharing wages, pay efficiency wages and use productivity-enhancing modern technology. In contrast, coefficients of dummy variables for transport and real estate and renting services are statistically insignificant. This is plausible as, like the industrial sector, these sub-sectors have significant organized and unorganized segments and employ large numbers of individuals in both skilled and unskilled jobs. Coefficients of dummy variables for wholesale and retail trade, hotels and restaurants and other social, community and personal services are negative and statistically significant at the 1 per cent level. For wholesale and retail trade and other social, community and personal services, this is only to be expected as both sectors are dominated by unorganized sector activity and largely employ people in unskilled jobs. For hotels and restaurants too, this is not surprising as except for in luxury hotels, individuals working in small restaurants and *dhabas*[14] are likely to earn low wages. Strikingly, those employed in education and health services earn significantly lower wages than those in the industrial sector. This is plausible, as the overall profitability of firms and the incidence of profit-sharing wages in the industrial sector may be relatively high.

---

[14] Small-scale roadside restaurants.

Table 6.7. *Quality of employment in terms of wages: A dividing line*

Dividing Line vis-à-vis the Industrial Sector

Worse-off or neither worse-off nor better-off in terms of earnings	*Better-off in terms of earnings*
Wholesale and Retail Trade	Communication Services
Hotels and Restaurants	Financial Services
Transport Services	Business Services
Real Estate and Renting Services	Public Administration and Defence
Education Services	
Health Services	
Other Social, Community and Personal Services	

For urban areas, the results are similar except for the fact that the coefficient of the dummy variable for transport services is positive and significant at the 5 per cent level. This is likely to reflect employment in air transport services, where pilots, engineers, technicians and flight crew receive high salaries from large private-sector companies. Moreover, unlike the industrial sector in urban areas, air transport services are unlikely to have a significant unorganized-sector component. For rural areas, there are some interesting differences. First, the coefficient on the dummy variable for business services is statistically insignificant. However, this result is not very meaningful as the number of people employed in this sector in rural areas in negligible. Second, the coefficient of the dummy variable for education services is negative but not statistically significant. This reflects the fact that, although teachers are paid poorly in general, their salaries are unlikely to be low relative to individuals employed in rural industrial activity such as mining and construction. Table 6.7 provides a summary of the results.[15]

This table reflects a dichotomy in the services sector – a set of sub-sectors characterized by relatively high wages and another set characterized by relatively low wages. This dichotomy is also captured in Figure 6.2, which shows that wages of individuals included in the sample are not normally distributed. There appears to be a set of individuals to the left of the distribution who earn relatively low wages and a set to the right who earn relatively high wages. The former are likely to be individuals employed in sub-sectors of services that are largely free-entry, whereas the latter are likely to be those employed in sub-sectors of services that have restricted entry.

[15] The coefficients on the personal characteristics, occupation affiliation dummies and the enterprise characteristics are statistically significant and have the expected signs.

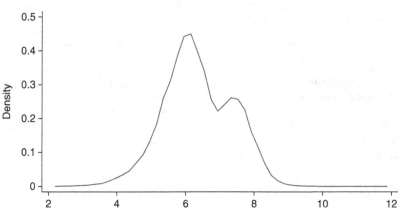

Figure 6.2. Free-entry and restricted-entry sub-sectors of services.
Source: Primary data from National Sample Survey Organisation, India

For the sample of 1993–94, we find two notable differences (see Appendix C, Table C.16). First, relative to the industrial sector, those employed in education and health services earn significantly more. This may be explained by fact that in 1993–94, when the process of economic liberalization was initiated, the overall profitability of the industrial sector may have been relatively low because of lack of competition. Moreover, it was dominated by public-sector enterprises which were less likely to use performance-based efficiency wages. Second, the coefficient on the dummy variable for business services is statistically insignificant. This may be attributable to the fact that business services such as software, business process outsourcing, engineering consultancy and accountancy were in their nascent stages of development at the time.

It is worth noting that the self-employed are excluded from the previous analysis as data on their wages are not available. Hence, we estimate the same regression model using household expenditure as a proxy for earnings, with the household head determining a household's sector of employment. Although this is not ideal as mixed incomes of the household are ignored, it is the only way to analyse incomes of the self-employed given the limitations of the dataset. Importantly, we find that the aforementioned conclusions are not changed in any notable way by the inclusion of workers other than wage earners.[16]

---

[16] Estimates available with the author.

6.7.3. Changes over Time

Unfortunately, we cannot carry out panel data analysis as the two surveys do not cover the same individuals. Still, the results of the cross-section analysis for two points in time reveal important trends over the ten-year period. For instance, on average, individual wages for certain service sub-sectors that were lower relative to the industrial sector in 1993–94 are higher in 2004–05, or vice versa. This reflects the relative development or stagnation of these service sub-sectors. For most sub-sectors of services, however, the results from 1993–94 and 2004–05 reinforce each other. This suggests that, relative to the industrial sector, the classification of service sub-sectors as ones providing "good" or "bad" jobs remains unchanged between 1993–94 and 2004–05.

Furthermore, we use the Blinder-Oaxaca decomposition technique to decompose the change in real wages[17] – for the all-India sample – between 1993–94 and 2004–05 into a part that is 'explained' by changes in a vector of explanatory variables and a part that cannot be 'explained' by these changes. Over the eleven-year period from 1993–94 to 2004–05, mean real wages increased by about 34.6 per cent. Table 6.8 presents a decomposition of this growth in mean real wages for the all-India sample, using two alternative decomposition formulae.

When the coefficients of 1993–94 are used, the effects of the change in mean characteristics of the labour force accounts for 27 per cent of the increase in real wages. This constitutes the 'explained' part of the decomposition. Conversely, 73 per cent of the increase in real wages is owing to the change in the income-generation mechanism – that is, the change in the coefficients of the mean characteristics and the intercept. This constitutes the 'unexplained' part of the decomposition. Using the coefficients of 2004–05 – when skill was better rewarded – the improved mean characteristics of the labour force account for 32 per cent of the real wage increase, and the sector dummy variables as a group for 3.7 per cent. At the same time, the change in coefficients[18] accounts for 68 per cent of the real wage increase, and the sector dummy variables group for –1.4 per cent. Hence, sector affiliation – both change in relative shares as well as change in sector-specific returns – affected real wages over the period from 1993–94 to

[17] Nominal wages are adjusted using the consumer price index for agricultural labourers in rural areas and the consumer price index for urban non-manual employees in urban areas.
[18] For the 'unexplained' part of the decomposition, the presence of dummy variables implies that there is a trade-off between the difference in intercepts and the part attributed to differences in slope coefficients. In the present exercise, the intercept term declined over the eleven years. This relates to the pay of those possessing the characteristics of the omitted categories – uneducated, unskilled women working in the industrial sector.

Table 6.8. *Decomposition of an increase in mean real wages: 1993–94 to 2004–05*

Percentage change owing to:	Based on the means of 2004–05 and coefficients of 1993–94	Based on means of 1993–94 and coefficients of 2004–05
Mean Characteristics		
Total	27.0	32.0
Assets (land owned)	0.0	0.0
Hours worked	2.7	2.6
Human capital variables (age, education, occupation)	21.4	25.7
Discrimination variables (gender, caste, religion)	0.0	0.0
Sector dummy variables	2.9	3.7
Coefficients		
Total	73.0	68.0
Assets (land owned)	0.1	0.1
Hours worked	22.5	22.5
Human capital variables (age, education, occupation)	33.4	32.4
Discrimination variables (gender, caste, religion)	17.0	17.0
Sector dummy variables	−1.5	−2.5
Intercept term	−1.4	−1.4

Source: Author's estimates based on primary data from National Sample Survey Organisation.

2004–05. However, net contribution of these changes is small because some sectors raised mean wages, while others lowered it.

6.8. Job Contracts and Social Security Benefits

6.8.1. Econometric Model

To analyse the effect of being employed in a particular sector on the probability of receiving a written job contract and social security benefits, we estimate Equation (6.5):

$$CONTRACT_i \text{ or } SOCIALSEC_i = \lambda + \alpha_1 AGE_i + \alpha_2 AGESQ_i$$
$$+ \alpha_3 LAND_i + \alpha_4 MALEDUM_i + \alpha_5 EDUDUM2_i$$
$$+ \alpha_6 EDUDUM3_i + \alpha_7 CASTEDUM_i$$
$$+ \alpha_8 RELIGIONDUM_i + \beta SECTORDUMMIES_i$$
$$+ DISTRICTDUMMIES_i + \varepsilon_i$$

Given binary dependent variables, we estimate the two equations using a Logit model for the sample of 2004–05. We define three cases for each equation: all-India, rural areas and urban areas. We cannot estimate the above equations for the sample of 1993–94 because it does not include data on contracts and social security benefits. Our variables of interest are the sector dummy variables and, as before, their coefficients represent the effect of being employed in a particular sub-sector of services, relative to industry, on the probability of getting a written job contract or receiving social security benefits. In estimating this relationship, we control for age, sex, education, land owned, caste, religion and district dummy variables. Similar to the case of wages, as a robustness check, we control for an individual's occupation affiliation as well as enterprise characteristics including the presence of unions, enterprise size, and public-private ownership. In addition, in Equation (6.6), we include a dummy variable for the self-employed because they do not receive explicit job contracts or social security benefits.

$$CONTRACT_i \; or \; SOCIALSEC_i = \lambda + \alpha_1 AGE_i + \alpha_2 AGESQ_i$$
$$+ \alpha_3 LAND_i + \alpha_4 MALEDUM_i + \alpha_5 EDUDUM2_i + \alpha_6 EDUDUM3_i$$
$$+ \alpha_7 CASTEDUM_i + \alpha_8 RELIGIONDUM_i + bSECTORDUMMIES_i$$
$$+ DISTRICTDUMMIES_i + \gamma_1 OCCDUMMIES_i$$
$$+ \gamma_2 SELFEMPDUM_i + \mu_1 PUBLICDUM_i$$
$$+ \mu_2 UNIONDUM_i + \mu_3 SCALEDUM_i + \varepsilon_i$$

6.8.2. Results

The detailed set of results is provided in Appendix C, Table C.17. Figures 6.3 and 6.4 report coefficients of the sector dummy variables and their statistical significance for the all-India sample, in the case of job contracts and social security benefits, respectively.

In the case of both job contracts and social security benefits and for all three samples – all-India, rural and urban – the marginal effects of dummy variables for communication, financial, business, public administration and defence, education and health services are positive and statistically significant – at the least at the 10 per cent level. This is intuitively robust, as these sub-sectors have greater educational requirements and larger organized segments relative to the industrial sector, which is likely to comprise a large number of unskilled workers employed in manufacturing, mining and construction. There is one exception: the case of business services in rural areas – both for job contracts and social security benefits – where the marginal effect of the dummy variable is statistically insignificant. Once again,

	All-India	Urban Areas	Rural Areas
0.3			
0.2	Finance*		Finance* Communication*
0.1	Business*, Education* Communication*, Health* Public administration*	Business* Education*, Health*, Finance* Communication* Public administration*	Education* Public administration* Health*, Business Real estate
Industry 0	Real estate Trade*, Hotels and restaurants*	Real estate, Transport Hotels and restaurants* Trade*	Trade Hotels and restaurants Other*
−0.1	Transport Other*	Other*	Transport
−0.2			
−0.3			

Figure 6.3. Variation in service sub-sector dummy variable coefficients for job contracts regression (2004–05).

	All-India	Urban Areas	Rural Areas
0.3			
0.2	Finance* Public administration*	Public administration* Finance*	Finance*
0.1	Communication* Education*, Health* Business*	Communication* Health* Business*	Public administration* Education* Health*, Communication*
Industry 0	Real estate* Hotels and restaurants*	Transport Real estate*	Hotels and restaurants Real estate*, Trade Business
−0.1	Trade* Other* Transport	Hotels and restaurants* Trade* Other*	Other* Transport
−0.2			
−0.3			

Figure 6.4. Variation in service sub-sector dummy variable coefficients for social security benefits regression (2004–05).

this result is not very meaningful as the number of people employed in this sector in rural areas is negligible.

In contrast, the marginal effect of the dummy variable for other social, community and personal services, wholesale and retail trade, and hotels and restaurants is negative and statistically significant at the least at the 5 per cent level. These services sub-sectors are largely free-entry sectors with extremely large unorganized segments. In the case of wholesale and retail trade and hotels and restaurants, however, these marginal effects become statistically insignificant for the sample of rural areas. This is plausible as individuals employed in wholesale trade units, small shops, small restaurants and *dhabas* in villages are not less likely to get job contracts or social security benefits relative to those employed in rural industrial activities such as mining, quarrying and construction.

The marginal effect of the dummy variable for real estate and renting services is negative and statistically significant in the case of social security benefits, but statistically insignificant in the case of job contracts. These results hold for all three samples – all-India, rural and urban. This implies that whereas people employed in real estate agencies or units renting out machinery and equipment have a significantly lower chance of getting social security relative to those employed in industry, they are no different in terms of their chances of getting a job contract.

Finally, in the case of both job contracts and social security benefits, the marginal effect of the dummy variable for transport services is statistically insignificant. This holds true for the all-India sample, rural areas and urban areas. It implies that individuals in transport services are no different from those employed in industry in terms of the likelihood of receiving job contracts or social security benefits. This result may be because of the presence of diverse segments within the transport services sector, which is similar to the industrial sector. In the transport services sector, air transport and the railways are dominated by organized-sector employment, whereas road and water transport segments are dominated by unorganized-sector employment. Table 6.9 provides a summary of the results from our econometric analysis.

6.9. Endogeneity and Selectivity Bias

It may be argued that the sector dummy variables, both in the wage and non-wage benefit (contracts and social security benefits) functions, are characterized by selectivity bias. For instance, there may be certain unobservable omitted variables such as specialized training or industry-specific skills which influence earnings of an individual – as also the probability of receiving a job contract and social security benefits – but are also correlated with his or her sector of employment. The same may be true of public-works programmes which place individuals in the agricultural or industrial

Table 6.9. *Quality of employment in terms of job contracts and social security benefits: A dividing line*

Dividing Line vis-à-vis the Industrial Sector

Worse-off or neither worse-off nor better-off	*Better-off*
Wholesale and Retail Trade	Communication Services
Hotels and Restaurants	Financial Services
Transport Services	Business Services
Real Estate and Renting Services	Public Administration and Defence
Other Social, Community and	Education Services
Personal Services	Health Services

Note: 'Better-off' because written job contracts provide security of employment, social security benefits provide individuals with income in times of emergency.

(includes construction activity) sectors and also influence the wage they receive. The National Rural Employment Guarantee Act (NREGA) of India may be relevant in this context. Of course, the NREGA, which was instituted in August 2005, does not affect the quality of the current set of empirical results, because the period under consideration concludes before that. In general, accounting for such endogeneity is important because the focus of our analysis is the influence of an individual's sector of employment on his or her wage and on the probability of receiving a job contract and social security benefits.

The inclusion of a large number of control variables – individual-specific, occupation-specific and firm-specific – reduces the possibility of the aforementioned selectivity bias but does not eliminate it. The ideal way to address the problem is instrumental variable estimation. Unfortunately, because we have twelve sector dummy variables, we would need at least twelve instruments. Finding twelve potential instrumental variables is extremely improbable, if not impossible, given that it is usually difficult to find even one good instrument (Wooldridge, 2002). Given this, we adopt a second-best solution. On the basis of the previously described results, we combine the eleven sub-sectors of services to form two distinct categories – "high job quality" services and "low job quality" services. For example, in the case of the earnings regression, high-wage services include communication, financial, business services and public administration services, whereas low-wage services include wholesale and retail trade, education, health, hotels and restaurants, transport, real estate and renting, and other social, community and personal services (see Table 6.7).[19] In the case of the job contract and social security benefits regressions, however, education and health services are included in the "high job quality" category of services (see Table 6.9).

Using this categorization, we have two potentially endogenous dummy variables for the services sector. A valid instrumental variable is one that is significantly correlated with an individual's sector of employment – one of low or high job quality – but one that is not correlated with omitted variables that affect his or her job quality (wages, contracts and social security benefits). Hence, we use (1) people employed in services as a proportion of all people employed, at the level of states, and (2) people employed in low-wage services as a proportion of all services, at the level of states as instruments. The two are likely to be highly correlated with an individual's sector of employment, and this is validated by the test for instrument relevance (see Appendix C, Table C.18 for the first-stage F-statistic). It may be argued that the two instrumental variables are correlated with overall income in the state, which in turn may be an important determinant of an individual's job quality. This suggests that our instruments will not meet the instrument exogeneity criteria. However, it must be noted that because district dummy variables are included, any state-specific variation in income is already controlled for. We cannot conduct a test of over-identifying restrictions because of the lack of a third suitable instrumental variable.

The results of the instrumental variable estimation, carried out only for the all-India sample, validate our earlier findings (see Appendix C, Table C.18). For instance, both in 1993–94 and 2004–05, relative to individuals employed in the industrial sector, those employed in the high-wage sub-sectors of services earn significantly more, whereas those employed in the low-wage sub-sectors of services earn significantly less.

6.10. Conclusion

To study the nature of employment being generated in the different sub-sectors of services in India, we carried out an econometric analysis of household survey data for two points in time: 1993–94 and 2004–05. The sample of 2004–05 was the focus of study as it includes data on all the variables of interest. We first found that access to employment in terms of educational requirements varies across the different sub-sectors of services.

[19] For the sample of 1993–94, education and health services are included in the high-wage category, while business services are included in the low-wage category.

Table 6.10. *Quality of employment across different sub-sectors of services*

Dividing Line vis-à-vis the Industrial Sector	
Worse-off or neither worse-off nor better-off	*Better-off*
Wholesale and Retail Trade	Communication Services
Hotels and Restaurants	Financial Services
Transport Services	Business Services
Real Estate and Renting Services	Public Administration and Defence
Other Social, Community and Personal Services	Education Services*
	Health Services*

Note: When considering wages alone, education and health services would be placed in the worse-off or neither worse-off nor better-off column.

For example, in certain sub-sectors, an individual's level of education has a significant effect on the probability of being employed. Subsequently, we found that services sub-sectors with low educational requirements have low overall quality of employment, relative to the industrial sector – where quality of employment was defined to include three variables that reflect quality of life: wages, the probability of getting a job contract and the probability of getting social security benefits. These include wholesale and retail trade, hotels and restaurants, transport, real estate and renting and other social, community and personal services. In contrast, our results reveal that services sub-sectors with high educational requirements have relatively higher quality of employment than the industrial sector. These include communication, financial, business, public administration and defence, education and health services. Table 6.10 provides a summary of the results from our analysis of these measures, based on the sample of 2004–05.

After standardizing for several individual, occupational and firm-specific characteristics, we find most service sub-sectors to be generally either 'good' or 'bad' employers; in other words, we see no 'compensating variation' where higher wages compensate for less job security or less social protection. This can also be seen in Table 6.11, which reports the impact of being employed for a 'good' employer or 'bad' employer (defined in Table 6.10), relative to the industrial sector, on each of the three parameters of job quality as determined by our regression analysis – that is, the coefficient on a service sub-sector dummy variable.

Education and health services are exceptions to the trend in this context. This is because whereas individuals employed in these sectors enjoy relatively high quality of employment in terms of job security and social protection, they do not offer relatively high wages. The fact that most sub-sectors

Table 6.11. *Coefficients on the services-sector dummy variables from the regression analysis for the all-India sample in 2004–05*

Sector	Wages	Job contract	Social security benefits
'Good' Employers (Mean across six sub-sectors of services)	0.06	0.45	0.42
'Bad' Employers (Mean across five sub-sectors of services)	–0.47	–0.38	–0.50

Source: Author's estimates based on primary data from National Sample Survey Organisation.

of services are generally 'good' or 'bad' employers may be attributable to the overall profitability of firms, profit-sharing wages and non-wage benefits, efficiency wages and sector-specific 'production functions' where the importance of technology and quality (as opposed to level) of employees' education may vary. This result may also relate to the theory of segmented markets where institutional factors such as the division between organized and unorganized economic activity are important.

Furthermore, comparing the results from our cross-section analysis at two points in time, we find that with the exception of a handful of service sub-sectors, their classification as "good" or "bad" employers – in terms of wages – remains unchanged during the ten-year period from 1993–94 to 2004–05. This shows the relative lack of improvement in the quality of employment, on average, for individuals employed in wholesale and retail trade, hotels and restaurants, transport, real estate and renting, and other social, community and personal services. Given that these sectors have large unorganized segments that employ unskilled labour in large numbers, this has possible implications for the country's income distribution. Finally, the juxtaposition of these results on quality of employment with data on quantity of employment (see Table 6.12) reveals an interesting story.

Table 6.12 shows that the sub-sectors of services which are characterised by low educational requirements and low quality of employment accounted for the largest shares in total services employment, both in 1993–94 and 2004–05. These include wholesale and retail trade, transport and other social, community and personal services. In contrast, Table 6.12 also shows that communication, financial and business services – sub-sectors characterized by high educational requirements and relatively high quality of employment – accounted for a very small proportion of total services employment, both in 1993–94 and 2004–05. These associations can be seen

Table 6.12. *Number of persons employed in different sub-sectors of services: 1993–94 and 2004–05*

Sector	Number Employed			As a Percentage of Total Employment in Services		Percentage Contribution to Increase in Employment
	1993–94	2004–05	Increase: 1993–94 to 2004–05	1993–94	2004–05	1993–94 to 2004–05
Wholesale and Retail Trade	23,071,570	35,431,315	12,359,745	36	38	43.7
Hotels and Restaurants	2,702,078	4,919,688	2,217,611	4	5	7.8
Transport Services	8,272,397	13,856,716	5,584,319	13	15	19.7
Communication Services	600,896	1,614,031	1,013,135	1	2	3.6
Financial Services	1,812,692	2,490,281	677,589	3	3	2.4
Real Estate and Renting Services	264,010	844,678	580,668	0.5	1	2.0
Business Services	823,482	2,834,967	2,011,485	1	3	7.1
Public Administration and Defence	8,364,519	7,313,423	-1,051,096	13	8	-3.7
Education Services	5,431,770	9,119,201	3,687,430	8	10	13.0
Health Services	2,630,858	3,071,370	440,512	4	3	1.5
Other Social, Community and Personal Services	9,897,141	10,657,002	759,861	15	12	2.7
Services Sector (aggregate)	63,871,414	92,152,672	28,281,257	100	100	100

Note: The sample figures have been extrapolated to provide All-India figures.
Source: National Sample Survey Organisation, Surveys on Employment.

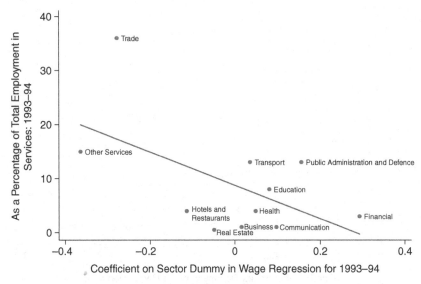

Figure 6.5. Quantity and quality of employment I (1993–94).
Source: Primary data from National Sample Survey Organisation, Surveys on Employment.

in Figures 6.5 and 6.6, which show the correlation between the coefficient on the sector dummy in the wage regression and the share of that sector in total services employment in 1993–94 and 2004–05, respectively. In both figures, a linear relationship is a good approximation, with the exception of wholesale and retail trade which appears to be an outlier. This is because the sub-sector takes up a lion's share of total services employment in both years.

Furthermore, it is the generally 'bad' employers that have the highest percentage contribution to the increase in total services employment during the period from 1993–94 to 2004–05. Whereas wholesale and retail trade accounts for a little less than half of the increase in total services employment, hotels and restaurants and transport services are the other major contributors. Business and education services are exceptions to the general trend as they are generally 'good' employers and also provide a high percentage contribution to the increase in total services employment during the period from 1993–94 to 2004–05. This association between the quality and quantity of employment can be seen in Figures 6.7 and 6.8, which correlate the percentage contribution of the sector to the increase in total services employment during the period from 1993–94 to 2004–05 with the

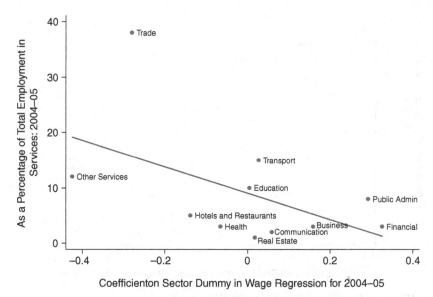

Figure 6.6. Quantity and quality of employment I (2004–05).
Source: Primary data from National Sample Survey Organisation, Surveys on Employment.

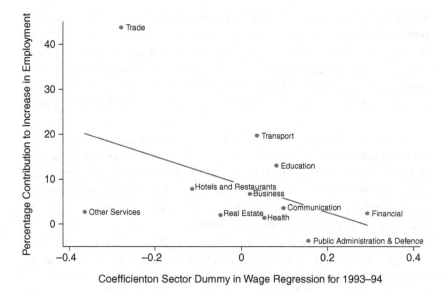

Figure 6.7. Quantity and quality of employment II (1993–94).
Source: Primary data from National Sample Survey Organisation, Surveys on Employment.

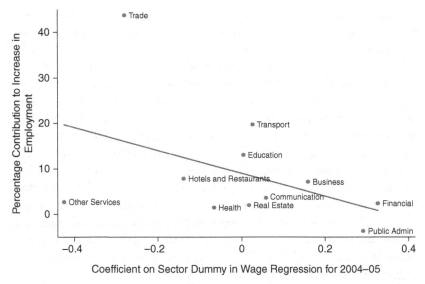

Figure 6.8. Quantity and quality of employment II (2004–05).
Source: Based on primary data from National Sample Survey Organisation, Surveys on Employment.

coefficient on the sector dummy variables from the wage regression for 1993–94 and 2004–05, respectively.

Once again, a linear relationship is a reasonable approximation, except for wholesale and retail trade and other social, community and personal services that appear to be outliers. With wholesale and retail trade, this is because it takes up a lion's share of the increase in total services employment. Surprisingly, however, other social, community and personal services, which is largely a free-entry sector with low quality of employment, does not contribute in a significant way to the increase in total services employment during the ten-year period under consideration. This may be attributable to the fact that this sub-sector is dichotomized between modern and traditional economic activity. In fact, data that is further disaggregated reveals that within this sub-sector, activities of membership organizations and recreational, cultural and sports activities saw a very small increase in employment.[20] In contrast, domestic servants, other personal services, sewage and refuse disposal, sanitation and other similar activities that constitute the mostly unorganized, free-entry segment with low quality of employment saw a large increase in employment during this period.

[20] Estimates available with the author.

In sum, barring a few exceptions, employment expansion within the service sector appears to be relatively more in sub-sectors where educational requirements are low and quality of employment is low – in other words, the low-end, "bad" employers. Given low employment elasticities of output for India's manufacturing sector (Gordon and Gupta, 2004), this fact may imply that a large amount of labour is being pushed into these service sub-sectors because of lack of employment opportunities in unskilled, labour-intensive manufacturing. Conversely, segments characterized by high educational requirements and high quality of employment are not creating a large number of jobs, with business and educational services being the exception. These results reinforce the findings of Mazumdar and Sarkar (2008), which show that a larger number of jobs in the services sector are being created in the bottom and topmost part of the income distribution, relative to the middle. Importantly, the results suggest that the welfare-enhancing effect of India's services-sector growth, in terms of benefits to a large cross-section of people, may be limited.

SEVEN

Labour Productivity in India's Urban
Informal Services Sector

A Comparison with Agriculture

7.1. Introduction

Chapter 6 showed that relative to the industrial sector, certain sub-sectors of services are characterized by low educational requirements and low quality of employment, where the latter is defined by wage and associated non-wage benefits. These include wholesale and retail trade, hotels and restaurants, transport services, real estate and renting services, and personal services. Furthermore, in developing a taxonomy for India's service sector, Chapter 5 showed that three of these sectors are classified as 'largely unorganized' and the remaining two as 'part organized, part unorganized'. Assuming that wages are linked to the productivity of workers, this evidence supports the extensive literature on dual-economy models, which argues that the urban informal sector (comprising services and industry) in developing countries is characterized by substantial underemployment, disguised unemployment and low levels of labour productivity. But according to these models, the same holds true for the agricultural sector. In other words, both are 'residual' sectors where individuals pour in to find jobs as a result of the lack of other employment opportunities.

The case of India is consistent with this literature (Nagaraj, 2007), given that the country's lack of employment creation in the manufacturing sector has been associated with increasing population pressure on farm land and a rapidly growing urban informal services sector consisting of hawkers, street vendors, domestic servants, service workers in small restaurants and *dhabas* and cycle-rickshaw pullers, among other occupations. So how do these urban informal service sector jobs compare with those in agriculture, in terms of productivity and, hence, wages?

In terms of theory, the Harris-Todaro model of rural-urban migration predicts that potential migrants choose between a relatively safe but low-paying option – which is to stay in the agricultural sector – and the gamble of moving to the urban (services) sector where they will either attain a high-paying formal (services) sector job or flow into an informal sector, where jobs or businesses pay – relatively speaking – a pittance. This equilibrium condition implies that the agricultural wage must exceed the wage in the urban informal (services) sector. But the data from India contradicts this prediction, thereby constituting an empirical puzzle.

Given the above, the object of this chapter is twofold. First, it aims to provide an explanation for these observed trends by carrying out an econometric analysis of macroeconomic and household survey data from India. In doing so, it focuses on the role of economic and social infrastructure, which is likely to be more widespread and of higher quality in urban areas relative to rural areas. Second, it attempts to reconcile the Harris-Todaro model of rural-urban migration with the numbers from India by developing a system of dynamic equations that capture the sequence of effects following an increase in urban infrastructure. Changes in the level of urban infrastructure – with rural infrastructure remaining constant – affect levels of labour productivity (and hence wages) in the agricultural and urban informal services sectors differentially and subsequently influence movement of labour across sectors, thereby altering their sizes. This movement of labour, in turn, affects levels of labour productivity. It is this set of dynamic effects which shows that the situation reflected in the data – that output per worker or wages in the urban informal services sector exceeds that in the agricultural sector – does not constitute long-run equilibrium for the Indian economy.

The scope of the chapter is limited to an analysis of data from India during the period from 1993–94 and 2004–05. The choice of years is determined by the following. First, the period from the early 1990s saw the most dramatic increase in the importance of the services sector. Second, while India's National Accounts Statistics do not disaggregate economic activity into formal and informal-sector components before 1993–94, 2004–05 is the most recent survey on employment for which data are available. Furthermore, the analysis in the chapter does not preclude the importance of other possible factors that may be driving the differential growth of labour productivity in the agricultural and urban informal services sectors.

The structure of the chapter is as follows. Section 7.2 provides a brief account of the implications from the literature on dual-economy models and how they relate to the object of our exercise. Section 7.3 presents an analytical framework to understand an individual's decision to migrate from rural to urban areas. This framework is a modified version of the

Harris-Todaro (1970) model. Section 7.4 presents data from India which constitute an empirical puzzle in the context of the modified Harris-Todaro (1970) model that defines our analytical framework. Using economic intuition and econometric analysis, Section 7.5 develops a hypothesis that helps to resolve this empirical puzzle. In light of this, Section 7.6 revisits the modified Harris-Todaro (1970) model to establish a new unique equilibrium for the economy. Section 7.7 develops a system of equations to analyse the stability of this new unique equilibrium. In doing so, it reconciles the macroeconomic data from India with the implications of the modified Harris-Todaro (1970) model. Section 7.8 presents conclusions. Such an exercise has not been attempted in the literature, either for India or elsewhere.

7.2. The Literature on Dual-Economy Models

7.2.1. Lewis Model

The literature on dual-economy models views economic development as the progressive transformation of a traditional rural sector (agriculture) into a modern urban sector (industry). Arthur Lewis (1954), for instance, placed the movement of labour from agriculture to industry and capital accumulation in the latter at the centre stage. The fundamental assumption made in the Lewis model is that unskilled labour is virtually unlimited in supply, being drawn from a vast agricultural sector. This is because large numbers of people per acre of arable land results in 'disguised unemployment' or underemployment, whereby a large surplus of labour in the agricultural sector can be removed with total output remaining practically constant. The model reconciles the coexistence of a marginal product of labour close to zero with a positive wage by arguing that the agricultural sector is characterized by a payment system based on the average product of labour, rather than its marginal product – in other words, family farms are likely to share equally the sum of incomes received by each of its members.

7.2.2. Harris-Todaro Model

While the class of models represented by the Lewis model argue that development is characterized by the transfer of labour from agriculture to the modern industrial sector, they assume that labour can move from one sector to another in accordance with its own wishes. In this context, models of rural-urban migration based on the work of Harris and Todaro (1970) assume importance. Migration from rural to urban areas is viewed as a response to significant wage gap between the urban formal sector and agriculture, with the former exceeding the latter. However, not everyone who migrates to urban areas can be absorbed into the formal sector where wages are not fully flexible. These individuals flow into an informal sector with exceedingly low wages (a wage below the agricultural supply price), but no barriers to entry.[1] Hence, potential migrants choose between a relatively safe but low-paying option, which is to stay in the agricultural sector, and the gamble of moving to urban sector where a high-paying formal job may or may not be attainable. Harris and Todaro (1970) view the urban informal sector as one in which jobs or businesses are easy enough to find but pay a pittance. This is perhaps indicative of the fact that, as in agriculture, low levels of labour productivity, substantial underemployment and a payment system based on income sharing characterize the urban informal sector.

7.2.3. How Do These Models Relate to Our Analytical Framework for India?

On the one hand, dual-economy models based on Lewis (1954) are important for our analysis as they describe the situation in agriculture in a land-scarce, labour-abundant economy like India even today. Organization of production in agriculture is characterized by family farms, and high population pressure on land results in low levels of labour productivity. This is indicative of a large amount of disguised unemployment or underemployment throughout the sector. On the other hand, rural-urban migration models based on Harris-Todaro (1970) are also important for our analytical framework, because we seek to explain the migration decisions made by potential migrants. Moreover, along with the rapid growth in India's software, business-process outsourcing, financial and telecommunication services segments, a fairly large informal services sector in urban areas has also developed simultaneously. Given the nature of activities performed in this sector, it is generally viewed as a low-wage, low-productivity sector with substantial underemployment or disguised unemployment.

7.3. Analytical Framework: A Modified Harris-Todaro Model

7.3.1. Equilibrium

For analytical simplicity, the urban sector in our framework is restricted to the service sector, which has seen remarkable growth in India during

---

[1]   In the original Harris-Todaro model, these individuals are unemployed.

the period from 1980–81 to 2009–10 (Chapter 1). We do not consider the manufacturing sector in our analysis as it has been characterized by jobless growth during the same time period. This is reflected in the very low employment elasticities of output for the manufacturing sector, which were close to zero (Bhalotra, 1998; Gordon and Gupta, 2004). Furthermore, for analytical simplicity, we do not consider the rural non-farm (services) sector. This may be justified by the fact that the size of the rural non-farm sector, although growing, is still relatively small, accounting for only about one-fourth of total employment in rural areas (Ranjan, 2007).[2]

The equilibrium in our model is analogous to the main idea in the Harris-Todaro model of rural-urban migration. Potential migrants choose between a relatively safe but low-paying option, which is to stay in the agricultural sector, and the gamble of moving to the urban services sector where a high-paying formal job may or may not be attainable owing to significant barriers to entry. Those who do not get a formal services-sector job will not be unemployed. Instead, they will flow into the informal sector, where jobs or businesses have no barriers to entry but pay, relatively speaking, a pittance. Examples include hawkers, street vendors, domestic servants and service workers in small restaurants.

A competitive equilibrium, by definition, needs to alleviate persistent migration between one sector and the other, for which the wages in the two sectors must be equalized (ignoring costs of migration). Hence, equilibrium requires that 'expected income' from migration to urban areas must be equal to the actual income received in agriculture. In our three-sector model of labour allocation – a modified Harris-Todaro model – this implies that equilibrium is given by the following equation:

$$w_a = c^f.w_s^f + (1 - c^f)w_s^i \qquad (7.1)$$

where c^f is the probability of finding a job in the formal services sector, $w_s^f = \bar{w}$ is the wage rate in the formal services sector, w_s^i is the wage rate in the informal services sector, and w_a is the wage in the agricultural sector.

The above condition implies that no individual will have an incentive to migrate from one sector to the other. For this equilibrium to hold, w_s^i must be less than w_a. This follows from the assumption that migrants are attracted by high-paying jobs in the formal services sector and hence place a psychological value on the probability of getting employed there. In

---

[2] In addition, the inclusion of these sectors will not make a notable difference to our final conclusions.

reality, however, costs of migration may prevent w_s^i from being depressed much below w_a.

7.3.2. Other Considerations

The Harris-Todaro model assumes that anyone migrating from rural areas can enter the urban formal sector irrespective of skills or education. This is plausible for the case of unskilled labour employed in manufacturing. However, it cannot be assumed that anyone migrating from the rural areas might be employed in any part of the services sector. This is attributable to high educational requirements which serve as a barrier to entry for potential job seekers in several segments of the sector. Such barriers to entry are especially important in the context of financial services and business services such as software development and business-process outsourcing, which are the visible dimension of the sector's dynamism. Hence, it may be argued that most agricultural workers do not have access to the dynamic end of the formal services sector. But Chapter 5 showed that the service sector is highly heterogeneous and covers a wide range of economic activities. In fact, there are a number of service sub-sectors – wholesale and retail trade, hotels and restaurants, transport, storage, real estate, communication and public administration – which have negligible educational requirements in several occupations and are likely to generate demand for unskilled labour. It is these service sub-sectors that are likely to employ unskilled migrants from rural areas.

Historically, in the development process, relatively unskilled farm workers migrated to cities and found initial employment in jobs with little skill content. Thereafter, experience thus gained enabled many to "graduate" to somewhat more skilled jobs, while their children's educational attainment in the urban areas exceeded that of the migrants (Krueger, 2007). In the context of the Harris-Todaro model, studies have argued that the search for formal sector employment in urban areas is more effective if an individual resides there (Fields, 1975; Mazumdar, 1975). This is attributable to being located in the area of job search or to the greater availability of relevant training in urban areas. Hence, urban informal-sector employment which is characterized by free entry may represent a 'transition' sector from where individuals can increase their chances of securing a formal sector job. Hence, we introduce the additional assumption that an individual who moves to a job in the informal services sector in an urban area increases his or her probability of getting a formal services sector job in the future.

Therefore, for individuals with a time horizon of one future period, rural-urban migration will occur until the point where:

$$w_a = q^f \left(\frac{w_s^f}{1+r} \right) + (1-q^f) \left(\frac{w_s^i}{1+r} \right) \tag{7.2}$$

where q^f is the adjusted probability of getting a job in the urban formal services sector (conditional on being employed in the urban informal services sector for one period; $0 < c^f < q^f < 1$) and 'r' is the rate which discounts future urban-sector wages to the present.

7.4. Empirical Puzzle?

In the Harris-Todaro model, as well as in our modified version of it, potential migrants choose between a relatively safe but low-paying option, which is to stay in the agricultural sector, and the gamble of moving to the urban services sector where they may either find a high-paying job in the formal sector or end up being employed in the informal sector which pays a pittance. This implies that in equilibrium, the agricultural wage must exceed the wage in the urban informal services sector. In reality, however, owing to costs of migration to urban areas, the urban informal services sector wage may not be far below the wage in the agriculture. Assuming that the payment system in the agricultural and informal service sectors is based on the average rather than the marginal product of labour, output per worker is a good approximation for the wage level. In this context, the data for India reveal the following.

Table 7.1 shows that during the period from 1993–94 to 2004–05, the level of output per worker in the informal services sector is consistently greater than the level of output per worker in agriculture. Table 7.2 shows that with the exception of Punjab and Haryana in 1993–94, this holds true at the level of states as well. Whereas the large productivity differences between industry and services on the one hand and agriculture on the other are well documented in the literature on India (Bosworth and Maertens, 2010), our findings represent a surprising trend.

The difference between output per worker in the informal services sector and output per worker in the agricultural sector is too large to be explained by costs of migration alone. One possible explanation goes back to the work of Sabot (1977), who argues that there is considerable internal differentiation among informal-sector activities, where entrance into some of them may be restricted by skill and capital requirements. This implies that the

Table 7.1. *Output per worker at the all-India level*
(rupees per annum at 1993–94 constant prices)

Year	Informal services sector	Agriculture	Ratio of informal services to agriculture
1993–94	36,277	14,962	2.4
1994–95	37,224	15,449	2.4
1995–96	39,468	15,060	2.6
1996–97	41,422	16,232	2.5
1997–98	43,068	15,573	2.8
1998–99	44,699	16,263	2.7
1999–2000	47,669	16,042	2.9
2000–01	48,389	15,562	3.1
2001–02	48,897	16,062	3.0
2002–03	51,072	14,510	3.5
2003–04	53,499	15,445	3.5
2004–05	56,975	14,994	3.8

Source: Central Statistical Organisation, National Accounts Statistics and Ministry of Labour and Employment, Government of India.

sector is not necessarily a reservoir of only very-low-income groups. In a study on Delhi in India, Banerjee (1986) argues that these activities constitute the non-wage informal sector. Several other empirical studies show that the informal economy is competitive, and earnings are not significantly different from those of urban unskilled formal sector workers and human capital is rewarded in the same way as in the formal sector (Burki and Abbas, 1991; Mitra, 1996). These studies, however, relate exclusively to the informal manufacturing sector, or do not distinguish between the manufacturing and service components of the informal sector. In one of the few surveys that distinguished between the two components, House (1984) shows that in Kenya, the informal services sector offered the lowest rewards because of low capital and skill intensity. Similarly, in a study on street vendors in Delhi, India, Dasgupta (2003) shows that human capital does not have a significant impact on informal service wages, and although average earnings in the sector are not the lowest in the economy, they are not comparable to wages in the urban formal unskilled sector (once characteristic differences between migrants and non-migrants are accounted for).

In the following section, we present an hypothesis which provides another possible explanation as to why output per worker in the urban informal services sector is notably higher that output per worker in the agricultural sector. Subsequently, we develop a system of equations for the economy to

Table 7.2. *Output per worker for fourteen major Indian states*
(rupees per annum at 1993–94 constant prices)

State	1993–94			2004–05		
	Informal services sector	Agriculture	Ratio of informal services to agriculture	Informal services sector	Agriculture	Ratio of informal services to agriculture
Andhra Pradesh	24,910	9,880	2.5	36,251	11,282	3.2
Bihar	19,494	7,056	2.8	23,376	7,613	3.0
Gujarat	32,410	12,024	2.7	51,840	13,111	3.9
Haryana	29,172	33,270	0.9	50,289	26,995	1.9
Karnataka	25,317	12,338	2.0	48,050	9,419	5.1
Kerala	30,832	18,271	1.7	44,537	14,939	2.9
Madhya Pradesh	28,781	9,705	2.9	31,036	8,265	3.7
Maharashtra	37,661	12,001	3.1	64,058	7,994	8.0
Orissa	20,179	9,466	2.1	30,200	7,966	3.8
Punjab	30,015	36,440	0.8	41,813	34,371	1.2
Rajasthan	26,859	8,595	3.1	30,060	11,204	2.7
Tamil Nadu	25,648	12,013	2.1	25,311	11,294	2.2
Uttar Pradesh	22,029	9,939	2.2	25,040	10,737	2.3
West Bengal	22,366	16,732	1.3	42,888	16,323	2.6

Source: Central Statistical Organisation, National Accounts Statistics and Ministry of Labour and Employment, Government of India.

help reconcile our modified version of the Harris-Todaro Model with the data under consideration.

7.5. Infrastructure and Labour Productivity: Empirical Analysis

The size and quality of infrastructure is likely to increase productivity in both the informal services sector and agriculture. For instance, better roads and electricity supply may reduce costs in the informal services sector on the supply side, thereby increasing productivity. Similarly, the presence of greater socio-economic overhead such as education and health services may render positive externalities for those employed in the informal services sector. At the same time, improved roads and transport services may increase agricultural productivity by facilitating the purchase of inputs and sale of output. Furthermore, education services and supply of electricity may enhance agricultural productivity by providing farmers with greater knowledge and the necessary tools to use modern agricultural technology, respectively. The positive relationship between infrastructure on the one hand and labour productivity in the agricultural and informal services sectors on the other is reflected in an analysis of the data. We carry out this analysis both at the state and household level.

7.5.1. State-Level Data

For fourteen major states over the period from 1993–94 to 2004–05, we estimate the following econometric model:

$$\ln(PRODY_{it}^{IS}) \ or \ \ln(PRODY_{it}^{AGR}) = \beta_1 INFRA_{it-1}$$
$$+ \beta_2 LIT_{it-1} + \beta_3 INVST_{it-1} + \beta_4 DEVEXP_{it-1} \qquad (7.3)$$
$$+ \eta_i + \mu_t + \varepsilon_{it}$$

where $PRODY^{IS}$ is the natural logarithm of output per worker in the informal services sector, $PRODY^{AGR}$ is the natural logarithm of output per worker[3] in agriculture, i indexes the state, t indexes the year, $INFRA$ is a relative infrastructure index[4] developed by the Centre for Monitoring the Indian Economy (CMIE), LIT is the literacy rate,[5] $INVST$ is loans extended by All-India Financial Institutions (as a percentage of state domestic product) to proxy for private investment,[6] $DEVEXP$ is government spending for development purposes[7] (as a percentage of state domestic product), η is a state-specific fixed effect and μ is a year-specific effect.

The fixed-effects formulation enables us to control for unobserved differences between states. This is important for if the fixed effects are correlated with the explanatory variables, their omission leads to an omitted variable bias. Moreover, it is important to include time-specific effects, as the mean of the output per worker series may increase or decrease over time. A further methodological concern relates to the endogeneity of the explanatory variables in the model – including the relative infrastructure index – owing to the possibility of reverse causality. For instance, it is not evident whether

---

[3] Derived using output data from National Accounts Statistics and employment data from the National Sample Survey Organisation's employment surveys.

[4] Index = 100 for the all-India level.

[5] Data are obtained from the National Human Development Report (2001).

[6] Data are obtained from various issues of the Report on Development Banking compiled by the Industrial Development Bank (IDBI) of India.

[7] Data are taken from various issues of the Handbook of Statistics compiled by the Reserve Bank of India (RBI).

Table 7.3. *Output per worker and infrastructure for fourteen major Indian states: 1993–94 to 2004–05*

Dependent Variable → Explanatory Variables ↓	Output per worker in agriculture	Output per worker in the informal services sector
Index of Economic and Social Infrastructure	0.011 (0.005) [0.021]	0.089 (0.027) [0.002]
Vector of Controls	Yes	Yes
State Fixed Effects	Yes	Yes
R-Squared	0.94	0.82

Note: The number of observations used is 168. The value in brackets refers to the standard error, whereas the value in the square brackets refers to the *p*-value.
Source: Author's regression estimates.

better infrastructure leads to higher labour productivity or if higher labour productivity leads to better infrastructure through its positive impact on economic growth. Given the lack of good instrumental variables, we use the explanatory variables, lagged by one year, to ensure that they are predetermined with respect to the dependent variable.

Regressing output per worker in the informal services sector on a relative infrastructure index – in a fixed-effects framework controlling for skill, private investment and state development expenditure – we find a statistically significant positive relationship. We find the same result for the agricultural sector (see Table 7.3). But the size of the coefficient shows that infrastructure has a greater impact on output per capita in the informal services sector than in agriculture. Unfortunately, India's National Accounts Statistics do not enable us to disaggregate informal economic activity into rural and urban components.

7.5.2. Individual-Level Data

To highlight the effect of infrastructure on the informal services sector in urban areas, we carry out a similar analysis at the level of the individual using household survey data – collected by India's National Sample Survey Organisation for 2004–05.[8] We use household per capita expenditure as a

---

[8] Although there is data for 1993–94 as well, we cannot carry out panel data analysis because the surveys under consideration do not cover the same individuals over time.

proxy for individual income because wage data in the surveys do not cover the self-employed – an important group of people both in agriculture and urban informal services. It is worth noting that the surveys do not classify a worker into the formal or informal sector. We define the informal sector to include individuals who do not receive either a written job contract or social security benefits, and who are employed in enterprises with less than ten workers. The 'use of electricity' is the proxy used for the level of infrastructure. Using these parameters, we estimate the following econometric model:

$$\ln(HHPCEXP_i^{IS}) \text{ or } \ln(HHPCEXP_i^{AGR}) = \lambda + \gamma ELECDUM_i$$
$$+\alpha_1 AGE_i + \alpha_2 AGESQ_i + \alpha_3 LAND_i + \alpha_4 MALEDUM_i$$
$$+\alpha_5 EDUDUM2_i + \alpha_6 EDUDUM3_i + \alpha_7 CASTEDUM_i \qquad (7.4)$$
$$+\alpha_8 RELIGIONDUM_i + \alpha_9 HRSWORKED_i$$
$$+\beta SECTORDUMMIES_i + DISTRICTDUMMIES_i + \varepsilon_i$$

where $HHPCEXP^{IS}$ is household per capita expenditure of individuals employed in the urban informal services sector, $HHPCEXP^{AGR}$ is household per capita expenditure of individuals employed in agricultural sector and $ELECDUM$ is a dummy variable which equals one when an individual is employed in an enterprise which uses electricity in its production process. The remaining are a set of control variables at the level of the individual – age, age-squared, gender, land possessed, hours worked, dummy variables for education, caste and religion – together with district dummy variables.

Despite the inclusion of a large number of control variables, coefficients estimated using OLS may be biased owing to reverse causality – in other words, while the use of electricity in production influences individual income (or expenditure), levels of individual income (or expenditure) also influence the likelihood of the use of electricity in production. Hence, we estimate the model using instrumental variables. Given that 'the use of electricity in production' is the potentially endogenous variable, a valid instrumental variable is one that is significantly correlated with it, but one that is not correlated with omitted variables that directly affect household per capita expenditure. Hence, we use the proportion of households in a "state" using electricity for production as an instrument for the use of electricity in production by an individual. The two are likely to be highly correlated, and this is validated by the test for instrument relevance (see Table 7.4 for the first-stage F-statistic). It may be argued, however, that the proportion of households in a "state" using electricity for production is correlated with overall income in the state (omitted variable), which, in turn, is an

Table 7.4. *Household per capita expenditure and infrastructure*
(2004–05): IV estimation

Dependent Variable→ Explanatory Variables ↓	Household per capita expenditure for individuals employed in agriculture	Household per capita expenditure for individuals employed in the urban informal services sector
Use of Electricity in Production	0.016	0.069
	(0.007)	(0.033)
	[0.033]	[0.039]
Vector of Control Variables	Yes	Yes
District Fixed Effects	Yes	Yes
R-Squared	0.61	0.62
Observations	1941	7814
First-stage F-Statistic	40.63	98.48
	[0.000]	[0.000]

Note: The value in brackets refers to the standard error, whereas the value in the square brackets refers to the p-value. The vector of control variables includes age, age-squared, gender, land possessed and dummy variables for education, caste and religion.

Source: Author's estimates using data from National Sample Survey Organisation, Surveys on Employment.

important determinant of individual income. This suggests that our instrument will not meet the instrument exogeneity criteria. However, it must be noted that because district dummy variables are included, any state-specific variation in income is already controlled for. We cannot conduct a test of over-identifying restrictions because of the lack of another suitable instrumental variable.

Table 7.4 shows that the 'use of electricity in production' has a statistically significant positive effect on household per capita expenditure of individuals employed in the urban informal services sector. Doing the same for the agricultural sector yields a similar result. Importantly, the size of the coefficient shows that infrastructure has a larger impact on household per capita expenditure of individuals (proxy for wages) employed in the urban informal services sector than in agriculture. This reinforces the result from the state-level analysis, which showed that infrastructure has a relatively large impact on output per worker in the informal services sector. As a large part of the informal services sector is located in urban areas, this is not entirely surprising given that in most developing countries, urban infrastructure is both more widespread and of a higher quality than rural infrastructure. In fact, in the household survey data under consideration, we find that as a percentage of total people employed, many more individuals in urban areas use electricity in production, relative to rural areas. This reflects better access to electricity in the former.

7.6. Modified Harris-Todaro Model: Equilibrium Revisited

7.6.1. Initial Equilibrium

Our modified version of the Harris-Todaro model – presented in Section 6.3 – established that (for individuals with a time horizon of one future period) rural-urban migration will occur till the point where expected income from migration to urban areas equals actual income received in agriculture – that is,

$$w_a = q^f \left(\frac{w_s^f}{1+r} \right) + (1 - q^f) \left(\frac{w_s^i}{1+r} \right) \tag{7.5}$$

where w^a is the agricultural supply price, w_s^f is the wage rate in the urban formal services sector, w_s^i is the wage rate in the urban informal services sector, q^f is the adjusted probability of getting a job in the urban formal services sector (conditional on being employed in the urban informal services sector for one period; $0 < c^f < q^f < 1$) and 'r' is the rate which discounts future urban sector wages to the present.

7.6.2. New Equilibrium

Now, suppose there is an increase in the level of economic and social infrastructure per capita in urban areas. This renders a positive externality for those working in urban areas – both in the formal and informal services sectors. Specifically, it increases labour productivity in both these sectors, and therefore, by assumption, also increases wage rates. Let us assume that there are absolute increases in both w_s^f and w_s^i. Note that we are discussing a supply (of informal services) relationship, where we do not consider demand issues – in other words, there is no consideration of relative price effects, which may alter the relative demand for informal and formal services.

$$\Rightarrow w_s^{f'} = \frac{w_s^f}{1+r} + x, \quad w_s^{i'} = \frac{w_s^i}{1+r} + y \tag{7.6}$$

where $x > y$.

The above equation implies that an increase in the level of infrastructure per capita in urban areas renders a greater positive externality for those employed in the formal services sector, relative to those employed in the informal services sector. This is because income levels are higher for individuals employed in the formal services sector, who are hence more likely to afford better-quality infrastructure.

An increase in w_s^f and w_s^i implies that there is an increase in expected urban income, which in turn induces more rural-urban migration to restore the equilibrium. In particular, this outflow of individuals from rural areas results in an increase in output per worker in the agricultural sector and hence in w^a. Hence, the new equilibrium condition is given by

$$w_a' = q^f w_s^{f'} + (1-q^f) w_s^{i'} \tag{7.7}$$

Inserting our post-externality conditions in the above equation, we get

$$w_a' = q^f \left(\frac{w_s^f}{1+r} + x \right) + (1-q^f) \left(\frac{w_s^i}{1+r} + y \right) \tag{7.8}$$

$$\Rightarrow w_a' = q^f \left(\frac{w_s^f}{1+r} \right) + (1-q^f) \left(\frac{w_s^i}{1+r} \right) + q^f x + y - q^f y \tag{7.9}$$

but, according to the initial equilibrium condition,

$$w_a = q^f \left(\frac{w_s^f}{1+r} \right) + (1-q^f) \left(\frac{w_s^i}{1+r} \right) \tag{7.10}$$

$$\Rightarrow w_a' = w_a + y + q^f (x - y)$$

At the outset, we defined 'y' as the increase in w_s^i.

$$\Rightarrow w_a' - w_a = w_s^{i'} - w_s^i + q^f (x - y) \tag{7.11}$$

$$\Rightarrow \dot{w}_a = \dot{w}_s^i + q^f (x - y) \tag{7.12}$$

where $x > y$.

The aforementioned condition identifies a new unique equilibrium, following the infrastructure externality effect. It shows that the change in wages received in the agricultural sector exceeds the change in wages received in the urban informal services sector in equilibrium. And if wage levels are linked to levels of labour productivity, this implies that in equilibrium, change in labour productivity in the agriculture exceeds the change in labour productivity in the urban informal services sector.

7.7. Reconciling the Data with the Modified Harris-Todaro Model: 'Dornbusch' Overshooting?

Investment in sectors such as electricity, telecommunication, roads, education and health is likely to be both risky and large. Hence, much of the social and economic infrastructure in developing countries is provided by governments (Jimenez, 1994). Given this and the set of empirical results presented in Section 7.5, we make the simplifying assumption that the government – which faces a budget constraint – invests all its designated resources in urban infrastructure and nothing in rural infrastructure. In our analytical framework, we considered the informal services sector located in urban areas and the agricultural sector located in rural areas. Because of the location difference, an increase in the level of urban infrastructure renders a positive externality for individuals employed in the urban informal services sector (i.e., makes people more productive at performing the same task), whereas agriculture remains unaffected. This may explain why the level of output per worker or wages in urban informal services is higher than in agriculture.

In the long run, however, the outcome may well be different as an increase in the level of urban infrastructure generates disequilibrium and so leads to several other changes. For one thing, assuming that wages equal output per worker, an increase in the level of urban infrastructure leads to a rise in expected urban income, thereby providing a greater incentive for people to migrate from rural to urban areas.[9] But given several entry barriers to formal services, rural-urban migration is likely to result in an increase in the size of the urban informal services sector which uses the available infrastructure. For another thing, over time, certain villages may get rural-urban link roads, their residents may use the services of schools and hospitals in neighbouring urban centres, and the wider distribution of electricity in urban areas may offer certain benefits for individuals employed in villages near urban centres. Hence, an increase in urban infrastructure may be associated with spillover effects that may benefit individuals employed in agriculture in the medium to long run.

---

[9]   Any increase in the formal services sector wage (exogenously given) will also induce rural-urban migration by increasing expected urban income.

7.7.1. System of Equations

Following the previous sections, consider the following system of equations.

$$\dot{p}_{is} = P_{is}\left(\alpha P_a - a\right) \tag{7.13}$$

$$\dot{p}_a = P_a\left(\beta P_{is} - b\right) \tag{7.14}$$

where $\dot{p}_{is}$ is the change in the level of output per worker in the urban informal services sector, $\dot{p}_a$ is the change in the level of output per worker in
agriculture, P_{is} is the level of output per worker in urban informal services,
P_a is the level of output per worker in agriculture, a and b are constant proportional growth rates that assumed to be positive, whereas α and β are
coefficients that are assumed to be positive.

Equations (7.13) and (7.14) are drawn from the Lotka-Volterra or
Predator-Prey models (Lotka, 1956), which consist of a pair of first-order
ordinary differential equations used to describe the dynamics of biologi-
cal systems in which two species interact. In the context of our modified
Harris-Todaro model, they represent the interaction between labour productivity levels in agriculture and urban informal services. The following is
an intuitive explanation for the system of equations.

Equation (7.13) shows that in the absence of the agricultural sector, the
rate of growth of output per worker in the urban informal services sector
declines at a constant proportional rate a. This is explained by the fact that
without an agricultural sector, a large proportion of the growing unskilled
labour force would be employed in the urban informal services sector,
thereby driving down labour productivity. Similarly, Equation (7.14) shows
that in the absence of the urban informal services sector, the rate of growth
of output per worker in the agriculture declines at a constant proportional
rate b.

In the presence of both sectors, adjustments need to be made. α and β
are coefficients to be interpreted as the effect of the labour productivity of
one sector on the labour productivity of the other, where the effects work
through exogenous changes in the level of infrastructure per capita and
resulting changes in rural-urban migration. Equation (7.13) shows that
output per worker in the agricultural sector has a positive effect on output
per worker in the urban informal services sector. This may be explained
by the following. An exogenous increase in the level of output per worker
(and hence wages) in agriculture, resulting from spillover effects of an
increase in urban infrastructure, does not affect movement of people, as

expected urban income remains the same and the model is assumed to have no reverse migration. With no increase in rural-urban migration, this, in turn, increases the level of infrastructure per capita available in urban areas, thereby increasing output per worker in urban informal services. Similarly, Equation (7.14) shows that output per worker in the informal services sector has a positive effect on output per worker in agriculture. This is because an exogenous increase in the level of output per worker in urban informal services (following an increase in the level of infrastructure per capita in urban areas), which implies an increase in the urban informal services wage, induces greater migration to urban areas and reduces population pressure on farmland, thereby resulting in an increase in the level of output per worker in agriculture.

7.7.2. Dynamics

In steady state, $\dot{p}_{is} = 0$ and $\dot{p}_{a} = 0$. This implies that there are two equilibria for the system, defined by Equations (7.13) and (7.14).

> (1) $[p_{is} = 0, p_{a} = 0]$ – Trivial Equilibrium
>
> (2) $[p_{is} = b/\beta, p_{a} = a/\alpha]$ – Non-Trivial Equilibrium

Given that output per worker in both the agricultural and urban informal services sectors are unlikely to be zero, we focus on the non-trivial equilibrium. $\dot{p}_{a} = 0$ and $\dot{p}_{is} = 0$ are the 'stationaries' – that is, lines (which are a loci of the combination of different values of p_{is} and p_{a}) along which the two functions equal zero. The non-trivial steady-state equilibrium enables us to determine the slopes of the functions, $\dot{p}_{a} = 0$ and $\dot{p}_{is} = 0$, in the (p_{is}, p_{a}) space (Figure 7.1). Any point in which the two functions of the system are simultaneously zero is called a 'singular point'. It represents a state of rest, or equilibrium of the system.

Figure 7.1 shows that the unique equilibrium for our system of equations is defined by the singular point E_{2}. In fact, Section 7.6 shows that this unique equilibrium is the point at which the change in the level of output per worker in agriculture exceeds that in urban informal services. The stability of this equilibrium is determined by the dynamics of the system, which, in turn, are based on the relationships set out in Equations (7.13) and (7.14).[10] The dynamics of the system are depicted by the arrows in Figure 7.1. These

---

10 $\dfrac{\partial \dot{p}_{is}}{\partial p_{a}} > 0$ and $\dfrac{\partial \dot{p}_{a}}{\partial p_{is}} > 0$.

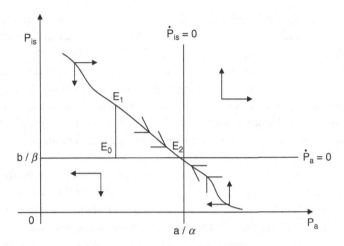

Figure 7.1. Phase-plane diagram.

arrows illustrate that our model has one 'stable arm', which means there is saddle point stability.

7.7.3. Implications for our Analytical Framework

In providing an explanation for the dynamics represented in the phase-plane diagram, it is important to emphasize that output per worker in the urban informal services sector is a 'jump' variable, whereas output per worker in agriculture is not. There are two reasons for this. First, an increase in the level of urban infrastructure per capita has an instantaneous effect on labour productivity in urban informal services but a lagged effect on labour productivity in agriculture. The lagged effect is attributable to the fact that a rise in urban infrastructure has no direct impact on agriculture which is located in rural areas, and spillover effects takes some time to set in. Second, an increase in the number of people migrating to urban areas has a lagged effect on labour productivity in both urban informal services and agriculture. This is because, given costs of migration and family concerns, the physical act of moving from rural to urban areas takes a while.

Suppose the initial equilibrium is at E_0. At this point, the level of output per worker in agriculture is greater than the level of output per worker in informal services. Now, suppose that the level of urban infrastructure increases permanently. In the long run, the economy will move from E_0 to E_2, where E_2 represents the unique steady-state equilibrium in which the change in the level of p_{is} is lower than that in p_a. The economy, however, cannot instantaneously jump from E_0 to E_2, as p_a is not a 'jump' variable, but changes only gradually. Hence, because there is no tendency for p_a to change in the first instance, p_{is} jumps onto the 'stable arm' of the system – from E_0 to E_1. Hence, even though p_a remains unchanged, the 'infrastructure shock' results in an instantaneous increase in the productivity of people employed in urban informal services. This situation may be indicative of the data which show that labour productivity in informal services, perceived as a free-entry residual sector, may actually be higher than labour productivity in agriculture.

Over time, however, the economic system will continue to move, through its intrinsic dynamics, from E_1 to E_2 along the 'stable arm', owing to several other changes that take place. An increase in the number of people migrating to urban areas in response to the 'infrastructure shock' increases employment in the urban informal services sector. This results in overcrowding – a larger number of people performing similar tasks with no real increase in total output – thereby dampening the initial increase in output per worker in urban informal services. Conversely, this increase in rural-urban migration reduces the population pressure on farmland, thereby resulting in an increase in the level of output per worker in agriculture.[11] In addition, agricultural productivity may also increase with a lag for the reason that the urban 'infrastructure shock' begins to have a positive, albeit small, impact on people working in rural areas that are in the immediate neighbourhood of urban centres. This indicates possible spillover effects. Finally, as more people migrate from rural to urban areas, the positive effect of infrastructure on output per worker in the urban informal services sector falls owing to a reduction in what is available for use per capita in urban areas. This is because the magnitude of benefit rendered by the economic and social overhead to those employed in urban areas is a decreasing function of the number of people using it.

Hence, p_{is} initially overshoots its long-run equilibrium level, after which it gradually falls alongside an increase in p_a following the path from E_1 to E_2 along the 'stable arm' of the system. Overshooting, which results from the requirement of the system that possesses 'saddle path' stability, is attributable to lagged effects. These lagged effects relate to the impact of an increase in urban infrastructure and the consequent rural-urban migration on labour productivity. The former has an instantaneous impact on urban informal services productivity but not on agricultural productivity, because spillover effects take some time to materialize. The latter has a lagged effect

---

[11] Assuming no fall in agricultural output owing to disguised unemployment.

on productivity in both sectors because, owing to family concerns and costs of migration, the physical act of moving from rural to urban areas takes a while. This result is analogous to the result of the model for exchange rate overshooting presented by Dornbusch (1976, 1980) in his seminal paper.

7.8. Conclusion

At the outset, we developed a modified version of the Harris-Todaro model for the Indian economy to help explain rural-urban migration at the level of the individual. In the Harris-Todaro model, relatively unskilled migrants have a realistic chance of finding a job in the urban formal sector owing to demand for unskilled workers in the labour-intensive manufacturing sector. The same is true of our model in which the urban formal sector consists only of services, because Chapter 5 showed that several segments of the services sector do have low educational barriers to entry.

As in the original model, this modified version predicts that wages in the urban informal services sector must lie below wages in the rural agricultural sector. Assuming that payment systems in these two sectors are based on the average product of labour, the data on India contradicts this prediction, as output per worker in informal services is much higher than output per worker in agriculture. The difference in magnitudes is too large to be explained by costs of migration alone. Guided by economic intuition and supported by empirical analysis, we found that an increase in social and economic infrastructure in urban areas is a potential explanation for the trends observed in the data. At the same time, assuming that the initial level of output per worker in urban informal services is less than the initial level of output per worker in agriculture, we showed that a higher level of output per worker in the urban informal services sector than in agriculture does not constitute long-run equilibrium for the economy. This is because in the long-run equilibrium, the change in output per worker in agriculture exceeds the change in output per worker in urban informal services.

In exploring this empirical puzzle, we analysed the dynamics of a system of equations, which helped to reconcile the Harris-Todaro model with the trends seen in the macroeconomic data for India. A positive 'infrastructure shock' in urban areas results in an instantaneous increase in the level of output per worker (and hence wages) in the urban informal services sector, leaving the agricultural sector unaffected. Over time, however, the 'infrastructure shock' increases 'expected urban income', which induces greater migration from rural to urban areas. This movement of labour between sectors alters their respective sizes and, hence, levels of productivity. In particular, the 'infrastructure externality' results in an increase in informal-services employment and a fall in agricultural-sector employment. This has implications for productivity levels. First, as more people enter urban areas in general, the positive effect of infrastructure falls owing to a reduction in what is available for use per capita. Second, as more people get employed in the urban informal-services sector, overcrowding occurs. Both these effects serve to reduce informal services productivity. At the same time, agricultural productivity increases as migration from rural areas reduces pressure on land. Finally, the 'infrastructure shock' in urban areas begins to have a small, positive impact on agricultural productivity by rendering an indirect benefit for people employed in rural areas that are in the immediate neighbourhood of urban centres.

In sum, following the 'infrastructure shock', the level of output per worker in the urban informal-services sector overshoots its long-run equilibrium level, after which it gradually falls alongside an increase in the level of output per worker in agriculture. This result relates to the famous exchange rate overshooting result presented by Dornbusch (1976). In our model, this results from the fact that both an increase in urban infrastructure and subsequent rural-urban migration have a lagged effect on rural sector productivity, but that the former has an instantaneous effect on urban formal services productivity. In fact, in long-run equilibrium, the change in output per worker in urban informal services is less than the change in output per worker in agriculture. And given that in our modified version of the Harris-Todaro model, the initial level of output per worker in informal services is less than the initial level of output per worker in agriculture, it implies that this will hold in the long run as well, thereby resolving the empirical puzzle.

The results of this chapter imply that public investment in economic and social infrastructure is an important determinant of labour productivity. For example, because of better infrastructure in urban relative to rural areas, hawkers or street vendors in an urban centre may be more productive than individuals working on a farm in agriculture. The results presented in this chapter also suggest that given the vast numbers employed in low-productivity occupations in agriculture, rapid absorption of unskilled labour into more productive activities, including the urban informal service sector, is important for India's growth process. This is especially true because the magnitude of investment required for improving the country's primary and secondary education implies that making even a quarter of the country's labour force employable in the fast-growing, skill-intensive services sector is at best a medium-term goal. Hence, the adoption of policies to boost gainful employment of low-skilled labour in the urban informal services sector so as to make it more dynamic is an important issue. Our results show that one way forward is large-scale investment in infrastructure such as roads, electricity, schools and hospitals and telecommunication. It reinforces the findings of Ghani (2010), who highlights the importance of appropriate infrastructure in making services-led growth work.

EIGHT

Conclusion

The aim of this chapter is to present and synthesize the main conclusions from each chapter of the book and to explore possible links between them. It also attempts to highlight the original contribution of the book to the literature on the subject. The conclusion draws attention, wherever possible, to relevant policy implications as well. In addition, the chapter suggests opportunities for further research in the area, with some focus on statistics that ought to be collected, compiled and made available to researchers. It is clear from Chapter 2 that there are conceptual problems, statistical limitations and measurement difficulties in attempting an analysis of the services sector, both in general and in the context of India's National Accounts Statistics. But this cannot and should not lead to the conclusion that any such exercise is not worthwhile.

The services sector accounts for an increasing proportion of output, and also employment, in most countries, including developing countries. Chapter 1 showed it accounted for as much as 57 per cent of India's GDP in 2010. Moreover, during the past three decades, the rate of growth of services has been higher than that of industry or agriculture. In fact, from 1980–81 to 2009–10, the share of the industrial sector in GDP remained almost constant, and hence the services sector picked up, almost completely, the decline in the share of the agricultural sector in GDP. This does not conform to stylized facts about structural change in the process of development in the now industrialized countries. It is also very different from the experience of other developing countries, such as China. Furthermore, during the same period, the increase in the share of the services sector in total employment was not commensurate to that in total output. This asymmetry makes India an outlier in the context of the rest of the world. In light of this, it is important to recognize the statistical problems, limitations and difficulties and to resolve them as far as possible, in order to understand the role of the services sector in the process of development.

8.1. Conclusions and Policy Implications

8.1.1. India's Services Sector Growth: Possible Explanations

The literature cites a number of potential explanations for the increasing importance of the services sector. Is it simply an increase in the relative price of services, indicative of the sector's relatively slow productivity growth? Or is it a statistical artifice whereby what was earlier subsumed in manufacturing or agriculture value added is now accounted for as service sector contributions to GDP? Chapter 1 showed that during the period from 1980 to 2010, the share of industry and services in total employment increased by about 8 percentage points each. However, over the same period, the share of the services sector in total output increased by about 21 percentage points while that of industry remained almost unchanged. It implies that, unlike the experience of the now industrialized countries, the services sector in India has not witnessed slower relative productivity growth. This was validated by our computation of implicit GDP price deflators in Chapter 3, which showed that during this period, the price of services did not increase notably, relative to either industry or agriculture. Furthermore, Chapter 3 demonstrated that increased 'contracting out' from the industrial to the services sector was not an important explanation for an increasing share of services in total output between 1980 and 2007. The two aforementioned findings suggest that the growth of India's services sector during the last three decades has been real rather than notional.

Chapter 3 showed that this real growth of the services sector may be attributable to a range of factors. In doing so, it first reviewed the existing literature on the subject to identify the potential factors. On the demand side, these include high income elasticity of demand for services that characterizes domestic households, government consumption, and international trade in services. On the supply side, policy liberalization and the availability of a pool of skilled labour may have made a contribution. The findings in the existing literature suggest that different factors may have been important for explaining the growth of different service sub-sectors. For instance, greater deregulation and privatization are likely to have induced growth in sectors – such as communication and financial services – that were state monopolies in the pre-reform period. The availability of skilled labour may have been a contributing factor to the growth of certain skill-intensive services – business, financial and community services, for example. The growth of India's services exports has been concentrated in the business services segment, and hence is likely to have had a significant effect on the growth of this service sub-sector over the last two and half decades. Finally, in the context of domestic demand, government consumption may be important for explaining any growth of the public administration sector, whereas household consumption is likely to have had an impact on growth of consumer services such as transport, communication, hotels and restaurants and personal services.

Subsequently, Chapter 3 combined the different factors that may have influenced the growth of the services sector, in both real and notional terms, in a regression exercise. This exercise ensures that the competing factors are not viewed in isolation, but rather analysed in unison. It followed a couple of studies in the literature using more recent data. It also included certain new variables – services exports disaggregated by service sub-sector being particularly noteworthy – and aimed to get around the problem of reverse causality in the context of certain factors. The results from the empirical estimation showed that final demand – arising from domestic households and exports to the rest of the world – and policy liberalization appear to be the most important for explaining the increasing share of the services sector in India's total output. Among these, the coefficient on the service exports variable was relatively small. The relatively small contribution of exports to the overall growth of the services sector may be attributable to the fact that services exports constituted less than 17 per cent of services GDP in 2008. But given that the volume of service exports is growing rapidly, their contribution to the growth of India's services sector is likely to increase in the years to come.

8.1.2. Highlighting the Role of Private Demand: Microeconomic Evidence

Macroeconomic data clearly suggest that private final demand is an important explanation for the growth of India's services sector (Banga, 2005; Gordon and Gupta, 2004; Rakshit, 2007). Unfortunately, the country's National Accounts data cannot distinguish precisely between the goods and services components under different expenditure heads. In addition, it is difficult to establish a causal effect of income on the share of services in the context of our regression framework at the all-India level in Chapter 3. Hence, to explore the importance of high income elasticity of demand for services as an explanation for the increasing share of the services sector in total output, it is important to move beyond the macroeconomic evidence. In Chapter 4, using consumption data for a sample of more than 120,000 households in India at two points in time – 1993–94 and 2004–05 – we estimated Engel curve-type relationships for six categories of services: education, health, entertainment, personal, communications and transport. These services accounted for about half of India's services GDP in 2005, and many of them were characterized by high rates of growth between 1993–94 and 2004–05. Importantly, the survey data used enabled us to capture expenditure on services per se rather than on services and goods for a category of service expenditure.

Employing two alternative estimators, we found upward-sloping Engel curves for each of the selected categories of services and for these services sector in the aggregate – both in 1993–94 and 2004–05. Given that we used a budget share specification for the estimation, this implies that these services take up a larger share of household budgets as incomes or expenditures increase, thereby suggesting that their expenditure elasticity of demand is greater than unity. In other words, education, health, entertainment, personal, communication and transport services are all 'luxury goods' – mirror images of Engel's Law for food. Non-linearities in the relationship between total expenditure and budget share allocated to different services were driven by outliers. This indicates that there is a consistent increase in the household budget share allocated to these services as total expenditure increases – they are luxury goods at all levels of income. The robustness of our results is further strengthened by the use of instrumental variable analysis, which facilitates the identification of a causal impact of total income or expenditure on the household budget share allocated to services.

We also extended our cross-sectional exercise to analyze changes over time. This is important because richer households may not necessarily be a good prediction for how poor households will spend their money when their income rises. A decomposition exercise showed that mean household expenditure was paramount in explaining increases in the mean household budget share allocated to services during the period from 1993–94 to 2004–05. Moreover, panel data analysis at the level of 'regions' revealed upward-sloping Engel curves. Given all of the above, our rigorous micro-econometric analysis lends credence to the view that high income elasticities of demand for services are an important explanation for the increasing importance of the services sector in India. The explanation for the high income elasticity of demand for services in India – unusual for a country of its level of development – may be attributable to increasing inequality of income and household preferences that have led to the introduction of a host of consumer services which households can spend on (Rakshit, 2007).

8.1.3. A Systematic Disaggregation of India's Services Sector

The micro-econometric analysis described earlier suggests that the different categories of services are similar if not homogenous inasmuch as they are all 'luxury goods'. But that is so only in a limited sense. In terms of economic characteristics, different service categories may differ considerably. Unfortunately, in the literature on the subject so far, economists have treated the services sector as a black box in much the same way as they treated technology for a long time. An analysis of the services sector at a disaggregated level is limited to documenting trends in output and employment (Banga, 2005; Gordon and Gupta, 2004). There are no studies exploring the heterogeneity across different service sub-sectors in terms of different characteristics that are relevant to economic development. The book explored that heterogeneity by developing a taxonomy to open the black box of services. In doing so, it makes an important contribution to understanding and knowledge. Chapter 5 disaggregated the services sector in India according to a set of attributes relevant to economic development, as guided by economic theory and analysis. The attributes were divided into five broad categories: structural characteristics (organized versus unorganized economic activity, public versus private provision, intermediate versus final demand), employment characteristics (educational barriers to entry for job seekers), factor-use characteristics (capital intensity and skill intensity), productivity-enhancing technology characteristics (potential to achieve economies of scale, contribution to technological progress and the incorporation of technological advance) and international trade characteristics. Of course, many of these attributes are related and interdependent.

Given this interdependence, we identified certain patterns across the different categories of characteristics in order to define a smaller set of archetype sub-sectors of services for the purpose of analysis (See Chapter 5). This is indicative of sub-sector-specific implications for economic growth, employment, balance of payments, the sustainability of services-led growth, poverty and inequality. The classification of sectors into categories of 'high', 'medium' and 'low' – across the different characteristics – was carried out on the basis of statistical analysis of available data.

In growth accounting exercises, economic growth can be decomposed into increases in factor accumulation (labour or capital) at given levels of productivity and increases in factor productivity. In the context of the earlier discussion, the taxonomy showed that wholesale and retail trade, hotels and restaurants, transport by other means, storage, real estate and renting and personal, recreational and entertainment services are characterized by 'low to medium' barriers to entry for employment and 'low to medium' productivity-enhancing technology characteristics. This implies that whereas these sectors are unlikely to be associated with economic growth via increases in factor productivity, they may be associated with growth through employment expansion, provided that it does not lead to a corresponding contraction of employment in other sectors of the economy.[1] In fact, Chapter 6 shows that it is some of these sectors that accounted for relatively large shares in total services employment during the period from 1993–94 to 2004–05. Storage services and real estate and renting services may also be associated with growth through increases in capital accumulation as they are 'high' capital intensity sectors.

In contrast, communication, financial and business services are characterized by 'medium to high' barriers to entry for employment and 'medium to high' productivity-enhancing technology characteristics. Hence, these sectors are likely to be associated with economic growth primarily via increases in factor productivity. Moreover, to a small extent, communication and business services may also be associated with growth through the accumulation of capital and labour. The remaining sub-sectors – railways, public administration and defence and community services – are characterized by 'medium' barriers to entry for employment and 'medium' productivity-enhancing technology characteristics. These sectors may be associated with economic growth either via increases in factor productivity or through employment expansion.

It is worth noting that the two channels outlined previously relate to changes within different sub-sectors of services. Economic growth may also occur through a transfer of resources such as labour from low to high productivity service sub-sectors. So, for example, taking an individual out of retail trade and placing him in business services could spur productivity growth. The lack of education, however, is likely to be a major hindrance in any such transfer of labour.

The taxonomy of services has important implications for the sustainability of the services-led growth as well. This is because the dichotomy between services and manufacturing that is traditionally assumed may not

---

[1] This qualification is applicable in subsequent paragraphs where the same argument is made.

necessarily hold because certain sub-sectors of services can be organized in ways that are close to modern manufacturing. For example, communication, business and financial services are characterized by 'medium to high' scope to achieve economies of scale, contribution to technological progress, and incorporation of technological advance to improve productivity. Given the preceding discussion, growth in the output of these service sub-sectors is likely to have a positive effect on their productivity and on average GDP growth. The business services sector, with its 'high' contribution to technological progress, may even improve the economy's overall productivity. The same may hold true for financial services, among others, which serve intermediate demand and hence can have productivity-enhancing spillover effects.

Finally, like the manufacturing sector, certain segments of the services sector can benefit the whole economy through international trade. According to the taxonomy, business services and to a lesser extent transport by other means, hotels and restaurants, communication, financial and community services are highly traded in international markets and hence can facilitate growth by boosting the country's productivity through learning-by-exporting effects, scale economies, transfer of technology and greater import competition. In fact, for services that are highly tradeable in international markets, government support in securing improved access is likely to be important. This is especially so given restrictions on movement of people across national boundaries and the recent backlash against outsourcing in several developed country markets. At the same time, like in the case of manufacturing, certain segments of the services sector may warrant some kind of 'infant services' protection if they generate positive externalities. Exports of services – which in India's case are driven by software services and business process outsourcing – also means that these foreign exchange earnings can finance the import of different commodities. Given all of the aforementioned factors, the sustainability of services-led growth does not appear as unfeasible as before. At the same time, growth impulses from other sectors cannot be underemphasized. This is especially so because the sustainability of this growth process is also likely to be a function of the amount of employment the services sector generates.

The question of employment is closely related to what this service-led growth process means for poverty and income inequality in the country. This is another implication of the taxonomy developed in Chapter 5. For example, it shows that wholesale and retail trade, hotels and restaurants, transport by other means and personal, recreational and entertainment services are characterized by 'low to medium' capital and skill intensity.

This suggests that these services sub-sectors that are likely to absorb a large unskilled workforce, and thereby to reduce poverty directly. In contrast, communication, financial and business services are characterized by 'medium to high' capital and skill intensity. Hence, employment expansion in these sectors is likely to be less relevant in terms of direct benefits to the relatively less well-off sections of society. It may, however, generate trickle-down effects.

Furthermore, the taxonomy shows that service sub-sectors that are classified with 'medium to high' productivity-enhancing technology characteristics are likely to create a small amount of employment opportunities, and are likely to favour capital and skilled labour over unskilled labour. Conversely, service sub-sectors with 'low to medium' productivity-enhancing technology characteristics are likely to create large-scale employment opportunities and favour unskilled labour over capital and skilled labour. This dichotomy suggests that in business services, for example, skilled workers and owners of capital are likely to benefit from productivity increases, whereas a large amount of unskilled labour in other sub-sectors of services – wholesale and retail trade, for example – may not benefit from such productivity increases. The resulting change in the relative earnings between different factor groups is likely to lead to higher income inequality.

8.1.4. Employment in India's Services Sector relative to Industry: Exploring the Heterogeneity

The taxonomy developed in Chapter 5 showed that educational barriers to entry for job seekers, skill intensity and productivity-enhancing technology characteristics vary considerably across different service sub-sectors. This suggests that individual earnings – and the nature of employment more generally – in the services sector may vary considerably across its different segments. But how does an individual employed in a particular service sub-sector compare to a similar individual employed in the industrial sector? This was the focus of Chapter 6.

Differences in wage levels and other non-wage benefits across formal and informal sectors of the economy are acknowledged by the literature. This is often based on empirical studies using small sample surveys of cities or districts (Banerjee, 1986; Dasgupta, 2003). But there is no analysis of the heterogeneity in wage and non-wage rewards by the industry of employment. The contribution of this chapter to the literature on the subject is to analyse the nature and quality of employment being generated in the different sub-sectors of services in India. We carried out an econometric analysis of household survey data for two points in time: 1993–94 and 2004–05. The second contribution of this chapter is that it moves beyond the usual small, city-specific surveys and utilizes a pan-India household survey database covering around 500,000 individuals.

The taxonomy in Chapter 5 showed that educational barriers to entry may be relatively high in some service sub-sectors and relatively low in others. That was the starting point. Using more rigorous tools of micro-econometrics, we found that access to employment in terms of educational requirements does vary across the different sub-sectors of services. For instance, in certain sub-sectors, the level of education of an individual has a significant effect on the probability of being employed. This result can be seen to represent the theories of 'human capital', or 'educational screening', or 'education as instrument of job competition'. Subsequently, we found that, relative to the industrial sector, sub-sectors of services with low educational requirements are characterized by lower quality of employment, where quality of employment was defined to include three variables that reflect quality of life: wages or earnings, the probability of getting a job contract and the probability of getting social security benefits. These include wholesale and retail trade, hotels and restaurants, transport, real estate and renting and other social, community and personal services. In contrast, our results revealed that services sub-sectors with high educational barriers to entry have relatively higher quality of employment. These include communication, financial, business, public administration and defence, education and health services. Hence, this set of results underscores the importance of secondary and tertiary education for people to benefit, in terms of wages and non-wage rewards, from the growth of service sub-sectors that provide a relatively higher quality of employment.

Moreover, we found that after standardizing for several possible factors, service sub-sectors appeared to be generally either 'good' or 'bad' employers. There is no 'compensating variation' according to which higher wages compensate for less job security or less social protection. The fact that certain sub-sectors of services are generally 'good' employers whereas others are generally 'bad' employers may be attributable to the overall profitability of firms, profit-sharing wage and non-wage benefits, efficiency wages, sector-specific 'production functions' where the importance of technology and quality (as opposed to level) of employees' education may vary. Segmentation between organised and unorganised economic activity may also be a factor. In fact, comparing the results from our cross-section analysis at two points in time, we found that the classification of most service sub-sectors as "good" or "bad" employers – in terms of wages – remains unchanged during the ten-year period from 1993–94 to 2004–05. This shows the relative lack of improvement in the quality of employment, on average, for individuals employed in wholesale and retail trade, hotels and restaurants, transport, real estate and renting and other social, community and personal services. Given that these sectors employ unskilled labour in large numbers, this has possible implications for the country's income distribution. In terms of implications for policy, an analysis of this heterogeneity in the nature of employment generated across different service sub-sectors is a vital point of reference for formulating policies on improving quality of employment – both in absolute and relative terms.

Our results on quality of employment, when juxtaposed with data on quantity of employment, reveal an interesting story. The sub-sectors of services which accounted for the largest shares in total services employment, both in 1993–94 and 2004–05, are the ones characterized by low educational requirements and relatively low quality of employment. Moreover, it is these generally 'bad' employers that had the highest percentage contribution to the increase in total services employment during that period. In sum, barring a few exceptions, employment expansion appears to be more in sub-sectors of services where educational barriers to entry are low and quality of employment is low. This matching of the empirics on the quality and quantity of employment across the different sub-sectors of services sheds some light on the welfare-enhancing impact of India's services sector growth. For instance, it suggests that because segments characterized by high quality of employment are not creating a large number of jobs for the unskilled, the direct benefits – in terms of a marked improvement in quality of life – of services-led growth to a cross-section of people may be limited.

The results of Chapter 6 have another important policy implication because sub-sectors of services where educational barriers to entry are low and quality of employment is low have relatively larger informal or unorganized segments (as shown in Chapter 5). Hence, better or more effective regulation of informal sector activity may result in better quality of employment for individuals employed in these sub-sectors. On the other hand, regulations, if and when introduced, might raise barriers to entry so that employment creation or expansion in these sectors could slow down.

8.1.5. Comparing Productivity and Wages between Urban Informal Services and Agriculture

In Chapter 6, we found that, relative to the industrial sector, individuals employed in certain service sub-sectors – wholesale and retail trade, hotels and restaurants, transport services, real estate and renting services and personal services – are characterized by lower educational requirements and lower wages. We also found that within the services sector, it is these segments that have generated the maximum employment opportunities over the last two and a half decades. At the same time, the results of Chapter 5 showed that the unorganized sector has a major presence in many of these service segments. This suggests that a large amount of labour is potentially being pushed into the services sector because of lack of employment opportunities in unskilled, labour-intensive manufacturing. It is plausible because alongside the success of the country's software, business process outsourcing and other professional services, a fairly large urban informal-services sector consisting of petty traders, service workers in small restaurants and *dhabas,* cycle-rickshaw pullers, street vendors, hawkers and domestic servants, among others, has developed simultaneously.

The above implies that the urban informal-services sector is a reservoir of low-wage occupations, where people are earning relatively less than those employed in the industrial sector. But how do their earnings compare with individuals employed in agriculture – also a 'residual' sector characterized by substantial underemployment, disguised unemployment and low levels of productivity? This makes for an interesting comparison. There has been no attempt in the literature to examine productivity differentials between service and non-service sectors in India and to find possible explanations for these existing differentials.

Chapter 7 provided a beginning. Using stylized facts for the Indian economy, it first developed a modified version of the Harris-Todaro model to help explain migration from rural to urban areas at the level of the individual. As in the original model, this modified version predicted that wages in the urban informal-services sector must lie below wages in the rural agricultural sector. But given the assumption that wages in these two sectors are based on the average product of labour, the data on India contradict this prediction, as output per worker in the informal-services sector is much higher than output per worker in agriculture. The difference in magnitudes is too large to be explained by costs of migration alone. Guided by economic intuition and supported by empirical analysis, we argued that an increase in social and economic infrastructure in urban areas could be driving the trends observed in the data. At the same time, assuming that the initial level of output per worker in agriculture exceeds the initial level of output per worker in urban informal services, we showed that a higher level of output per worker in the urban informal-services sector than in agriculture does not constitute long-run equilibrium for the economy. This is because in the long-run equilibrium, the change in output per worker in agriculture exceeds the change in output per worker in urban informal services.

In exploring this empirical puzzle, we analysed the dynamics of a system of equations, which helped to reconcile the Harris-Todaro model with the trends seen in the data for India. An increase in the level of infrastructure in urban areas results in an instantaneous increase in the level of output per worker in the urban informal-services sector, leaving the agricultural sector unaffected. This reflects the trends seen in the data. Over time, however, the 'infrastructure shock' increases 'expected urban income', which induces greater migration from rural to urban areas. This movement of labour between sectors alters their respective sizes and, hence, levels of productivity. In particular, the 'infrastructure externality' results in an increase in informal-services employment and a fall in agricultural-sector employment. This has implications for productivity levels. First, as more people enter urban areas in general, the positive effect of infrastructure falls owing to a reduction in what is available for use per capita. Second, as more people get employed in the urban informal-services sector, this results in underemployment. Both these effects serve to reduce productivity in the informal-services sector. At the same time, productivity in agriculture increases as migration from rural areas reduces pressure on land. Finally, the 'infrastructure shock' in urban areas begins to have a small, positive impact on agricultural productivity by rendering an indirect benefit for people employed in rural areas that are in the immediate neighbourhood of urban centres. In sum, following the 'infrastructure shock', the level of output per worker in the informal-services sector overshoots its long-run equilibrium level, after which it gradually falls alongside an increase in the level of output per worker in agriculture.

This result relates to the famous exchange rate overshooting results presented by Dornbusch (1976). Overshooting results from the fact that the system is characterized by lagged effects. In our model, these lagged effects relate to the impact of an increase in urban infrastructure and of the consequent rural-urban migration on labour productivity. The former has an instantaneous impact on urban informal-services productivity, but not on agricultural productivity because spillover effects take some time to materialize. The latter has a lagged effect on productivity in both sectors, because owing to family concerns and costs of migration, the physical act of moving from rural to urban areas takes a while. In fact, in long-run equilibrium, the change in output per worker in urban informal services is less than the change in output per worker in agriculture. And given that in our modified version of the Harris-Todaro model, the initial level of output per worker in informal services is less than the initial level of output per worker in agriculture, it implies that this will hold in the long run as well, thereby resolving the empirical puzzle.

The findings of the chapter imply that given the vast numbers employed in low-productivity occupations in agriculture, a more rapid absorption of unskilled labour into more productive activities, including even some in the urban informal service sector, is important for India's growth process. This is especially true because the magnitude of investment required for improving the country's primary and secondary education implies that making large numbers of people employable in the fast-growing, skill-intensive services sector is a medium- to long-term goal. The result is that the adoption of policies to boost gainful employment of low-skilled labour in the urban informal-services sector so as to make it more dynamic is an important issue. One way forward, as suggested by the results of Chapter 6, is large-scale investment in infrastructure, such as roads, electricity, railways and telecommunication; because of better infrastructure in urban areas, workers in urban informal services may be more productive than those working on a farm in agriculture. Other possible policy measures could include the development of an effective credit delivery system (Rakshit, 2007), the provision of supply side financial services (Rakshit, 2007) and governments maintaining a high rate of growth of aggregate demand, thereby giving small enterprises a greater opportunity to survive and expand than would be the case in a static macroeconomic environment (Dasgupta and Singh, 2005).

8.1.6. The Whole: Greater Than the Sum of Its Parts

For a country of its level of economic development, the rapidly increasing share of the services sector in India's total output does not conform to the historical experience of the now industrialized countries as well many other developing countries, such as China. This book has shown that the growth of India's services sector during the last three decades has been real rather than notional, attributable, in large part, to a high income elasticity of domestic household demand, policy liberalization and growing service exports. The old literature on structural change would question the sustainability of a services-led growth process, because the sector traditionally was not associated with growth-promoting characteristics. But with significant advancement in technology, today's world is very different from the time in which these economists lived and worked; many services now closely resemble modern manufacturing. Exploring the heterogeneity of the services sector, the taxonomy developed in this book showed that certain subsectors can exploit economies of scale, incorporate technological advance to enhance productivity, be traded in international markets, have productivity spillovers to other sectors and even contribute to technological progress. In this context, the growth of business, financial, communication and community services becomes crucial.

But the sustainability of this services-led growth process is also a function of the employment it creates. In India, the growth of services employment has not been commensurate with the growth of services output. However, this aggregate finding does not reveal the complete picture. The services sector has created employment opportunities, but those have been concentrated in a few sub-sectors – wholesale and retail trade, hotels and restaurants, transport services and personal services, for example. These services are likely to have directly benefitted the less well-off sections of society. In contrast, employment expansion in financial, communication and business services either has been limited or biased in favour of the skilled. Importantly, this book showed that, by and large, sectors that constituted a large part of the increase in total services employment are characterized by low educational requirements, wages and other non-wage benefits – and vice versa – relative to the industrial sector. This suggests that to make large numbers of unskilled people in sectors such as wholesale and retail trade better off, their quality of employment needs to be improved. At the same time, greater investment in education at all levels needs to be undertaken to facilitate the employment of more people in the skill-biased service sectors that are characterized by a relatively high quality of employment. However, educating a large population – where the number of young people is growing exponentially – is an objective that is unlikely to be achieved quickly. Hence, in the meantime, given the huge population pressure on farmland, efforts to improve the productivity of a large number of unskilled people employed in a growing informal-services sector is the need of the hour. This is especially important given that, on average, individuals employed in India's urban informal-services sector appear to be more productive that those working in agriculture. The book shows that investment in infrastructure is one way forward in this context. Of course, this result does not preclude the importance of progress in the two other sectors of the economy: the expansion of an unskilled labour-intensive manufacturing sector and productivity improvements in the agricultural sector.

8.2. Future Research

In recent years, a fairly vast literature has emerged on services. However, it concentrates only on a few themes and aspects. Empirical research on the services sector is limited and incomplete primarily because of the lack of reliable, timely and easily interpretable data. Chapter 2 showed that this largely relates to the statistical difficulties associated with measuring services output in National Accounts Statistics, adjusting for price change over a period of time to compute reliable constant price estimates and making comparisons between services and other sectors of the economy.

This book was able to circumvent or manage some of these constraints. In Chapters 4 and 6, the analysis relied entirely on household survey data. In Chapter 5, the analysis was based on sample survey data for households and firms, with some data from National Accounts Statistics, and the problems associated with the latter were reduced because the focus was on the services sector alone. In Chapter 7, the analysis of differences in productivity between agriculture and urban informal services relied in part on employment data from sample surveys and in part on output data from National Accounts Statistics. Fortunately, evidence presented in Chapter 3 suggests that the price of services, relative to agriculture, did not increase significantly during the period under review.

It is hoped that this book has filled some of the gaps in the literature. At the same time, it has opened up opportunities for further research in this area, both in the context of India and other developing countries. For some unanswered questions, there is a need for new data on services to be collected, compiled and made available to researchers. The following are a few suggestions.

First and foremost, methods used by national accountants to estimate output for different service sub-sectors must be improved. This is especially important in the context of deflating services sector output, because prevailing price indices include only agricultural commodities and manufactured goods. Methods adopted by National Accounts Statistics in developed countries could be a starting point. A more precise deflation of service output would be particularly relevant for any analysis which compares the services sector with other sectors in the economy. For instance, in the taxonomy developed in Chapter 5, it would be useful to know how business services compare with the industrial sector in the context of incorporation of technological advance to improve productivity.

Second, any analysis of the service sector's heterogeneity, such as that carried out in Chapter 5, can be significantly enhanced by the availability of data on a number of variables at a more disaggregated level. This includes, for example, estimates of capital stock, as well as the division between public and private provision, and organized and unorganized economic activity, derived from India's National Accounts Statistics. It also includes data on international trade in services, which are not available at a level of disaggregation consistent with data on value added and employment.

Third, existing pan-India household surveys conducted by the National Sample Survey Organisation (NSSO) are invaluable in that they provide data at the microeconomic level to complement that at the macroeconomic level. However, these surveys do not follow the same individuals or households over time. The results in Chapters 4 and 6 are illustrative, but they need to be complemented by research that analyses changes in household consumption expenditure, employment and wages over time. Hence, the availability of data – albeit on smaller scale – that tracks down the same households over a period of time would significantly enhance any analysis of the services sector. Furthermore, several service categories – such as wholesale and retail trade and financial services – are not covered in household surveys collecting data on consumer expenditure. Hence, the collection of firm or household-level data would facilitate much needed research on these services at the microeconomic level.

In addition to the previously described themes, the book sets the stage for some additional research questions relating to the services sector. It outlines the importance of the urban informal service sector in providing gainful employment opportunities for the unskilled. A more in-depth analysis of the informal-services sector, relating to issues of employment and productivity, is needed. Can this sector be made more dynamic? If so, how? Can parts of today's urban informal-services sector become tomorrow's formal sector in terms of productivity? An examination of a growing rural informal-services sector may be equally important. In this endeavour, existing data can be complemented by new field surveys focusing on different occupational groups such as hawkers, domestic servants, petty traders and service workers in hotels and restaurants. Next, in explaining the growth of India's services sector, the book identifies domestic demand, service exports and increased liberalization as important factors. A comparison with other developing countries, such as China, in this regard would be most fruitful. Is high income elasticity of household final demand for services particularly high in India? If so, why? Similarly, is the rise of India as a major exporter of certain services a solitary example in the developing world? What about countries in Asia and Africa? Finally, one overriding end-product of this book is the detailed documentation of heterogeneity that characterizes the services sector. To develop sub-sector specific policy recommendations, future research must focus on carrying out detailed case studies of individual segments of the service sector.

APPENDICES

Index of Tables

Appendix A

Appendix B

B.1. Engel Curves: Tobit Model

B.2. Marginal Effects: Tobit Model

B.3. Engel Curves: Tobit Model (Non-Linearities)

B.4. Engel Curves: Censored Quantile Regressions

B.4.1. 2004–05

B.4.2. 1993–94

Appendix C

C.1. Educational Requirements

C.1.1. Logit Model

Appendices

C.1.2. Multinomial Logit Model

C.2. Wages, Contracts and Social Security Benefits

Appendix A

Table A.1. *Estimating value added in the services sector in India's national accounts statistics: Sources and methods*

Sector	Public sector component	Private organized sector component	Private unorganized sector component
Wholesale and Retail Trade	Budget documents and annual reports of government corporations	Corporate sector – sample surveys carried out by the Reserve Bank of India; co-operative credit societies – information records at the National Bank of Agricultural and Rural Development; maintenance and repair of motor vehicles and household goods – product of value added per worker in benchmark year (based on enterprise surveys) and number of workers (based on employment surveys)	Product of value added per worker in benchmark year (based on enterprise surveys) and number of workers (based on employment surveys)
Hotels and Restaurants	Same as above	Sample surveys carried out by the Reserve Bank of India	Same as above

(*continued*)

Table A.1 (*continued*)

Sector	Public sector component	Private organized sector component	Private unorganized sector component
Transport	Same as above	Annual reports and accounts of private companies	Same as above
Storage	Same as above	Annual Survey of Industries (ASI)	Same as above
Communication	Same as above	Product of value added per worker in benchmark year (based on enterprise surveys) and number of workers (based on employment surveys)	Same as above
Financial Services	Same as above	Annual reports and accounts of private companies	Value added in the activities of unorganized non-banking financial undertakings and own-account moneylenders is assumed to be one-third of value added in the organized segment of the sector
Real Estate, Ownership of Dwellings and Renting Services	–	Real estate and renting – product of value added per worker in benchmark year (based on enterprise surveys) and number of workers (based on employment surveys); ownership of dwellings – gross rental less the cost of repair and maintenance (gross rental is obtained by multiplying the number of dwellings, based on the population census, by the gross rental per dwelling which obtained from consumer expenditure surveys)	Real estate and renting – same as above

(*continued*)

Table A.1 (*continued*)

Sector	Public sector component	Private organized sector component	Private unorganized sector component
Business Services	–	Product of value added per worker in benchmark year (based on enterprise surveys) and number of workers (based on employment surveys); for software and other computers-related services – data from the National Association of Software and Services Companies (NASSCOM) (Rath et al, 2007)	Product of value added per worker in benchmark year (based on enterprise surveys) and number of workers (based on employment surveys
Public Administration and Defence	Budget documents	–	–
Other Social, Community and Personal Services	Budget documents and annual reports of government corporations	Product of value added per worker in benchmark year (based on enterprise surveys) and number of workers (based on employment surveys)	Product of value added per worker in benchmark year (based on enterprise surveys) and number of workers (based on employment surveys)

Source: Central Statistical Organisation, National Accounts Statistics: Sources and Methods, 2007.

Table A.2. *Methods of estimating constant price estimates of value added in the services sector: India's National Accounts Statistics*

Sector	Public Sector Component	Private Organized Sector Component	Private Unorganized Sector Component
Wholesale and Retail Trade	Base year estimates are moved forward with a quantum index which is obtained on the basis of the quantities of different products purchase and sale of public sector companies	For the 'corporate sector' and for the 'maintenance and repair of motor vehicles', current price estimates are deflated using the GDP implicit deflator (GDP excluding that of trade, hotels and restaurants). For 'co-operative societies', base year estimates are moved forward with an index of deflated sales (value of sales at current prices deflated using wholesale price indices of non-food and manufactured goods).	Base year estimates are moved forward by an index of gross trading income which is based on the volume of goods evaluated at constant prices
Hotels and Restaurants	Same as above	Current price estimates are deflated using the GDP implicit deflator (GDP excluding that of trade, hotels and restaurants)	Same as above
Railways	Base year estimates are moved forward with a combined indicator of passenger kilometres and tonne kilometres.		
Air transport	Base year estimates are moved forward with an air transport volume index.	Base year estimates are moved forward with a combined index of passenger and cargo traffic handled at airports.	

Mechanized road transport	Base year estimates are moved forward with a quantum index of passenger kilometres.	Product of base year labour input moved forward with an index of registered vehicles, and base year value added per worker
Non-mechanized road transport		Base year estimates are moved forward with the growth rate of workforce.
Water transport	Base year estimates are moved forward with an index of cargo handled at major ports	Base year estimates are moved forward with an average compound growth rate of workforce.
	Base year estimates are moved forward with an index of cargo handled at major ports.	
Supporting and auxiliary transport activities	Current price estimates are deflated with the consumer price index for industrial workers	Base year estimates are moved forward with the average compound growth rate of employment
Storage	Current price estimates are deflated with a physical storage index	For other private storage facilities, base year estimates are moved forward with the average compound growth rate of employment.
	For private cold storage facilities, current price estimates are deflated with an index of agricultural production.	
Communication	Base year estimates are moved forward using a combined weighted index of the number of money orders, telegrams, telephones and postal articles handled	Same as left
	Current price estimates are deflated using the consumer price index for agricultural labourers and that for industrial workers for rural and urban areas respectively	

(continued)

Table A.2 (continued)

Sector	Public Sector Component	Private Organized Sector Component	Private Unorganized Sector Component
Financial Services			
Commercial Banks	Current price estimates are deflated by the implicit GDP deflator of commodity producing sectors	Current price estimates are deflated by the implicit GDP deflator of commodity producing sectors	
Insurance	Current price estimates are deflated using the wholesale price index	Current price estimates are deflated using the wholesale price index	
Non-banking financial enterprises	Current price estimates are deflated using the wholesale price index		Current price estimates are deflated using the wholesale price index
Banking department of the Reserve Bank	Current price estimates are deflated using the implicit GDP deflator for commercial banks		
Post office savings bank	Current price estimates are deflated by the consumer price index		
Cooperative credit societies	Base year estimates are moved forward by an average of deposits deflated using the wholesale price index and changes in membership		
Real Estate, Ownership of Dwellings and Renting Services	For real estate and renting services, current price estimates are deflated with the consumer price index for agricultural labourers and that for industrial workers for rural	Same as left	For real estate and renting services, same as left

	and urban areas respectively. For ownership of dwellings, base year estimates are moved forward by multiplying the rent per household of the base year with the projected residential census houses of subsequent years and subtracting from there the costs of repairs and maintenance at constant prices.		
Business Services	Current price estimates are deflated with the consumer price index for agricultural labourers and that for industrial workers for rural areas and urban areas, respectively	Same as left	Same as left
Public Administration and Defence	Current price estimates are deflated by the consumer price index for industrial workers	–	–
Other Social, Community and Personal Services	Current price estimates are deflated with the consumer price index for agricultural labourers and that for industrial workers for rural and urban areas, respectively	Same as left	Same as left

Source: Central Statistical Organisation, National Accounts Statistics: Sources and Methods, 2007.

Appendix B

Note

The following tables consist of the author's regression estimates based on primary data from India's National Sample Survey Organisation's surveys on Consumer Expenditure. They are divided into the following sections:

B.1. Engel Curves: Tobit Model
B.2. Marginal Effects: Tobit Model
B.3. Engel Curves: Tobit Model (Non-Linearities)
B.4. Engel Curves: Censored Quantile Regressions
   - B.4.1. 2004–05
   - B.4.2. 1993–94

Regressions in each of the five sections use the same set of control variables. The first table in Sections B.1.1 and B.1.2 reports coefficients (and standard errors) for each variable included in these regressions. For reasons of space, subsequent tables do not report coefficients (and standard errors) on variables not directly relevant to our analysis. Instead, this set of variables is referred to as 'vector of controls'. In each section, the 'vector of controls' consists of the following: household size, dummy variables for household caste and religion, age-sex categories, and age, gender and level of education of household head.

B.1. Engel Curves: Tobit Model

Table B.1. *Engel curve for services – Tobit*

Dependent Variable: Proportion of Household Expenditure Spent on Services (aggregate)					
Explanatory Variables ↓	All-India 1993–94	Rural 1993–94	Urban 1993–94	All-India 2004–05	Rural 2004–05	Urban 2004–05
Log of Household Expenditure	0.0369*** [0.00046]	0.0315*** [0.00046]	0.0382*** [0.00089]	0.0717*** [0.0007]	0.0594*** [0.0009]	0.0827*** [0.0013]
Constant	−0.197*** [0.0053]	−0.157*** [0.0074]	−0.207*** [0.0090]	−0.459*** [0.0083]	−0.384*** [0.011]	−0.540*** [0.014]
Household Size	0.004*** [0.00013]	0.003*** [0.00012]	0.005*** [0.00029]	0.009*** [0.00022]	0.006*** [0.00026]	0.011*** [0.00042]
Caste Dummy	−0.004*** [0.00055]	−0.002*** [0.00049]	−0.007*** [0.0013]	−0.014*** [0.00090]	−0.009*** [0.0011]	−0.016*** [0.0016]
Religion Dummy	0.003*** [0.00060]	0.003*** [0.00063]	0.004*** [0.0011]	0.006*** [0.0010]	0.004*** [0.0013]	0.006*** [0.0017]
Age of Household Head	0.00005** [0.00002]	0.00008*** [0.00002]	0.000005 [0.00005]	0.0002*** [0.00004]	0.00009** [0.00005]	0.0005*** [0.00007]
Household Head Male Dummy	0.009*** [0.00091]	0.005*** [0.00090]	0.013*** [0.0018]	0.013*** [0.0015]	0.015*** [0.0018]	0.011*** [0.0026]
Household Head Education Dummy 2	0.017*** [0.00055]	0.011*** [0.00055]	0.019*** [0.0011]	0.0252*** [0.00087]	0.0216*** [0.00099]	0.0328*** [0.0017]
Household Head Education Dummy 3	0.034*** [0.00092]	0.021*** [0.0013]	0.035*** [0.0015]	0.0840*** [0.0015]	0.0723*** [0.0020]	0.0883*** [0.0025]
Proportion of Males Aged 0–4	0.001 [0.0033]	0.004 [0.0031]	−0.008 [0.0069]	−0.0121** [0.0056]	0.0004 [0.0064]	. −0.034*** [0.011]
Proportion of Females Aged 0–4	−0.001 [0.0034]	0.002 [0.0031]	−0.013* [0.0070]	−0.012** [0.0057]	0.00002 [0.0065]	−0.036*** [0.011]
Proportion of Males Aged 5–9	0.031*** [0.0033]	0.016*** [0.0031]	0.046*** [0.0067]	0.0228*** [0.0053]	0.0209*** [0.0061]	0.0259** [0.010]

(*continued*)

Appendix B

Table B.1 (continued)

Explanatory Variables ↓	All-India 1993–94	Rural 1993–94	Urban 1993–94	All-India 2004–05	Rural 2004–05	Urban 2004–05
Proportion of Females Aged 5–9	0.019*** [0.0034]	0.009*** [0.0032]	0.028*** [0.0069]	0.0134** [0.0055]	0.00543 [0.0063]	0.0269** [0.011]
Proportion of Males Aged 10–14	0.034*** [0.0031]	0.027*** [0.0029]	0.039*** [0.0063]	0.0303*** [0.0049]	0.0302*** [0.0057]	0.0348*** [0.0092]
Proportion of Females aged 10–14	0.019*** [0.0033]	0.010*** [0.0031]	0.028*** [0.0065]	0.0148*** [0.0052]	0.0169*** [0.0060]	0.0182* [0.0097]
Proportion of Males Aged 15–19	0.059*** [0.0029]	0.036*** [0.0029]	0.074*** [0.0057]	0.0739*** [0.0047]	0.0620*** [0.0056]	0.0888*** [0.0083]
Proportion of Females Aged 15–19	0.018*** [0.0032]	0.008** [0.0031]	0.031*** [0.0062]	0.0303*** [0.0051]	0.0260*** [0.0060]	0.0411*** [0.0091]
Proportion of Males Aged 20–24	0.049*** [0.0029]	0.032*** [0.0030]	0.058*** [0.0055]	0.0633*** [0.0045]	0.0564*** [0.0057]	0.0666*** [0.0079]
Proportion of Females Aged 20–24	0.006* [0.0031]	0.003 [0.0030]	0.007 [0.0061]	0.0159*** [0.0050]	0.00843 [0.0059]	0.0246*** [0.0089]
Proportion of Males Aged 25–60	0.022*** [0.0026]	0.024*** [0.0026]	0.015*** [0.0051]	0.0096** [0.0041]	0.0317*** [0.0050]	−0.0150** [0.0072]
Proportion of Females Aged 25–60	−0.011*** [0.0025]	−0.008*** [0.0023]	−0.016*** [0.0049]	0.00525 [0.0036]	0.0110*** [0.0042]	−0.00786 [0.0068]
Proportion of Males Aged 61 and Older	0.042*** [0.0037]	0.028*** [0.0035]	0.056*** [0.0073]	0.0231*** [0.0056]	0.0402*** [0.0065]	
Proportion of Females Aged 61 and Older						
District Dummy Variables	Yes	Yes	Yes	Yes	Yes	Yes
Observations	115,192	69,119	46,073	124,640	79,295	45,345

Note: Standard errors in brackets; ***p<0.01, **p<0.05, *p<0.1.
A dummy variable for urban areas is interacted with the district dummy variable in the all-India sample.

Table B.2. *Engel curve for education services – Tobit*

Dependent Variable: Proportion of Household Expenditure Spent on Education Services

Explanatory Variables ↓	All-India 1993–94	Rural 1993–94	Urban 1993–94	All-India 2004–05	Rural 2004–05	Urban 2004–05
Log of Household Expenditure	0.0236*** [0.00042]	0.0135*** [0.00031]	0.0268*** [0.00083]	0.0458*** [0.0007]	0.0358*** [0.0008]	0.0527*** [0.0011]
Constant	−0.262*** [0.0051]	−0.135*** [0.0050]	−0.332*** [0.0092]	-0.538*** [0.0082]	−0.442*** [0.0103]	−0.637*** [0.0139]
Vector of Control Variables	Yes	Yes	Yes	Yes	Yes	Yes
District Dummy Variables	Yes	Yes	Yes	Yes	Yes	Yes
Observations	115,192	69,119	46,073	124,640	79,295	45,345

Note: Standard errors in brackets; ***p<0.01, **p<0.05, *p<0.1.
A dummy variable for urban areas is interacted with the district dummy variable in the all-India sample.

Table B.3. *Engel curve for health services – Tobit*

Dependent Variable: Proportion of Household Expenditure Spent on Health Services

Explanatory Variables ↓	All-India 1993–94	Rural 1993–94	Urban 1993–94	All-India 2004–05	Rural 2004–05	Urban 2004–05
Log of Household Expenditure	0.0391*** [0.00083]	0.0368*** [0.00089]	0.0415*** [0.0015]	0.0743*** [0.0013]	0.0837*** [0.0017]	0.0682*** [0.0020]
Constant	−0.309*** [0.0091]	−0.278*** [0.013]	−0.344*** [0.015]	−0.780*** [0.0159]	−0.884*** [0.0242]	−0.702*** [0.0230]
Vector of Control Variables	Yes	Yes	Yes	Yes	Yes	Yes
District Dummy Variables	Yes	Yes	Yes	Yes	Yes	Yes
Observations	115,192	69,119	46,073	124,640	79,295	45,345

Note: Standard errors in brackets; ***p<0.01, **p<0.05, *p<0.1.
A dummy variable for urban areas is interacted with the district dummy variable in the all-India sample.

Table B.4. *Engel curve for entertainment services – Tobit*

Dependent Variable: Proportion of Household Expenditure Spent on Entertainment Services

Explanatory Variables ↓	All-India 1993–94	Rural 1993–94	Urban 1993–94	All-India 2004–05	Rural 2004–05	Urban 2004–05
Log of Household Expenditure	0.0105*** [0.00022]	0.0099*** [0.00030]	0.0079*** [0.00033]	0.0223*** [0.0002]	0.0205*** [0.0003]	0.0178*** [0.0004]
–	–0.081*** [0.0025]	–0.079*** [0.0040]	–0.061*** [0.0034]	–0.193*** [0.00284]	–0.193*** [0.00402]	–0.148*** [0.00388]
Vector of Control Variables	Yes	Yes	Yes	Yes	Yes	Yes
District Dummy Variables	Yes	Yes	Yes	Yes	Yes	Yes
Observations	115,192	69,119	46,073	124,640	79,295	45,345

Note: Standard errors in brackets; ***p<0.01, **p<0.05, *p<0.1.
A dummy variable for urban areas is interacted with the district dummy variable in the all-India sample.

Table B.5. *Engel curve for personal services – Tobit*

Dependent Variable: Proportion of Household Expenditure Spent on Personal Services

Explanatory Variables ↓	All-India 1993–94	Rural 1993–94	Urban 1993–94	All-India 2004–05	Rural 2004–05	Urban 2004–05
Log of Household Expenditure	0.0123*** [0.00015]	0.0121*** [0.00021]	0.0121*** [0.00024]	0.0057*** [0.0001]	0.0034*** [0.0002]	0.0081*** [0.0003]
Constant	–0.082*** [0.0018]	–0.086*** [0.0033]	–0.075*** [0.0025]	–0.037*** [0.0017]	–0.022*** [0.0022]	–0.051*** [0.0029]
Vector of Control Variables	Yes	Yes	Yes	Yes	Yes	Yes
District Dummy Variables	Yes	Yes	Yes	Yes	Yes	Yes
Observations	115192	69119	46073	124640	79295	45345

Note: Standard errors in brackets; ***p<0.01, **p<0.05, *p<0.1.
A dummy variable for urban areas is interacted with the district dummy variable in the all-India sample.

Table B.6. *Engel curve for communication services – Tobit*

Dependent Variable: Proportion of Household Expenditure Spent on Communication Services

Explanatory Variables ↓	All-India 1993–94	Rural 1993–94	Urban 1993–94	All-India 2004–05	Rural 2004–05	Urban 2004–05
Log of Household Expenditure	0.0171*** [0.0002]	0.0091*** [0.0002]	0.0206*** [0.0004]	0.0330*** [0.0003]	0.0308*** [0.0004]	0.0323*** [0.0004]
Constant	−0.137*** [0.0025]	−0.075*** [0.0030]	−0.159*** [0.0038]	−0.266*** [0.0031]	−0.257*** [0.0042]	−0.254*** [0.0047]
Vector of Control Variables	Yes	Yes	Yes	Yes	Yes	Yes
District Dummy Variables	Yes	Yes	Yes	Yes	Yes	Yes
Observations	115,192	69,119	46,073	124,640	79,295	45,345

Note: Standard errors in brackets; ***p<0.01, **p<0.05, *p<0.1.
A dummy variable for urban areas is interacted with the district dummy variable in the all-India sample.

Table B.7. *Engel curve for transport services – Tobit*

Dependent Variable: Proportion of Household Expenditure Spent on Transport Services

Explanatory Variables ↓	All-India 1993–94	Rural 1993–94	Urban 1993–94	All-India 2004–05	Rural 2004–05	Urban 2004–05
Log of Household Expenditure	0.0194*** [0.00032]	0.0197*** [0.00038]	0.0196*** [0.00057]	0.0283*** [0.0003]	0.0288*** [0.0004]	0.0322*** [0.0005]
Constant	−0.139*** [0.0037]	−0.131*** [0.0060]	−0.142*** [0.0059]	−0.189*** [0.0035]	−0.190*** [0.0046]	−0.219*** [0.0059]
Vector of Control Variables	Yes	Yes	Yes	Yes	Yes	Yes
District Dummy Variables	Yes	Yes	Yes	Yes	Yes	Yes
Observations	115,192	69,119	46,073	124,640	79,295	45,345

Note: Standard errors in brackets; ***p<0.01, **p<0.05, *p<0.1.
A dummy variable for urban areas is interacted with the district dummy variable in the all-India sample.

B.2. Marginal Effects: Tobit Model

Table B.8. *Marginal effect from Engel curve for education services – Tobit*

Dependent Variable: Proportion of Household Expenditure on Education Services

Explanatory Variable ↓	All-India conditional expectation	Rural conditional expectation	Urban conditional expectation	All-India unconditional expectation	Rural unconditional expectation	Urban unconditional expectation
Log of Household Expenditure (1993–94)	0.007	0.004	0.008	0.008	0.005	0.010
Log of Household Expenditure (2004–05)	0.014	0.011	0.017	0.018	0.014	0.022

Table B.9. *Marginal effect from Engel curve for health services – Tobit*

Dependent Variable: Proportion of Household Expenditure on Health Services

Explanatory Variable ↓	All-India conditional expectation	Rural conditional expectation	Urban conditional expectation	All-India unconditional expectation	Rural unconditional expectation	Urban unconditional expectation
Log of Household Expenditure (1993–94)	0.007	0.006	0.008	0.007	0.006	0.008
Log of Household Expenditure (2004–05)	0.017	0.016	0.018	0.017	0.017	0.018

Table B.10. *Marginal effect from Engel curve for entertainment services – Tobit*

Dependent Variable: Proportion of Household Expenditure on Entertainment Services

Explanatory Variable ↓	All-India conditional expectation	Rural conditional expectation	Urban conditional expectation	All-India unconditional expectation	Rural unconditional expectation	Urban unconditional expectation
Log of Household Expenditure (1993–94)	0.002	0.001	0.002	0.002	0.001	0.002
Log of Household Expenditure (2004–05)	0.006	0.004	0.007	0.008	0.005	0.010

Table B.11. *Marginal effect from Engel curve for personal services – Tobit*

Dependent Variable: Proportion of Household Expenditure on Personal Services

Explanatory Variable ↓	All-India conditional expectation	Rural conditional expectation	Urban conditional expectation	All-India unconditional expectation	Rural unconditional expectation	Urban unconditional expectation
Log of Household Expenditure (1993–94)	0.005	0.004	0.006	0.007	0.006	0.008
Log of Household Expenditure (2004–05)	0.004	0.002	0.005	0.005	0.003	0.007

Table B.12. *Marginal effect from Engel curve for communication services – Tobit*

Dependent Variable: Proportion of Household Expenditure on Communication Services

Explanatory Variable ↓	All-India conditional expectation	Rural conditional expectation	Urban conditional expectation	All-India unconditional expectation	Rural unconditional expectation	Urban unconditional expectation
Log of Household Expenditure (1993–94)	0.003	0.001	0.005	0.003	0.001	0.005
Log of Household Expenditure (2004–05)	0.011	0.009	0.013	0.014	0.010	0.019

Table B.13. *Marginal effect from Engel curve for transport services – Tobit*

Dependent Variable: Proportion of Household Expenditure on Transport Services

Explanatory Variable ↓	All-India conditional expectation	Rural conditional expectation	Urban conditional expectation	All-India unconditional expectation	Rural unconditional expectation	Urban unconditional expectation
Log of Household Expenditure (1993–94)	0.009	0.009	0.009	0.012	0.012	0.012
Log of Household Expenditure (2004–05)	0.016	0.015	0.018	0.023	0.022	0.025

B.3. Engel Curves: Tobit Model (Non-linearities)

Table B.14. *Engel curve for education services – Tobit with non-linearities*

Dependent Variable: Proportion of Household Expenditure on Education Services						
Explanatory Variables ↓	All-India 1993–94	Rural 1993–94	Urban 1993–94	All-India 2004–05	Rural 2004–05	Urban 2004–05
Log of Household Expenditure	0.111*** [0.0044]	0.0642*** [0.0033]	0.135*** [0.0088]	0.178*** [0.0070]	0.158*** [0.0084]	0.225*** [0.012]
Log of Household Expenditure Squared	−0.006*** [0.0003]	−0.003*** [0.0002]	−0.007*** [0.0006]	−0.008*** [0.0004]	−0.007*** [0.0005]	−0.01*** [0.0007]
Constant	−0.584*** [0.017]	−0.318*** [0.013]	−0.736*** [0.034]	−1.067*** [0.029]	−0.927*** [0.035]	−1.336*** [0.051]
Vector of Controls	Yes	Yes	Yes	Yes	Yes	Yes
District Dummy Variables	Yes	Yes	Yes	Yes	Yes	Yes
Observations	115,192	69,119	46,073	124,640	79,295	45,345

Note: Standard errors in brackets; ***p<0.01, **p<0.05, *p<0.1.
A dummy variable for urban areas is interacted with the district dummy variable in the all-India sample.

Table B.15. *Engel curve for health services – Tobit with non-linearities*

Dependent Variable: Proportion of Household Expenditure on Health Services

Explanatory Variables ↓	All-India 1993–94	Rural 1993–94	Urban 1993–94	All-India 2004–05	Rural 2004–05	Urban 2004–05
Log of Household Expenditure	0.087*** [0.0081]	0.092*** [0.0085]	0.064*** [0.015]	0.349*** [0.014]	0.342*** [0.018]	0.364*** [0.023]
Log of Household Expenditure Squared	−0.003*** [0.0005]	−0.004*** [0.0006]	−0.001 [0.0010]	−0.017*** [0.0008]	−0.015*** [0.0011]	−0.017*** [0.0014]
Constant	−0.483*** [0.031]	−0.474*** [0.033]	−0.427*** [0.059]	−1.870*** [0.058]	−1.898*** [0.075]	−1.899*** [0.097]
Vector of Controls	Yes	Yes	Yes	Yes	Yes	Yes
District Dummy Variables	Yes	Yes	Yes	Yes	Yes	Yes
Observations	115,192	69,119	46,073	124,640	79,295	45,345

Note: Standard errors in brackets; ***p<0.01, **p<0.05, *p<0.1.

A dummy variable for urban areas is interacted with the district dummy variable in the all-India sample.

Table B.16. *Engel curve for entertainment services – Tobit with non-linearities*

Dependent Variable: Proportion of Household Expenditure on Entertainment Services						
Explanatory Variables ↓	All-India 1993–94	Rural 1993–94	Urban 1993–94	All-India 2004–05	Rural 2004–05	Urban 2004–05
Log of Household Expenditure	0.017*** [0.0021]	0.017*** [0.0027]	0.002 [0.0029]	0.0979*** [0.0028]	0.0902*** [0.0037]	0.0936*** [0.0040]
Log of Household Expenditure Squared	−0.000*** [0.0001]	−0.000*** [0.0002]	0.0004* [0.0002]	−0.004*** [0.0001]	−0.004*** [0.0002]	−0.004*** [0.0002]
Constant	−0.105*** [0.0080]	−0.106*** [0.011]	−0.041*** [0.011]	−0.497*** [0.012]	−0.472*** [0.016]	−0.453*** [0.016]
Vector of Controls	Yes	Yes	Yes	Yes	Yes	Yes
District Dummy Variables	Yes	Yes	Yes	Yes	Yes	Yes
Observations	115,192	69,119	46,073	124,640	79,295	45,345

Note: Standard errors in brackets; ***p<0.01, **p<0.05, *p<0.01.

Dependent variable: Proportion of household expenditure on entertainment services

A dummy variable for urban areas is interacted with the district dummy variable in the all-India sample.

Table B.17. *Engel curve for personal services – Tobit with non-linearities*

Explanatory Variables ↓	All-India 1993–94	Rural 1993–94	Urban 1993–94	All-India 2004–05	Rural 2004–05	Urban 2004–05
Log of Household Expenditure	−0.0006 [0.001]	−0.004** [0.001]	−0.0012 [0.002]	−0.008*** [0.0013]	0.002 [0.0016]	−0.020*** [0.0023]
Log of Household Expenditure Squared	0.001*** [0.0001]	0.001*** [0.0001]	0.0008*** [0.0001]	0.00089*** [0.00008]	0.00009 [0.0001]	0.0017*** [0.0001]
Constant	−0.036*** [0.0052]	−0.030*** [0.0071]	−0.026*** [0.0083]	0.0178*** [0.0053]	−0.0165** [0.0065]	0.0597*** [0.0095]
Vector of Controls	Yes	Yes	Yes	Yes	Yes	Yes
District Dummy Variables	Yes	Yes	Yes	Yes	Yes	Yes
Observations	115,192	69,119	46,073	124,640	79,295	45,345

Note: Standard errors in brackets; ***p<0.01, **p<0.05, *p<0.1.

Dependent variable: Proportion of household expenditure on personal services

A dummy variable for urban areas is interacted with the district dummy variable in the all-India sample.

Table B.18. *Engel curve for communication services – Tobit with non-linearities*

Explanatory Variables ↓	All-India 1993–94	Rural 1993–94	Urban 1993–94	All-India 2004–05	Rural 2004–05	Urban 2004–05
Log of Household Expenditure	0.015*** [0.0021]	0.013*** [0.0018]	0.008** [0.0037]	0.140*** [0.0031]	0.176*** [0.0041]	0.101*** [0.0047]
Log of Household Expenditure Squared	0.000 [0.00014]	−0.000** [0.00012]	0.001*** [0.00024]	−0.006 [0.0002]	−0.009 [0.0002]	−0.004 [0.0003]
Constant	−0.131*** [0.0082]	−0.088*** [0.0071]	−0.113*** [0.014]	−0.696*** [0.013]	−0.833*** [0.017]	−0.533*** [0.020]
Vector of Controls	Yes	Yes	Yes	Yes	Yes	Yes
District Dummy Variables	Yes	Yes	Yes	Yes	Yes	Yes
Observations	115,192	69,119	46,073	124,640	79,295	45,345

Note: Standard errors in brackets; ***p<0.01, **p<0.05, *p<0.1.

A dummy variable for urban areas is interacted with the district dummy variable in the all-India sample.

Table B.19. *Engel curve for transport services – Tobit with non-linearities*

Dependent Variable: Proportion of Household Expenditure on Transport Services

Explanatory Variables ↓	All-India 1993–94	Rural 1993–94	Urban 1993–94	All-India 2004–05	Rural 2004–05	Urban 2004–05
Log of Household Expenditure	0.048*** [0.0030]	0.045*** [0.0036]	0.045*** [0.0054]	−0.00003 [0.0029]	0.029*** [0.0037]	−0.035*** [0.0049]
Log of Household Expenditure Squared	−0.002*** [0.0002]	−0.002*** [0.0002]	−0.002*** [0.0004]	0.0017*** [0.0001]	−0.00002 [0.0002]	0.004*** [0.0003]
Constant	−0.242*** [0.011]	−0.220*** [0.014]	−0.238*** [0.021]	−0.079*** [0.012]	−0.191*** [0.015]	0.048** [0.020]
Vector of Controls	Yes	Yes	Yes	Yes	Yes	Yes
District Dummy Variables	Yes	Yes	Yes	Yes	Yes	Yes
Observations	115,192	69,119	46,073	124,640	79,295	45,345

Note: Standard errors in brackets; ***p<0.01, **p<0.05, *p<0.1.

A dummy variable for urban areas is interacted with the district dummy variable in the all-India sample.

B.4. Engel Curves: Censored Quantile Regressions

B.4.1. 2004–05

Table B.20. *Engel curve for services – censored quantile regressions (2004–05)*

Dependent Variable: Proportion of Household Expenditure on Services (aggregate)									
Explanatory Variables	All-India			Rural			Urban		
	35th Percentile	50th Percentile	85th Percentile	35th Percentile	50th Percentile	85th Percentile	35th Percentile	50th Percentile	85th Percentile
Log of Household Expenditure	0.0571***	0.0711***	0.106***	0.0448***	0.0574***	0.0951***	0.0749***	0.0895***	0.114***
	[0.0004]	[0.0004]	[0.0009]	[0.0004]	[0.0004]	[0.0011]	[0.0008]	[0.0008]	[0.0019]
Constant	−0.346***	−0.417***	−0.568***	−0.265***	−0.331***	−0.505***	−0.472***	−0.545***	−0.624***
	[0.0031]	[0.0035]	[0.0082]	[0.0032]	[0.0037]	[0.0092]	[0.0067]	[0.0069]	[0.0162]
Vector of Control Variables	Yes	Yes	Yes	Yes	Yes	Yes	Yes	Yes	Yes
District Dummy Variables	Yes	Yes	Yes	Yes	Yes	Yes	Yes	Yes	Yes
Observations	121,483	122,287	123,774	78,353	78,512	78,955	43,784	44,227	45,004

Note: Standard errors in brackets; ***p<0.01, **p<0.05, *p<0.1.
A dummy variable for urban areas is interacted with the district dummy variable in the all-India sample.

Table B.21. *Engel curve for education services – censored quantile regressions (2004–05)*

Dependent Variable: Proportion of Household Expenditure on Education Services

Explanatory Variables →	All-India			Rural			Urban		
	35th Percentile	50th Percentile	85th Percentile	35th Percentile	50th Percentile	85th Percentile	35th Percentile	50th Percentile	85th Percentile
Log of Household Expenditure	0.0155*** [0.00021]	0.0222*** [0.00020]	0.0436*** [0.00037]	0.00728*** [0.00019]	0.0127*** [0.00020]	0.0325*** [0.00034]	0.0227*** [0.00049]	0.0293*** [0.00054]	0.0467*** [0.00089]
Constant	-0.165*** [0.0026]	-0.217*** [0.0024]	-0.356*** [0.0038]	-0.0719*** [0.00228]	-0.116*** [0.00231]	-0.254*** [0.00353]	-0.251*** [0.0061]	-0.304*** [0.0064]	-0.415*** [0.0088]
Vector of Control Variables	Yes	Yes	Yes	Yes	Yes	Yes	Yes	Yes	Yes
District Dummy Variables	Yes	Yes	Yes	Yes	Yes	Yes	Yes	Yes	Yes
Observations	43,812	61,298	98,906	31,254	40,236	62,272	19,712	25,462	37,868

Note: Standard errors in brackets; ***p<0.01, **p<0.05, *p<0.1.
A dummy variable for urban areas is interacted with the district dummy variable in the all-India sample.

Table B.22. *Engel curve for health services – censored quantile regressions (2004–05)*

Dependent Variable: Proportion of Household Expenditure on Health Services									
Explanatory Variables	All-India			Rural			Urban		
	35th Percentile	50th Percentile	85th Percentile	35th Percentile	50th Percentile	85th Percentile	35th Percentile	50th Percentile	85th Percentile
Log of Household Expenditure			0.0165*** [0.00025]			0.0189*** [0.00032]			0.0140*** [0.00040]
Constant			-0.089*** [0.0021]			-0.107*** [0.00257]			-0.069*** [0.00344]
Vector of Control Variables			Yes			Yes			Yes
District Dummy Variables			Yes			Yes			Yes
Observations			118,786			75,199			42,746

Note: Standard errors in brackets; ***p<0.01, **p<0.05, *p<0.1.
There are no entries for the 35th and 50th percentiles because of the presence of a large number of households with zero expenditure.
A dummy variable for urban areas is interacted with the district dummy variable in the all-India sample.

Table B.23. *Engel curve for entertainment services – censored quantile regressions (2004–05)*

Dependent Variable: Proportion of Household Expenditure on Entertainment Services

Explanatory Variables →	All-India			Rural			Urban		
	35th Percentile	50th Percentile	85th Percentile	35th Percentile	50th Percentile	85th Percentile	35th Percentile	50th Percentile	85th Percentile
Log of Household Expenditure			0.0186*** [0.00018]			0.0160*** [0.00022]			0.00690*** [0.00035]
Constant			-0.117*** [0.0017]			-0.110*** [0.00218]			-0.0186*** [0.00312]
Vector of Control Variables			Yes			Yes			Yes
District Dummy Variables			Yes			Yes			Yes
Observations			118,696			71,949			45,337

Note: Standard errors in brackets; ***p<0.01, **p<0.05, *p<0.1.
There are no entries for the 35th and 50th percentiles due to the presence of a large number of households with zero expenditure.
A dummy variable for urban areas is interacted with the district dummy variable in the all-India sample.

Table B.24. *Engel curve for personal services – censored quantile regressions (2004–05)*

Dependent Variable: Proportion of Household Expenditure on Personal Services

Explanatory Variables →	All-India			Rural			Urban		
	35th Percentile	50th Percentile	85th Percentile	35th Percentile	50th Percentile	85th Percentile	35th Percentile	50th Percentile	85th Percentile
Log of Household Expenditure	0.0006*** [0.00010]	0.0015*** [0.00012]	0.0097*** [0.00029]	−0.00012 [0.00013]	0.000164 [0.00015]	0.007*** [0.00035]	0.0016*** [0.00015]	0.0034*** [0.0002]	0.0125*** [0.00046]
Constant	0.0007 [0.00086]	0.0002 [0.00098]	−0.025*** [0.0023]	0.004*** [0.00109]	0.008*** [0.00121]	−0.013*** [0.00283]	−0.004*** [0.00135]	−0.011*** [0.00176]	−0.034*** [0.00383]
Vector of Control Variables	Yes	Yes	Yes	Yes	Yes	Yes	Yes	Yes	Yes
District Dummy Variables	Yes	Yes	Yes	Yes	Yes	Yes	Yes	Yes	Yes
Observations	124,640	124,640	124,633	79,295	79,295	79,294	45,330	45,328	45,324

Note: Standard errors in brackets; ***p<0.01, **p<0.05, *p<0.1.
A dummy variable for urban areas is interacted with the district dummy variable in the all-India sample.

Table B.25. *Engel curve for communication services – censored quantile regressions (2004–05)*

Dependent Variable: Proportion of Household Expenditure on Communication Services									
Explanatory Variables →	All-India			Rural			Urban		
	35th Percentile	50th Percentile	85th Percentile	35th Percentile	50th Percentile	85th Percentile	35th Percentile	50th Percentile	85th Percentile
Log of Household Expenditure		0.0270*** [0.00027]	0.0401*** [0.00023]		0.0168*** [0.000222]	0.0327*** [0.000247]		0.0342*** [0.000354]	0.0412*** [0.000428]
Constant		−0.205*** [0.0026]	−0.258*** [0.0021]		−0.126*** [0.000206]	−0.214*** [0.00217]		−0.249*** [0.00340]	−0.254*** [0.00406]
Vector of Control Variables		Yes	Yes		Yes	Yes		Yes	Yes
District Dummy Variables		Yes	Yes		Yes	Yes		Yes	Yes
Observations		46,490	98,442		24,459	60,590		29,551	40,631

Note: Standard errors in brackets; ***p<0.01, **p<0.05, *p<0.1.

There are no entries for the 35th percentile because of the presence of a large number of households with zero expenditure.

A dummy variable for urban areas is interacted with the district dummy variable in the all-India sample.

Table B.26. *Engel curve for transport services – censored quantile regressions (2004–05)*

Dependent Variable: Proportion of Household Expenditure on Transport Services

Explanatory Variables →	All-India			Rural			Urban		
	35th Percentile	50th Percentile	85th Percentile	35th Percentile	50th Percentile	85th Percentile	35th Percentile	50th Percentile	85th Percentile
Log of Household Expenditure	0.0193*** [0.00019]	0.0239*** [0.00020]	0.0421*** [0.00048]	0.0160*** [0.00022]	0.0205*** [0.00025]	0.0438*** [0.00069]	0.0262*** [0.00040]	0.0317*** [0.00041]	0.0445*** [0.00089]
Constant	-0.134*** [0.0017]	-0.155*** [0.0018]	-0.231*** [0.0042]	-0.107*** [0.00199]	-0.128*** [0.00221]	-0.237*** [0.0058]	-0.191*** [0.00369]	-0.219*** [0.00383]	-0.254*** [0.00814]
Vector of Control Variables	Yes	Yes	Yes	Yes	Yes	Yes	Yes	Yes	Yes
District Dummy Variables	Yes	Yes	Yes	Yes	Yes	Yes	Yes	Yes	Yes
Observations	109,351	119,125	124,089	72,604	77,005	78,940	37,370	41,884	45,076

Note: Standard errors in brackets; ***p<0.01, **p<0.05, *p<0.1.
A dummy variable for urban areas is interacted with the district dummy variable in the all-India sample.

B.4.2. 1993–94

Table B.27. *Engel curve for services – censored quantile regressions (1993–94)*

Dependent Variable: Proportion of Household Expenditure on Services (aggregate)

Explanatory Variables →	All-India			Rural			Urban		
	35th Percentile	50th Percentile	85th Percentile	35th Percentile	50th Percentile	85th Percentile	35th Percentile	50th Percentile	85th Percentile
Log of Household Expenditure	0.0221*** [0.00019]	0.0284*** [0.00023]	0.0460*** [0.00062]	0.0173*** [0.00020]	0.0233*** [0.00028]	0.0391*** [0.00077]	0.0278*** [0.00039]	0.0350*** [0.00043]	0.0531*** [0.0012]
Constant	−0.123*** [0.0016]	−0.149*** [0.0019]	−0.195*** [0.0049]	−0.095*** [0.0016]	−0.121*** [0.0022]	−0.166*** [0.0059]	−0.162*** [0.0033]	−0.191*** [0.0036]	−0.224*** [0.0100]
Vector of Control Variables	Yes	Yes	Yes	Yes	Yes	Yes	Yes	Yes	Yes
District Dummy Variables	Yes	Yes	Yes	Yes	Yes	Yes	Yes	Yes	Yes
Observations	115,192	115,192	115,192	69,119	69,119	69,119	46,073	46,073	46,073

Note: Standard errors in brackets; ***p<0.01, **p<0.05, *p<0.1.
A dummy variable for urban areas is interacted with the district dummy variable in the all-India sample.

Table B.28. *Engel curve for education services – censored quantile regressions (1993–94)*

Dependent Variable: Proportion of Household Expenditure on Education Services

Explanatory Variables	All-India			Rural			Urban		
	35th Percentile	50th Percentile	85th Percentile	35th Percentile	50th Percentile	85th Percentile	35th Percentile	50th Percentile	85th Percentile
Log of Household Expenditure		0.000*** [0.00001]	0.0029*** [0.00006]		0.000*** [0.0000001]	0.001*** [0.00003]		0.002*** [0.00007]	0.003*** [0.00017]
Constant		-0.003*** [0.00008]	-0.017*** [0.00053]		-0.000*** [0.00001]	-0.006*** [0.00027]		-0.014*** [0.00059]	-0.025*** [0.0015]
Vector of Control Variables		Yes	Yes		Yes	Yes		Yes	Yes
District Dummy Variables		Yes	Yes		Yes	Yes		Yes	Yes
Observations		115,192	115,192		69,119	69,119		46,073	46,073

Note: Standard errors in brackets; ***p<0.01, **p<0.05, *p<0.1.

There are no entries for the 35th percentile because of the presence of a large number of households with zero expenditure.

A dummy variable for urban areas is interacted with the district dummy variable in the all-India sample.

Table B.29. *Engel curve for health services – censored quantile regressions (1993–94)*

Dependent Variable: Proportion of Household Expenditure on Health Services

Explanatory Variables	All-India			Rural			Urban		
	35th Percentile	50th Percentile	85th Percentile	35th Percentile	50th Percentile	85th Percentile	35th Percentile	50th Percentile	85th Percentile
Log of Household Expenditure			0.007*** [0.000201]			0.006*** [0.00029]	0.004*** [0.00028]		
Constant			-0.041*** [0.00171]			-0.024*** [0.0022]	-0.003 [0.0023]		
Vector of Control Variables			Yes			Yes	Yes		
District Dummy Variables			Yes			Yes	Yes		
Observations			115,192			69,119	46,073		

Note: Standard errors in brackets; ***p<0.01, **p<0.05, *p<0.1

There are no entries for the 35th and 50th percentiles because of the presence of a large number of households with zero expenditure

A dummy variable for urban areas is interacted with the district dummy variable in the all-India sample.

Table B.30. *Engel curve for entertainment services – censored quantile regressions (1993–94)*

Dependent Variable: Proportion of Household Expenditure on Entertainment Services

Explanatory Variables	All-India			Rural			Urban		
	35th Percentile	50th Percentile	85th Percentile	35th Percentile	50th Percentile	85th Percentile	35th Percentile	50th Percentile	85th Percentile
Log of Household Expenditure			0.005*** [0.000116]			0.004*** [0.00016]			0.002*** [0.00022]
Constant			-0.025*** [0.00115]			-0.027*** [0.0016]			-0.005*** [0.0020]
Vector of Control Variables			Yes			Yes			Yes
District Dummy Variables			Yes			Yes			Yes
Observations			108,294			57,717			45,823

Note: Standard errors in brackets; ***p<0.01, **p<0.05, *p<0.1.
There are no entries for the 35th and 50th percentiles because of the presence of a large number of households with zero expenditure.
A dummy variable for urban areas is interacted with the district dummy variable in the all-India sample.

257

Table B.31. *Engel curve for personal services – censored quantile regressions (1993–94)*

Dependent Variable: Proportion of Household Expenditure on Personal Services

Explanatory Variables →	All-India			Rural			Urban		
	35th Percentile	50th Percentile	85th Percentile	35th Percentile	50th Percentile	85th Percentile	35th Percentile	50th Percentile	85th Percentile
Log of Household Expenditure	0.003*** [0.000069]	0.0027*** [0.000060]	0.012*** [0.00018]	0.003*** [0.00008]	0.001*** [0.00008]	0.009*** [0.00023]	0.002*** [0.00010]	0.004*** [0.000099]	0.015*** [0.00035]
Constant	-0.020*** [0.00066]	-0.016*** [0.00054]	-0.059*** [0.0014]	-0.021*** [0.00079]	-0.010*** [0.000071]	-0.046*** [0.0017]	-0.016*** [0.00094]	-0.021*** [0.00087]	-0.065*** [0.0028]
Vector of Control Variables	Yes	Yes	Yes	Yes	Yes	Yes	Yes	Yes	Yes
District Dummy Variables	Yes	Yes	Yes	Yes	Yes	Yes	Yes	Yes	Yes
Observations	105,895	113,049	114,333	58,380	67,420	68,352	44,967	45,571	45,861

Note: Standard errors in brackets; ***p<0.01, **p<0.05, *p<0.1.
A dummy variable for urban areas is interacted with the district dummy variable in the all-India sample.

Table B.32. *Engel curve for communication services – censored quantile regressions (1993–94)*

Dependent Variable: Proportion of Household Expenditure on Communication Services

Explanatory Variables	All-India			Rural			Urban		
	35th Percentile	50th Percentile	85th Percentile	35th Percentile	50th Percentile	85th Percentile	35th Percentile	50th Percentile	85th Percentile
Log of Household Expenditure			0.028*** [0.00015]			0.002*** [0.000048]			0.002*** [0.000060]
Constant			-0.189*** [0.0013]			-0.014*** [0.00038]			-0.011*** [0.00045]
Vector of Control Variables			Yes			Yes			Yes
District Dummy Variables			Yes			Yes			Yes
Observations			20,763			31,848			46,073

Note: Standard errors in brackets; ***p<0.01, **p<0.05, *p<0.1.
There are no entries for the 35th and 50th percentiles because of the presence of a large number of households with zero expenditure.
A dummy variable for urban areas is interacted with the district dummy variable in the all-India sample.

Table B.33. *Engel curve for transport services – censored quantile regressions (1993–94)*

Dependent Variable: Proportion of Household Expenditure on Transport Services

Explanatory Variable	All-India			Rural			Urban		
→	35th Percentile	50th Percentile	85th Percentile	35th Percentile	50th Percentile	85th Percentile	35th Percentile	50th Percentile	85th Percentile
Log of Household Expenditure	0.0039*** [0.000045]	0.0083*** [0.000011]	0.016*** [0.00038]	0.010*** [0.00030]	0.013*** [0.00020]	0.017*** [0.00043]	0.004*** [0.00010]	0.008*** [0.00021]	0.016*** [0.00067]
Constant	−0.023*** [0.00037]	−0.046*** [0.00091]	−0.059*** [0.0031]	−0.064*** [0.0026]	−0.076*** [0.0017]	−0.068*** [0.0034]	−0.028*** [0.00085]	−0.049*** [0.0017]	−0.052*** [0.0057]
Vector of Control Variables	Yes	Yes	Yes	Yes	Yes	Yes	Yes	Yes	Yes
District Dummy Variables	Yes	Yes	Yes	Yes	Yes	Yes	Yes	Yes	Yes
Observations	115,192	115,192	115,192	39,198	58,349	69,025	46,073	46,073	46,073

Note: Standard errors in brackets; ***p<0.01, **p<0.05, *p<0.1.
A dummy variable for urban areas is interacted with the district dummy variable in the all-India sample.

Appendix C

Note

The following tables consist of the author's regression estimates based on primary data from India's National Sample Survey organisation's surveys on employment. They are divided into the following sections:

C.1. Educational Requirements
- C.1.1. Logit Model
- C.1.2. Multinomial Logit Model

C.2. Wages, Contracts and Social Security Benefits

The first table in each section reports coefficients (and standard errors) for each variable included in the regression. For reasons of space, subsequent tables do not report coefficients (and standard errors) on variables not directly relevant to our analysis. Instead, this set of variables is referred to as 'vector of controls'. In the three sections, the 'vector of controls' consists of the following.

C.1 – Table C.1 to C.15

Vector of Controls = age, age-squared, male dummy variable, land owned

C.2 – Table C.16 to C.18

Vector of Controls = age, age-squared, male dummy variable, land owned, hours worked, dummy variables for caste and religion (dummy variable for the self-employed is also included when the dependent variable is the probability of getting a job contract or social security benefits)

C.1. Educational Requirements for Job Seekers (Marginal Effects)

C.1.1. Logit Model

Table C.1. *Educational requirements for job seekers – wholesale and retail trade*

Dependent Variable – Probability of Being Employed in Wholesale and Retail Trade						
Explanatory Variables ↓	All-India 1993–94	Rural 1993–94	Urban 1993–94	All-India 2004–05	Rural 2004–05	Urban 2004–05
Age	−0.00003 [0.00004]	0.00009*** [0.000035]	−0.000654*** [0.00012]	−0.00416*** [0.00052]	−0.00037 [0.00065]	−0.00913*** [0.00084]
Age-Squared	0.000001 [0.0000005]	−0.000001** [0.00000045]	0.00000845*** [0.0000015]	0.00005*** [0.0000065]	0.00001 [0.0000083]	0.00011*** [0.000010]
Male Dummy	0.00778*** [0.00034]	0.00264*** [0.00025]	0.0185*** [0.0011]	0.112*** [0.0039]	0.0786*** [0.0047]	0.153*** [0.0065]
Land Owned	−0.000968*** [0.000078]	−0.000399*** [0.000076]	−0.000494*** [0.00017]	−0.000006*** [0.0000012]	0.000001 [0.00000093]	−0.000005** [0.0000027]
Education Dummy 2	−0.00636*** [0.00025]	−0.00247*** [0.00020]	−0.00922*** [0.00074]	−0.0727*** [0.0029]	−0.0587*** [0.0036]	−0.0733*** [0.0049]
Education Dummy 3	−0.00710*** [0.00036]	−0.00122** [0.00050]	−0.00777*** [0.00099]	−0.0357*** [0.0044]	−0.0611*** [0.0066]	−0.0470*** [0.0064]
Constant	−0.0449*** [0.0035]	−0.0218*** [0.0028]	−0.0799*** [0.0060]	−0.314*** [0.024]	−0.317*** [0.032]	−0.281*** [0.037]
District Dummy Variables	Yes	Yes	Yes	Yes	Yes	Yes
Observations	488,221	325,086	159,389	95,346	52,865	42,481

Note: Standard error in brackets; ***p<0.01, **p<0.05, *p<0.1.

Table C.2. *Educational requirements for job seekers – hotels and restaurants*

Dependent Variable – Probability of Being Employed in Hotels and Restaurants

Explanatory Variables ↓	All-India 1993–94	Rural 1993–94	Urban 1993–94	All-India 2004–05	Rural 2004–05	Urban 2004–05
Education Dummy 2	−0.000383*** [0.000043]	−0.000225*** [0.000074]	−0.00107*** [0.00015]	−0.00647*** [0.0010]	−0.00453*** [0.0011]	−0.0111*** [0.0016]
Education Dummy 3	−0.000498*** [0.000057]		−0.00139*** [0.00017]	−0.0323*** [0.0019]	−0.0243*** [0.0027]	−0.0440*** [0.0027]
Constant	−0.00187*** [0.00026]	−0.000943*** [0.00030]	−0.00620*** [0.00087]	−0.0689*** [0.0078]	−0.0465*** [0.0089]	−0.0877*** [0.012]
Vector of controls	Yes	Yes	Yes	Yes	Yes	Yes
District Dummy Variables	Yes	Yes	Yes	Yes	Yes	Yes
Observations	434,229	84,885	142,099	95,065	52,537	42,324

Note: Standard error in brackets; ***p<0.01, **p<0.05, *p<0.1.

Table C.3. *Educational requirements for job seekers – transport services*

Dependent Variable – Probability of Being Employed in Transport Services

Explanatory Variables ↓	All-India 1993–94	Rural 1993–94	Urban 1993–94	All-India 2004–05	Rural 2004–05	Urban 2004–05
Education Dummy 2	−0.0358*** [0.00064]	−0.0213*** [0.00055]	−0.0239*** [0.0017]	−0.00605*** [0.0012]	−0.00097 [0.0014]	−0.0150*** [0.0020]
Education Dummy 3	−0.00446*** [0.0012]	−0.00669*** [0.0014]	−0.0619*** [0.0028]	−0.0492*** [0.0023]	−0.0451*** [0.0034]	−0.0569*** [0.0031]
Constant	−0.160*** [0.0084]	−0.0937*** [0.0072]	−0.193*** [0.021]	−0.286*** [0.0088]	−0.262*** [0.012]	−0.312*** [0.013]
Vector of controls	Yes	Yes	Yes	Yes	Yes	Yes
District Dummy Variables	Yes	Yes	Yes	Yes	Yes	Yes
Observations	488,221	328,494	159,727	95,346	52,865	42,481

Note: Standard error in brackets; ***p<0.01, **p<0.05, *p<0.1.

Table C.4. *Educational requirements for job seekers – communication services*

Dependent Variable – Probability of Being Employed in Communication Services

Explanatory Variables ↓	All-India 1993–94	Rural 1993–94	Urban 1993–94	All-India 2004–05	Rural 2004–05	Urban 2004–05
Education Dummy 2	0.0105*** [0.00027]	0.00401*** [0.00021]	0.0167*** [0.00088]	0.0125*** [0.00052]	0.00968*** [0.00058]	0.0154*** [0.00098]
Education Dummy 3	0.0110*** [0.00041]	0.00537*** [0.00038]	0.00960*** [0.0012]	0.0127*** [0.00060]	0.00904*** [0.00073]	0.0165*** [0.0010]
Constant	−0.0454*** [0.0027]	−0.0222*** [0.0020]	−0.0759*** [0.0074]	−0.0435*** [0.0038]	−0.107*** [0.0086]	−0.0440*** [0.0053]
Vector of controls	Yes	Yes	Yes	Yes	Yes	Yes
District Dummy Variables	Yes	Yes	Yes	Yes	Yes	Yes
Observations	488,221	321,066	159,727	93,901	52,017	41,091

Note: Standard error in brackets; ***p<0.01, **p<0.05, *p<0.1.

Table C.5. *Educational requirements for job seekers – financial services*

Dependent Variable – Probability of Being Employed in Financial Services

Explanatory Variables ↓	All-India 1993–94	Rural 1993–94	Urban 1993–94	All-India	Rural	Urban
Education Dummy 2	0.000191*** [0.000056]	−0.00001 [0.000010]	0.000227 [0.00022]	0.00998*** [0.00047]	0.00629*** [0.00045]	0.0147*** [0.0010]
Education Dummy 3	0.000650*** [0.000081]	−0.000002 [0.000024]	0.00139*** [0.00026]	0.0167*** [0.00063]	0.00955*** [0.00066]	0.0261*** [0.0011]
Constant	−0.00521*** [0.00051]	−0.000405*** [0.00013]	−0.0154*** [0.0018]	−0.124*** [0.0078]	−0.0804*** [0.0075]	−0.198*** [0.013]
Vector of controls	Yes	Yes	Yes	Yes	Yes	Yes
District Dummy Variables	Yes	Yes	Yes	Yes	Yes	Yes
Observations	458,728	270,325	151,525	94,896	52,479	42,051

Note: Standard error in brackets; ***p<0.01, **p<0.05, *p<0.1.

Table C.6. *Educational requirements for job seekers – real estate and renting services*

Dependent Variable – Probability of Being Employed in Real Estate and Renting Services

Explanatory Variables ↓	All-India 1993–94	Rural 1993–94	Urban 1993–94	All-India 2004–05	Rural 2004–05	Urban 2004–05
Education Dummy 2	0.00006 [0.00005]	0.0000865*** [0.000032]	–0.00039*** [0.00015]	0.00185*** [0.00038]	0.00157*** [0.00040]	0.00145** [0.00065]
Education Dummy 3	0.000142** [0.000069]	0.00006 [0.00007]	–0.000300* [0.00018]	0.00180*** [0.00048]	0.00149*** [0.00056]	0.00113 [0.00077]
Constant	–0.00295*** [0.00037]	–0.000840*** [0.00024]	–0.00821*** [0.0010]	–0.0271*** [0.0038]	–0.0490*** [0.0054]	–0.0329*** [0.0053]
Vector of controls	Yes	Yes	Yes	Yes	Yes	Yes
District Dummy Variables	Yes	Yes	Yes	Yes	Yes	Yes
Observations	434,968	194,279	141,370	90,915	49,557	40,439

Note: Standard error in brackets; ***p<0.01, **p<0.05, *p<0.1.

Table C.7. *Educational requirements for job seekers – business services*

Dependent Variable – Probability of Being Employed in Business Services

Explanatory Variables ↓	All-India 1993–94	Rural 1993–94	Urban 1993–94	All-India 2004–05	Rural 2004–05	Urban 2004–05
Education Dummy 2	0.00571*** [0.00015]	0.00177*** [0.00011]	0.0173*** [0.00055]	0.00958*** [0.00056]	0.00402*** [0.00040]	0.0154*** [0.0014]
Education Dummy 3	0.00936*** [0.00026]	0.00267*** [0.00018]	0.0312*** [0.00070]	0.0190*** [0.00065]	0.00692*** [0.00056]	0.0333*** [0.0013]
Constant	–0.0268*** [0.0015]	–0.00716*** [0.00068]	–0.111*** [0.0076]	–0.0313*** [0.0029]	–0.0496*** [0.0059]	–0.0484*** [0.0057]
Vector of controls	Yes	Yes	Yes	Yes	Yes	Yes
District Dummy Variables	Yes	Yes	Yes	Yes	Yes	Yes
Observations	488,221	318,440	159,492	93,783	51,603	41,702

Note: Standard error in brackets; ***p<0.01, **p<0.05, *p<0.1.

Table C.8. *Educational requirements for job seekers – public administration*

Dependent Variable – Probability of Being Employed in Public Administration and Defence					
Explanatory Variables ↓	All-India 1993–94	Rural 1993–94	Urban 1993–94	All-India 2004–05	Rural 2004–05	Urban 2004–05
Education Dummy 2	0.000674*** [0.000051]	0.000225*** [0.000034]	0.00233*** [0.00017]	0.0377*** [0.0012]	0.0330*** [0.0013]	0.0396*** [0.0021]
Education Dummy 3	0.00113*** [0.00010]	0.000402*** [0.000069]	0.00389*** [0.00028]	0.0466*** [0.0013]	0.0347*** [0.0017]	0.0560*** [0.0022]
Constant	−0.00222*** [0.00029]	−0.000863*** [0.00018]	−0.00770*** [0.00088]	−0.304*** [0.0070]	−0.257*** [0.0093]	−0.364*** [0.011]
Vector of controls	Yes	Yes	Yes	Yes	Yes	Yes
District Dummy Variables	Yes	Yes	Yes	Yes	Yes	Yes
Observations	462,075	273,602	149,065	95,346	52,865	42,481

Note: Standard errors in brackets; ***p<0.01, **p<0.05, *p<0.1.

Table C.9. *Educational requirements for job seekers – education services*

Dependent Variable – Probability of Being Employed in Education Services					
Explanatory Variables ↓	All-India 1993–94	Rural 1993–94	Urban 1993–94	All-India 2004–05	Rural 2004–05	Urban 2004–05
Education Dummy 2	0.000362*** [0.000050]	0.000130*** [0.000033]	0.00175*** [0.00019]	0.0620*** [0.0011]	0.0715*** [0.0016]	0.0407*** [0.0017]
Education Dummy 3	0.000621*** [0.00010]	0.000252*** [0.000075]	0.00293*** [0.00041]	0.107*** [0.0018]	0.123*** [0.0030]	0.0816*** [0.0022]
Constant	−0.00106*** [0.00020]	−0.000540*** [0.00016]	−0.00536*** [0.0010]	−0.171*** [0.0064]	−0.191*** [0.0099]	−0.115*** [0.0074]
Vector of controls	Yes	Yes	Yes	Yes	Yes	Yes
District Dummy Variables	Yes	Yes	Yes	Yes	Yes	Yes
Observations	460,397	281,107	146,594	95,346	52,865	42,481

Note: Standard error in brackets; ***p<0.01, **p<0.05, *p<0.1.

Table C.10. *Educational requirements for job seekers – health services*

Dependent Variable – Probability of Being Employed in Health Services

Explanatory Variables ↓	All-India 1993–94	Rural 1993–94	Urban 1993–94	All-India 2004–05	Rural 2004–05	Urban 2004–05
Education Dummy 2	0.000224*** [0.000042]	0.000006 [0.000041]	0.000512*** [0.00012]	0.0169*** [0.00067]	0.0162*** [0.00073]	0.0151*** [0.0013]
Education Dummy 3	0.000135** [0.000062]	0.000142** [0.000060]	−0.00009 [0.00018]	0.0270*** [0.00075]	0.0247*** [0.0010]	0.0278*** [0.0012]
Constant	−0.00147*** [0.00024]	−0.00074** [0.00031]	−0.00312*** [0.00061]	−0.0655*** [0.0045]	−0.0568*** [0.0054]	−0.0718*** [0.0074]
Vector of controls	Yes	Yes	Yes	Yes	Yes	Yes
District Dummy Variables	Yes	Yes	Yes	Yes	Yes	Yes
Observations	366,534	114,165	126,922	95,346	52,865	42,372

Note: Standard error in brackets; ***p<0.01, **p<0.05, *p<0.1.

Table C.11. *Educational requirements for job seekers – other social, community and personal services*

Dependent Variable – Probability of Being Employed in Other Social, Community and Personal Services

Explanatory Variables ↓	All-India 1993–94	Rural 1993–94	Urban 1993–94	All-India 2004–05	Rural 2004–05	Urban 2004–05
Education Dummy 2	−0.135*** [0.00096]	−0.0756*** [0.00072]	−0.136*** [0.0027]	−0.0277*** [0.0015]	−0.0248*** [0.0020]	−0.0310*** [0.0020]
Education Dummy 3	−0.244*** [0.0014]	−0.143*** [0.0013]	−0.281*** [0.0032]	−0.0634*** [0.0026]	−0.0584*** [0.0045]	−0.0707*** [0.0029]
Constant	−0.265*** [0.011]	−0.153*** [0.0083]	−0.203*** [0.029]	−0.0632*** [0.012]	−0.0847*** [0.017]	−0.0320** [0.015]
Vector of controls	Yes	Yes	Yes	Yes	Yes	Yes
District Dummy Variables	Yes	Yes	Yes	Yes	Yes	Yes
Observations	488,221	328,494	159,727	95,346	52,586	42,481

Note: Standard error in brackets; ***p<0.01, **p<0.05, *p<0.1.

C.1.2. Multinomial Logit Model

Table C.12. *Educational requirements in different service sub-sectors relative to industry, 2004–05*

Dependent Variable: Probability of Being Employed in a Particular Sector (All-India)
(Base Outcome: Being employed in the Industrial Sector)

Explanatory Variables ↓	Agriculture	Wholesale and retail trade	Hotels and restaurants	Transport services	Communication services	Financial services
Education Dummy 2	−0.198*** [0.0028]	0.0162 [0.0037]	0.0029 [0.0059]	0.0074 [0.0064]	0.0078*** [0.00030]	0.0062*** [0.00027]
Education Dummy 3	−0.465*** [0.0072]	0.0149 [0.0033]	0.0012 [0.0015]	0.0046 [0.0014]	0.0125*** [0.00051]	0.0128*** [0.00059]
Constant	0.802*** [0.0092]	−0.170*** [0.0059]	−0.0388*** [0.0022]	−0.150*** [0.0030]	−0.0216*** [0.0012]	−0.0244*** [0.0013]
Vector of Controls	Yes	Yes	Yes	Yes	Yes	Yes
District Dummy Variables	Yes	Yes	Yes	Yes	Yes	Yes
Observations	98,455	98,455	98,455	98,455	98,455	98,455

Note: Standard error in brackets; ***$p<0.01$, **$p<0.05$, *$p<0.1$.

Table C.13. *Educational requirements in different service sub-sectors relative to industry, 2004–05*

Dependent Variable: Probability of Being Employed in a Particular Sector (All-India)
(Base Outcome: Being employed in the Industrial Sector)

Explanatory Variables ↓	Real estate and renting services	Business services	Public administration and defence	Education services	Health services	Other social, community and personal services
Education Dummy 2	0.0017*** [0.0002]	0.0061*** [0.0003]	0.0383*** [0.0007]	0.0382*** [0.0006]	0.0122*** [0.0004]	−0.0109*** [0.0011]
Education Dummy 3	0.0035*** [0.0003]	0.0149*** [0.0006]	0.0836*** [0.0014]	0.075*** [0.0014]	0.0292*** [0.0009]	−0.0179*** [0.0025]
Constant	−0.0123*** [0.00094]	−0.0171*** [0.0010]	−0.222*** [0.0035]	−0.102*** [0.0025]	−0.0368*** [0.0015]	−0.0390*** [0.0033]
Vector of controls	Yes	Yes	Yes	Yes	Yes	Yes
District Dummy Variables	Yes	Yes	Yes	Yes	Yes	Yes
Observation	98,455	98,455	98,455	98,455	98,455	98,455

Note: Standard error in brackets; ***p<0.01, **p<0.05, *p<0.1.

Table C.14. *Educational requirements in different service sub-sectors relative to industry, 1993–94*

Dependent Variable: Probability of Being Employed in a Particular Sector (All-India)
(Base Outcome: Being employed in the Industrial Sector)

Explanatory Variables ↓	Agriculture	Wholesale and retail trade	Hotels and restaurants	Transport services	Communication services	Financial services
Education Dummy 2	−0.275*** [0.00182]	0.00082 [0.00183]	0.00072 [0.00135]	0.00086 [0.00091]	0.00239*** [0.000105]	0.00624*** [0.000179]
Education Dummy 3	−0.532*** [0.00498]	0.00028 [0.00181]	0.000287 [0.000914]	0.00052 [0.000806]	0.00334*** [0.000167]	0.0121*** [0.000413]
Constant	0.647*** [0.00566]	−0.136*** [0.00302]	−0.0254*** [0.00115]	−0.128*** [0.00168]	−0.00972*** [0.000533]	−0.0205*** [0.000740]
Vector of Controls	Yes	Yes	Yes	Yes	Yes	Yes
District Dummy Variables	Yes	Yes	Yes	Yes	Yes	Yes
Observations	487,853	487,853	487,853	487,853	487,853	487,853

Note: Standard error in brackets; ***p<0.01, **p<0.05, *p<0.1.

Table C.15. *Educational requirements in different service sub-sectors
relative to industry, 1993–94*

Dependent Variable: Probability of Being Employed in a Particular Sector (All-India)
(Base Outcome: Being employed in the Industrial Sector)

Explanatory Variables ↓	Real estate and renting services	Business services	Public administration and defence ·	Education services	Health services	Other social, community and personal services
Education Dummy 2	0.00114*** [0.0000871]	0.00350*** [0.000119]	0.0687*** [0.000579]	0.0212*** [0.000366]	0.00927*** [0.000204]	−0.0205*** [0.000802]
Education Dummy 3	0.00199*** [0.000140]	0.00769*** [0.000294]	0.117*** [0.00109]	0.0343*** [0.000695]	0.0155*** [0.000392]	−0.0257*** [0.00199]
Constant	−0.00552*** [0.000400]	−0.00922*** [0.000432]	−0.194*** [0.00237]	−0.0456*** [0.00100]	−0.0228*** [0.000753]	−0.0183*** [0.00241]
Vector of Controls	Yes	Yes	Yes	Yes	Yes	Yes
District Dummy Variables	Yes	Yes	Yes	. Yes	Yes	Yes
Observation	487,853	487,853	487,853	487,853	487,853	487,853

Note: Standard error in brackets; ***p<0.01, **p<0.05, *p<0.1.

C.2. Wages, Contracts and Social Security Benefits

Table C.16. *Wage function (OLS)*

Dependent Variable: Log of Weekly Earnings

Explanatory Variables ↓	All-India 1993–94	Rural 1993–94	Urban 1993–94	All-India 2004–05	Rural 2004–05	Urban 2004–05
Trade Dummy	−0.278***	−0.279***	−0.270***	−0.145***	−0.162***	−0.147***
	[0.0190]	[0.0371]	[0.0232]	[0.0131]	[0.0249]	[0.0152]
Hotels Dummy	−0.114***	−0.0125**	−0.143***	−0.0762***	−0.0186***	−0.0979***
	[0.0329]	[0.0384]	[0.0394]	[0.0199]	[0.0394]	[0.0228]
Transport Dummy	0.0363	0.0246	0.0631	0.0138	0.010	0.128**
	[0.0245]	[0.0231]	[0.0191]	[0.0207]	[0.0257]	[0.0143]
Communication Dummy	0.0985**	0.0414**	0.124**	0.0369***	0.0184*	0.079**
	[0.0409]	[0.0359]	[0.0529]	[0.0238]	[0.0268]	[0.0207]
Finance Dummy	0.293***	0.355***	0.265***	0.150***	0.163***	0.130***
	[0.0244]	[0.0489]	[0.0294]	[0.0206]	[0.0380]	[0.0239]
Real Estate Dummy	−0.0492	−0.0454	−0.0683	0.0166	0.0734	−0.00589
	[0.115]	[0.195]	[0.145]	[0.0540]	[0.122]	[0.0588]
Business Dummy	0.016	0.0032	0.537	0.145***	−0.0151	0.168***
	[0.0473]	[0.107]	[0.0553]	[0.0244]	[0.0596]	[0.0264]
Public Administration Dummy	0.156***	0.235***	0.133***	0.103***	0.124***	0.0956***
	[0.0131]	[0.0218]	[0.0170]	[0.0131]	[0.0212]	[0.0166]
Education Dummy	0.0814***	0.242***	0.0551*	−0.182***	−0.012	−0.184***
	[0.0201]	[0.0310]	[0.0172]	[0.0158]	[0.0244]	[0.0208]
Health Dummy	0.0496*	0.115**	0.0342*	−0.194***	−0.166***	−0.195***
	[0.0284]	[0.0503]	[0.0156]	[0.0203]	[0.0346]	[0.0247]
Others Dummy	−0.364***	−0.303***	−0.373***	−0.179***	−0.187***	−0.226***
	[0.0163]	[0.0249]	[0.0219]	[0.0145]	[0.0251]	[0.0177]
Agriculture Dummy	−0.177***	−0.132***	−0.0768*	−0.161***	−0.132***	−0.170***
	[0.0227]	[0.0258]	[0.0432]	[0.0235]	[0.0287]	[0.0430]
Vector of Controls	Yes	Yes	Yes	Yes	Yes	Yes
District Dummy Variables	Yes	Yes	Yes	Yes	Yes	Yes
Occupation Dummy Variables	Yes	Yes	Yes	Yes	Yes	Yes
Enterprise Characteristics	No	No	No	Yes	Yes	Yes
Constant	2.559***	2.838***	2.022***	3.337***	3.415***	3.269***
	[0.0272]	[0.0316]	[0.0494]	[0.0288]	[0.0429]	[0.0386]
Observations	71,618	41,459	30,159	46,085	20,150	25,935
R-squared	0.521	0.503	0.437	0.667	0.648	0.694

Note: Standard error in brackets; ***$p<0.01$, **$p<0.05$, *$p<0.1$.

Appendix C

Table C.17. *Job contract and social security benefit function*
(marginal effect from Logit, 2004–05)

Dependent Variable: Probability of getting a Written Job Contract and Social Security Benefits

Explanatory Variables ↓	All-India Benefits	Rural Benefits	Urban Benefits	All-India Contract	Rural Contract	Urban Contract
Trade Dummy	−0.106*** [0.018]	−0.0326 [0.028]	−0.127*** [0.026]	−0.0784*** [0.015]	−0.0365 [0.024]	−0.0943*** [0.019]
Hotels Dummy	−0.0633** [0.028]	−0.0252 [0.041]	−0.105** [0.042]	−0.0734*** [0.022]	−0.0491 [0.037]	−0.0730** [0.030]
Transport Dummy	−0.148 [0.090]	−0.153 [0.095]	−0.0293 [0.11]	−0.104 [0.069]	−0.120 [0.081]	−0.0243 [0.077]
Communication Dummy	0.0568* [0.023]	0.0421* [0.016]	0.0887* [0.041]	0.0737*** [0.017]	0.110*** [0.022]	0.058* [0.026]
Finance Dummy	0.130*** [0.021]	0.164*** [0.030]	0.101*** [0.032]	0.105*** [0.015]	0.163*** [0.023]	0.0694*** [0.020]
Real Estate Dummy	−0.0496*** [0.012]	−0.0394*** [0.015]	−0.0657*** [0.020]	−0.011 [0.0095]	0.00817 [0.013]	−0.0193 [0.014]
Business Dummy	0.0372* [0.022]	−0.0539 [0.047]	0.0386* [0.023]	0.0942*** [0.017]	0.0632 [0.048]	0.0936*** [0.021]
Public Administration Dummy	0.106*** [0.013]	0.0962*** [0.015]	0.128*** [0.023]	0.0399*** [0.0091]	0.0762*** [0.012]	0.0148* [0.014]
Education Dummy	0.0447*** [0.015]	0.0610*** [0.019]	0.0346* [0.016]	0.0805*** [0.011]	0.0984*** [0.015]	0.0646*** [0.017]
Health Dummy	0.0486** [0.020]	0.0448* [0.026]	0.0563* [0.032]	0.0639*** [0.015]	0.0719*** [0.020]	0.0644*** [0.021]
Others Dummy	−0.135*** [0.020]	−0.147*** [0.028]	−0.137*** [0.030]	−0.114*** [0.015]	−0.0896*** [0.022]	−0.107*** [0.021]
Agriculture Dummy	−0.129*** [0.032]	−0.115*** [0.035]	−0.122* [0.064]	−0.109*** [0.025]	−0.0704** [0.029]	−0.131*** [0.045]
Vector of Controls	Yes	Yes	Yes	Yes	Yes	Yes
District Dummy Variables	Yes	Yes	Yes	Yes	Yes	Yes
Occupation Dummy Variables	Yes	Yes	Yes	Yes	Yes	Yes
Self-Employment Dummy Variable	Yes	Yes	Yes	Yes	Yes	Yes
Enterprise Characteristics	Yes	Yes	Yes	Yes	Yes	Yes
Constant	−1.382*** [0.044]	−1.118*** [0.058]	−1.669*** [0.071]	−0.623*** [0.035]	−0.581*** [0.049]	−0.653*** [0.050]
Observations	49,388	26,007	23,347	49,388	26,007	23,319

Note: Standard error in brackets; ***p<0.01, **p<0.05, *p<0.1.

Table C.18. *All-India sample (instrumental variable estimation)*

Dependent variable: Probability of getting a written job contract and social security benefits

Dependent Variable → Explanatory Variables ↓	Wages (IV) 2004–05	Wages (IV) 1993–94	Job Contract (IV) 2004–05	Social Security Benefits (IV) 2004–05
Agriculture Dummy	−0.364 [0.521]	−0.554 [0.493]	−0.112 [0.091]	−0.143 [0.101]
Low Job Quality Services Dummy	−0.825*** [0.057]	−0.132*** [0.017]	−0.329*** [0.085]	−0.136* [0.080]
First stage F-statistic:	*21.8 [0.000]*	*17.2 [0.000]*		
High Job Quality Services Dummy	0.685** [0.097]	0.424*** [0.033]	0.205* [0.112]	0.211* [0.112]
First stage F-statistics:	*69.7 [0.000]*	*44.1 [0.000]*		
Vector of Controls	Yes	Yes	Yes	Yes
District Dummy Variables	Yes	Yes	Yes	Yes
Constant	3.999*** [0.314]	2.471*** [0.145]	1.018*** [0.052]	1.179*** [0.103]
Observations	46,085	71,618	46,759	46,759

Note: Standard error in brackets (for the first stage F-Statistics, p-values in the brackets); ***p<0.01, **p<0.05, *p<0.1.

The regressions for job contracts and social security benefits are estimated using the *mvprobit* command in Stata. It does not report a first-state F-statistic.

Source: Author's regression estimates.

Appendix D

1. Engel Curve in a "Budget Share" Specification

$$\frac{E}{Y} = \alpha + \beta \log Y$$

where E is household expenditure on services and Y is total household expenditure

Differentiating with respect to time

$$\frac{Y(dE/dt) - E(dY/dt)}{Y^2} = \beta . \frac{1}{Y} . \frac{dY}{dt}$$

$$\Rightarrow \frac{Y\dot{E} - E\dot{Y}}{Y} = \beta \dot{Y}$$

$$\Rightarrow \beta \dot{Y} = \dot{E} - \frac{E\dot{Y}}{Y}$$

$$\Rightarrow \dot{E} = \left(\beta + \frac{E}{Y} \right) \dot{Y}$$

$$\Rightarrow \hat{\beta} = \frac{\dot{E}}{\dot{Y}} - \frac{E}{Y}$$

$$\hat{\beta} > 0 \Rightarrow \frac{\dot{E}}{E} > \frac{\dot{Y}}{Y}$$

that is, percentage change in expenditure on services is greater than percentage change in total household expenditure.

2. Engel Curve in an "Absolute Levels" Specification

$$\log E = \alpha + \beta \log Y$$

where E is household expenditure on services and Y is total household expenditure

Differentiating with respect to time

$$\frac{1}{E} \cdot \frac{dE}{dt} = \beta . \frac{1}{Y} \cdot \frac{dY}{dt}$$

$$\Rightarrow \frac{\dot{E}}{E} = \beta . \frac{\dot{Y}}{Y}$$

$$\Rightarrow \hat{\beta} = \frac{\left(\dot{E} / E \right)}{\left(\dot{Y} / Y \right)}$$

$$\hat{\beta} > 1 \Rightarrow \frac{\dot{E}}{E} > \frac{\dot{Y}}{Y}$$

Hence, $\hat{\beta} > 0$ in the "budget share" specification is equivalent to the expenditure elasticity of demand being greater than 1 in the "absolute levels" specification.

Bibliography

Abraham, V. (2007), "Growth and Inequality of Wages in India: Recent Trends and Patterns", *The Indian Journal of Labour Economics*, Volume 50, Number 4, pp. 927–941.

Agarwal, P. (2006), "Higher Education Services in India and Trade Liberalization", in Chanda, R. (ed.), *Trade in Services in India: Prospects and Strategies*, Wiley-India, New Delhi.

Allen, R.G.D. and Bowley, A.L. (1935), *Family Expenditure: A Study of its Variation*, P.S. King and Son, London.

Amin, M. and Mattoo, A. (2008), "Human Capital and the Changing Structure of the Indian Economy", World Bank Policy Research Working Paper Number 4576, World Bank, Washington D.C.

Arrow, K. (1973), "Higher Education as a Filter", *Journal of Public Economics*, Volume 2, Issue 3, pp. 193–216.

Balakrishnan, P. and Parameswaran, M. (2007), "Understanding Economic Growth in India: A Prerequisite", *Economic and Political Weekly*, July 14.

Balasubramanyam, V.N. and Balasubramanyam, A. (1997), "International Trade in Services: The Case of India's Computer Software", *The World Economy*, Volume 20, Issue 6, pp. 829–843.

Banerjee, B. (1986), *Rural to Urban Migration and the Urban Labour Market*, Himalaya Publishing House, New Delhi.

Banga, R. (2005a), "Critical Issues in India's Service-Led Growth", *ICRIER Working Paper Series*, Number 171, Indian Council for Research on International Economic Relations, New Delhi.

(2005b), "Role of Services in the Growth Process: A Survey", *ICRIER Working Paper Series*, Number 159, Indian Council for Research on International Economic Relations, New Delhi.

Banga, R. and Goldar, B.N. (2004), "Contribution of Services to Output Growth Productivity in Indian Manufacturing: Pre and Post Reform", *ICRIER Working Paper Series*, Number 139, Indian Council for Research on International Economic Relations, New Delhi.

Banks, J., Blundell, R. and Lewbel, A. (1997), "Quadratic Engel Curves and Consumer Demand", *Review of Economics and Statistics*, Volume 79, pp. 527–539.

Basu, S., Fernald, J.G. and Shapiro, M.D. (2001), "Productivity Growth in the 1990s: Technology, Utilization or Adjustment?", *NBER Working Paper Series*, Working Paper Number 8359, National Bureau of Economic Research, Massachusetts.

Basu, K. and Maertens, A. (2009), "The Growth of Industry and Services in South Asia", in Ghani, E. and Ahmed, S. (eds.), *Accelerating Growth and Job Creation in South Asia*, Oxford University Press, Oxford.

Baumol, W.J. (1967), "Macroeconomics of Unbalanced Growth: The Anatomy of Urban Crisis", *American Economic Review*, Volume 57, Number 3, pp. 415–426.

Beaston, M. (2000), "Job Quality and Forms of Employment: Concepts and the UK Statistical Evidence", Invited Paper at the Joint ECE-Eurostat-ILO Seminar on Measurement of the Quality of Employment, 3–5 May, Geneva.

Beatty, T (2006), "Zero Expenditures and Engel Curve Estimation", Selected Paper presented at the American Agricultural Association Annual Meeting, 23–26 July, Long Beach, California.

Becker, G.S. (1964), *Human Capital: A Theoretical and Empirical Analysis with Special Reference to Education*, The University of Chicago Press, Chicago.

Bhagwati, J. (1984), "Splintering and Disembodiment of Services and Developing Nations", *The World Economy*, Volume 7, Issue 2, pp. 133–144.

Bhagwati, J.N. and Srinivasan, T.N. (1977), "Education in a 'Job-Ladder' Model and the Fairness-in-Hiring Rule", *Journal of Public Economics*, Volume 7, pp. 1–22.

Bhalla, S. (2003), "The Restructuring of the Unorganised Sector in India", Institute of Human Development, New Delhi, Report on a Project funded by the Planning Commission, Government of India.

Bhalotra, S. (1998), "The Puzzle of Jobless Growth in Indian Manufacturing", *Oxford Bulletin of Economics and Statistics*, Volume 60, Number 1, pp. 5–32.

Bhattacharya, B.B. and Mitra, A. (1990), "Excess Growth of the Tertiary Sector in Indian Economy: Issues and Implications", *Economic and Political Weekly*, November 3, Bombay.

Bhushan, S. (2004), "Trade in Education Services under GATS: Implications for Higher Education in India", *Economic and Political Weekly*, June 5.

Bierens, H. and Pott-Buter, H.A. (1990), "Specification of Household Expenditure Functions and Equivalence Scales by Nonparametric Regression", *Econometric Reviews*, Volume 9, pp. 123–210.

Black, D.A., Noel, B.J. and Wang, Z. (1999), "On-the-job Training, Establishment Size, and Firm-Size: Evidence for Economies of Scale in the Production of Human Capital", *Southern Economic Journal*, Volume 66, Number 1, pp. 82–100.

Blunch, N.H. and Verner, D. (1999), "Sector Growth and the Dual Economy Model – Evidence from Cote D'Ivoire, Ghana and Zimbabwe", *World Bank Policy Research Working Paper Series*, Working Paper Number 2175, The World Bank.

Bosworth, B., Collins, S.M. and Virmani, A. (2007), "Sources of Growth in the Indian Economy", *NBER Working Paper Series*, Working Paper Number w12901, February.

Bosworth B. and Maertens A. (2010), "The Role of the Service Sector in Economic Growth and Employment in South Asia", in Ghani. E. (ed.), *The Service Revolution in South Asia*, Oxford University Press, Oxford.

Bullard, D. (2008), "Estimating Wage Differentials for the Western Region: Using the March Current Population Survey Supplement", Working Paper, Department of Employment, State of Wyoming.

Burki, A. and Abbas, Q. (1991), "Earnings Function in Pakistan's Urban Informal Sector: A Case Study", *The Pakistan Development Review*, Volume 30, Number 4, pp. 695–706.

Cabral, L. (2000), *Introduction to Industrial Organisation*, MIT Press, Massachusetts.

Canadian Services Coalition (2007), "Canada and India: Trade and Investment Opportunities in the Services Sector", India Paper, March.

Canning, D. and Bennathan, E. (2000), "The Social Rate of Return on Infrastructure Investments", *World Bank Policy Research Working Paper Series*, Working Paper Number 2390, World Bank, Washington, DC.

Caplan, D. (1998), "Measuring the Output of Non-Market Services", *Economic Trends*, Volume 539, pp. 45–49.

Central Statistical Organisation (CSO) (1999), *Working Force Estimates 1993-94: A Methodological Note*, Ministry of Statistics and Programme Implementation, Government of India.

  (2006), New Series of *National Accounts Statistics: Base Year 1999–2000*, Ministry of Statistics and Programme Implementation, Government of India.

  (2007a), *National Accounts Statistics: Sources and Methods*, Ministry of Statistics and Programme Implementation, Government of India.

  (2007b), *National Accounts Statistics: Back Series (1950–51 to 1999–2000)*, Ministry of Statistics and Programme Implementation, Government of India.

  (2008), *National Accounts Statistics: In the Accounting Framework of System of National Accounts 1993*, Ministry of Statistics and Programme Implementation, Government of India.

Central Statistical Organisation. *Input Output Transactions Table*, Various Issues, Ministry of Statistics and Programme Implementation, Government of India.

  National Account Statistics, Various Issues, Ministry of Statistics and Programme Implementation, Government of India.

Chakraborty, A.B. and Das, A, (2007), "Banking Sector's Output in National Accounts: Measurement Issues", *Economic and Political Weekly*, September 15.

Chakraborty, C. and Nunnenkamp, P. (2008), "Economic Reforms, FDI, and Economic Growth in India: A Sector Level Analysis", *World Development*, Volume 36, Number 7, pp. 1192–1212.

Chanda, R. (2001), "Trade in Health Services", *ICRIER Working Paper Series*, Number 70, Indian Council for Research on International Economic Relations, New Delhi.

  (2002), *Globalization of Services: India's Opportunities and Constraints*, Oxford University Press, New Delhi.

  (2005), "Trade in Financial Services: India's Opportunities and Constraints", *ICRIER Working Paper Series*, Number 171, Indian Council for Research on International Economic Relations, New Delhi.

  (2006), "Services and India", in Basu, K. (ed.), *The Oxford Companion to Economics in India*, Oxford University Press, New Delhi.

  (2008), "India and Services Outsourcing in Asia", *The Singapore Economic Review*, Volume 52, Number 3, pp. 1–29.

  (2009), "Global Economic Crisis and Protectionism in Services for India's IT-ITeS Exports and the GATS", ICRIER Policy Brief, September, Volume 1, Number 1.

Chenery, H.B. (1960), "Patterns of Industrial Growth", *American Economic Review*, Volume 57, pp. 415–426.

280 Bibliography

Clark, A.E. (1996), "Job Satisfaction in Britain", *British Journal of Industrial Relations*, Volume 34, Issue 2, pp. 189–217.

(1998), "Measures of Job Satisfaction: What Makes a Good Job? Evidence from OECD Countries", OECD Labour Market and Social Policies, Occasional Paper Number 34.

Clark, A.E. and Oswald, A.J. (1996), "Satisfaction and Comparison Income", *Journal of Public Economics*, Volume 61, Number 3, pp. 133–155.

Clark, C. (1940), *The Conditions of Economic Progress*, McMillan and Co. Ltd., London.

Coase, R.H. (1937), "The Nature of the Firm", *Economica*, Volume 4, Number 16, pp. 386–405.

Commander, S., Chanda, R., Kangasniemi, M. and Winters, L.A. (2008), "The Consequences of Globalization: India's Software Industry and Cross-Border Labour Mobility", *The World Economy*, Volume 31, Issue 2, pp. 187–211.

Dasgupta, S. (2003), "Structural and Behavioural Characteristics of Informal Services Employment: Evidence from a Survey in New Delhi", *Journal of Development Studies*, Volume 39, Number 3, pp. 51–80.

Dasgupta, S. and Singh, A. (2005), "Will Services be the New Engine of Indian Economic Growth?", *Development and Change*, Volume 36, Number 6, pp. 1035–1057.

(2006), "Manufacturing, Services and Premature De-Industrialization in Developing Countries: A Kaldorian Empirical Analysis", *Working Paper Series*, Working Paper Number 327, Centre for Business Research, University of Cambridge.

Deaton, A. (1997), *The Analysis of Household Surveys: A Microeconometric Approach to Development Policy*, John Hopkins University Press, Baltimore.

Deaton, A. and Irish, M. (1984), "Statistical Models for Zero Expenditures in Budget Shares", *Journal of Public Economics*, Volume 23, pp. 59–80.

Dev, S.M. (2000), "Economic Reforms, Poverty, Income Distribution and Employment", *Economic and Political Weekly*, March 4.

(2002), "Pro-Poor Growth in India: What Do We Know about the Employment Effects of Growth 1980–2000?", Working Paper 161, Overseas Development Institute, London.

Dewan, S. and Peek, P. (2007), "Beyond the Employment/Unemployment Dichotomy: Measuring the Quality of Employment in Low Income Countries," Working Paper Number 83, Policy Integration and Statistics Department, ILO, Geneva.

Dickens, W.T. and Katz, L.F. (1987), "Industry Wage Differences and Theories of Wage Determination", *NBER Working Paper Series*, Working Paper Number 2271, Cambridge, Massachusetts.

Doeringer, P.B. and Piore, M.J. (1971), *Internal Labour Markets and Manpower Analysis*, Lexington, Massachusetts, D.C. Health and Company.

Dollar, D. and Kraay, A. (2004), "Trade, Growth and Poverty", *Economic Journal*, Volume 114, pp. F22–F49.

Dornbusch, R. (1976), "Expectations and Exchange Rate Dynamics", *Journal of Political Economy*, Volume 84, pp. 1161–1176.

(1980), *Open Economy Macroeconomics*, Basic Books, New York.

Easterlin, R.A. (2001), "Income and Happiness: Towards a Unified Theory", *Economic Journal*, Volume 111, pp. 465–484.

(2009), "The Two Waves of Services Sector Growth", *NBER Working Paper Series*, Working Paper Number 14968, National Bureau of Economic Research, Cambridge, Massachusetts.

Eichengreen, B. and Gupta, P. (2010), "The Service Sector as India's Road to Economic Growth", *ICRIER Working Paper Series*, Number 249, Indian Council for Research on International Economic Relations, New Delhi.

Engel, E. (1857), "Die Productions – und Consumptionsverhaeltnisse des Koenigsreichs Sachsen", Zeitschrift des Statistischen Bureaus des Koniglich Sachsischen Ministeriums des Inneren, Number 8 und 9, Reprinted in the Appendix of Engel (1895).

(1895), "Die Lebenskosten Belgischer Arbeiter-Familien Fruher and Jetzt", *International Statistical Institute Bulletin*, Volume 9, pp. 1–74.

Erikson, R. and Aberg, R. (1987), *Welfare in Transition: A Survey of Living Conditions in Sweden 1968–1981*, Clarendon Press, Oxford.

Falvey, R.E. and Gemmell, N. (1996), "Are Services Income-Elastic? Some New Evidence", *Review of Income and Wealth*, Series 42, Number 3, pp. 257–269.

Fields, G.S. (1975), "Rural-Urban Migration, Urban Employment and Underemployment, and Job Search Activity in LDCs", *Journal of Development Economics*, Volume 2, Number 2, pp. 165–187.

Fisher, A.G.B (1935), *The Clash of Progress and Security*, Macmillan and Co. Ltd., London.

Freeman, R.B. (1978), "Job Satisfaction as an Economic Variable", *American Economic Review*, Volume 68, Number 2, pp. 135–141.

Frey, B.S. and Stutzer, A. (2002), "What Can Economists Learn from Happiness Research?", *Journal of Economic Literature*, Volume 40, pp. 402–435.

Gemmell, N., Lioyd, T. and Marinan M. (1998) "Dynamic Sectoral Linkages and Structural Change in a Developing Economy", Centre for Research in Economic Development and International Trade (CREDIT) Research Paper Number 98/3, University of Nottingham.

Gerxhani, K. (2004), "The Informal Sector in Developed and Less Developed Countries: A Literature Survey", *Public Choice*, Volume 120, Number 3–4, pp. 267–300.

Ghani, E. (2010), *The Service Revolution in South Asia*, Oxford University Press, India.

Ghose, A. K. (1999), "Current Issues of Employment Policy in India", *Economic and Political Weekly*, September 4.

Gibson, J. and Stillman, S. (2009), "Why Do Big Firms Pay Higher Wages? Evidence from an International Database", *Review of Economics and Statistics*, Volume 91, Number 1, pp. 213–218.

Giri, B.K., Roy, A. and Mukhopadhyay, S.K. (2007), "Calculation of Gross Value Added in the Unorganised Sector: An Alternative Approach to Measuring Labour Inputs", *Economic and Political Weekly*, September 15.

Gondolfo, G. (1997), *Economic Dynamics*, 3rd Edition, Springer-Verlag, Berlin.

Gordon, J. and Gupta, P. (2004), "Understanding India's Services Revolution", *IMF Working Paper Series*, Working Paper Number 171, Washington, DC.

Grajek, M. (2007), "Estimating Network Effects and Compatibility in Mobile Telecommunications", *ESMT Research Working Paper Series*, Working Paper Number 07–001, European School of Management and Technology, Berlin.

Griliches, Z. (1992), *Output Measurement in the Service Sectors*, The University of Chicago Press, Chicago.

Griliches, Z. and Siegel, D. (1992), "Purchased Services, Outsourcing, Computers and Productivity in Manufacturing", in Griliches, Z. (ed.), *Output Measurement in the Service Sectors*, The University of Chicago Press, Chicago.

Gustavsen, G.W., Jolliffe, D. and Rickertsen, K. (2008), "Censored Quantile Regressions and Purchases of Ice Cream", Selected Paper presented at the American Agricultural Economics Association Annual Meeting, 27–29 July, Orlando, Florida.

Gustavsen, G.W. and Rickertsen, K. (2004), "For Whom Reduced Prices Count: A Censored Quantile Regression Analysis of Vegetable Demand", Selected Paper presented at the American Agricultural Economics Association Annual Meeting, 1–4 July, Denver, Colorado.

Hansda, S.K. (2001), "Sustainability of Services-led Growth: An Input-Output Analysis of the Indian Economy", *RBI Occasional Working Paper Series*, Volume 22, Working Paper Number 1, 2 and 3, Reserve Bank of India, Bombay.

Härdle, W. and Jerison, M. (1991), "Cross Section Engel Curves over Time", *Recherches Economiques de Louvain*, Volume 57, pp. 391–431.

Harris J. and Todaro, M. (1970), "Migration, Unemployment & Development: A Two-Sector Analysis", *American Economic Review*, Volume 60, Number 1, pp. 126–142.

Hausman, J.A., W. K. Newey, and J. L. Powell (1995), "Nonlinear Errors in Variables: Estimation of Some Engel Curves", *Journal of Econometrics*, Volume 65, pp. 205–253.

Heckman, J.J. (1979), "Sample Selection Bias as a Specification Error", *Econometrica*, Volume 47, Number 1, pp. 153–161.

Heeks, R. (2000), "The Approach of Senior Public Officials to Information Technology related Reform: Lessons from India", *Public Administration and Development*, Volume 20, pp. 197–205.

Hicks, J. (1939), *Value and Capital*, Oxford University Press, Oxford.

Hill, P. (1996), "The Services of Financial Intermediaries: FISIM Revisited", Paper Presented at the Brookings Institution Workshop on Measuring Banking Output, Washington, DC, 20 November.

Hill, T.P. (1977), "On Goods and Services", *Review of Income and Wealth*, Volume 23, pp. 315–338.

House, W.J. (1984), "Nairobi's Informal Sector: Dynamic Entrepreneurs or Surplus Labour?", *Economic Development and Cultural Change*, Volume 32, Number 2, pp. 277–302.

Illeris, S. and Philippe, J. (1993), "Introduction: The Role of Services in Regional Economic Growth", *The Service Industries Journal*, Volume 13, Number 2, pp. 3–10.

Inman, R.P. (1985), *Managing the Service Economy Prospects and Problems*, Cambridge University Press, Cambridge.

Jackson, A. and Kumar, P. (1998), "Measuring and Monitoring the Quality of Jobs and the Work Environment in Canada", Paper presented at the Centre for the Study of Living Standards Conference on the State of Living Standards and Quality of Life in Canada, 30–31 October, Ottawa.

Jain, R. (2004), "A Review of Telecom Regulatory Authority of India's Tariff and Interconnection Regulations", in *India Infrastructure Report 2004*, Oxford University Press India, Delhi.

Jha, R. (2000), "Reducing Poverty and Inequality in India: Has Liberalization Helped?", Research Paper 204, World Institute for Development Economics Research, Helsinki.

Jimenez, E. (1994), "Human and Physical Infrastructure: Public Investment and Pricing Policies and Developing Countries", *World Bank Policy Research Working Paper Series*, Working Paper Number 1281, World Bank, Washington, DC.

Johri, R. (2005), "Work Values and the Quality of Employment: A Literature Review", Working Paper, August, Department of Labour, Government of New Zealand.

Joseph, M., Soundararajan, N., Gupta, M. and Sahu, S. (2008), "Impact of Organised Retailing on the Unorganised Sector", *ICRIER Working Paper Series*, Working Paper Number 222, Indian Council for Research on International Economic Relations, New Delhi.

Joshi, S. (2004), "Tertiary Sector-Driven Growth in India: Impact on Employment and Poverty", *Economic and Political Weekly*, September 11.

(2006), "FDI in India's Service Sector: Determinants and Implications," in Chanda, R. (ed.), *Trade in Services and India*, Wiley India, New Delhi, pp. 51–81.

Kaldor, N. (1966), *Causes of Slow Rate of Growth in the United Kingdom*, Cambridge University Press, Cambridge.

(1967), *Strategic Factors in Economic Development*, Cornell University Press, Ithaca, New York.

Kansal, S.M. (1992), "Contribution of 'Other Services' Sector to Gross Domestic Product in India: An Evaluation", *Economic and Political Weekly*, September 19.

Kar, A., Singh, G. and Kulshreshtha, A.C. (2003), "Estimates of Value Added Per Worker from Enterprise Surveys: Cross-Validating Results", *Economic and Political Weekly*, December 27.

Kim, J.I. and Kim, J.D. (2003), "Liberalization of Trade in Services and Productivity Growth in Korea", in Ito, T. and Krueger, A. (eds.), *Trade in Services in the Asia-Pacific Region*, University of Chicago Press, Chicago.

Kingdon, G. (2005), "Where Has All the Bias Gone? Detecting Gender Bias in the Intrahousehold Allocation of Educational Expenditure", *Economic Development and Cultural Change*, Volume 53, pp. 409–451.

Knight, J.B. (1979), "Job Competition, Occupational Production Functions and Filtering Down", *Oxford Economic Papers*, Volume 31, Number 2, pp. 187–204.

Knight, J.B. and Sabot, R.H. (1987), "The Rate of Return on Educational Expansion", *Economics of Education Review*, Volume 6, Issue 3, pp. 255–262.

Kochhar, K., Kumar, U., Rajan, R. and Subramanian, A. (2006), "India's Patterns of Development: What Happened, What Follows?", *NBER Working Paper Series*, Working Paper Number, 12023, National Bureau of Economic Research, Cambridge, Massachusetts.

Koenker, R. and Basett, G. (1978), "Regression Quantiles", *Econometrica*, Volume 46, pp. 33–50.

Koenker, R. and Hallock, K. (2001), "Quantile Regression", *Journal of Economic Perspectives*, Volume 15, Number 4, pp. 143–156.

Kongsamut, P., Rebelo, S. and Xie, D. (2001), "Beyond Balanced Growth", *Review of Economic Studies*, Volume 68, Number 4, pp. 869–882.

Kotwal, A., Ramaswami, B. and Wadhwa, W. (2010), "Economic Liberalization and Indian Economic Growth: What's the Evidence?", *BREAD Research Working Paper Series*, Working Paper Number 294, Duke University.

Kravis, I., Heston, A. and Summers, R. (1982), "The Share of Services in Economic Growth", in Adams, G. and Hickman, B. (eds.), *Global Econometrics: Essays in Honour of Lawrence Klein*, University of Pennsylvania, Philadelphia.

Krueger, A. (2007), "The Missing Middle", *Stanford Institute for Economic Policy Research Working Paper Series*, Working Paper Number 343, Stanford University, Palo Alto, California.

Krueger, A. and Summers, L. (1987), "Reflections on the Inter-Industry Wage Structure", in Lang. K. and Leonard, J.S. (eds.), *Unemployment and the Structure of Labor Markets*, Blackwell Publishing, Oxford.

(1988), "Efficiency Wages and the Inter-Industry Wage Structure", *Econometrica*, Volume 56, pp. 259–293.

Kulshreshtha, A.C. and Singh, G. (1999), "Services Sector in National Accounts: Methodology, Data Quality, Gaps and Possibilities of Improvement", *The Journal of Income and Wealth*, Volume 21, Number 2.

Kulshreshtha, A.C., Singh, G. and Kar, A. (2002a), "Enterprise Surveys in the Improvement of Indian National Accounts Statistics", *The Journal of Income and Wealth*, Volume 24, Number 1.

Kulshreshtha, A.C., Singh, G., Kar, A. and Mishra, R.L. (2002b), "Workforce in the Indian National Accounts Statistics", *The Journal of Income and Wealth*, Volume 22, Number 2.

Kumar, N. and Joseph, K.J. (2005), "Export of Software and Business Process Outsourcing from Developing Countries: Lessons from the Indian Experience", *Asia-Pacific Trade and Investment Review*, Volume 1, Number 1, pp. 91–110.

Kuznets, S. (1971), *Economic Growth of Nations: Total Output and Production Structure*, Harvard University Press, Cambridge, Massachusetts.

Lancaster, G., Maitra, P. and Ray, R. (2008), "Household Expenditure Patterns and Gender Bias: Evidence from Selected Indian States", *Oxford Development Studies*, Volume 36, Number 2, pp. 133–157.

Layard, R. (1980), "Human Satisfactions and Public Policy", *Economic Journal*, Volume 90, Number 363, pp. 737–750.

(2005), *Happiness: Lessons from a New Science*, Penguin Books, London.

Lee, D. and Wolpin, K.I. (2006) "Inter-Sectoral Labor Mobility and the Growth of the Service Sector", *Econometrica*, Volume 74, Number 1, pp. 1–46.

Lequiller, F. and Blades, D. (2006), *Understanding National Accounts*, OECD Publishing, Paris.

Leschke, J., Watt, A. and Finn, M. (2008), "Putting a Number on Job Quality: Constructing a European Job Quality Index", *European Trade Union Institute Working Paper Series*, Working Paper Number 2008.03.

Leser, C.E.V. (1963), "Forms of Engel Functions", *Econometrica*, Volume 31, pp. 694–703.

Letourneux, V. (1998), "Precarious Employment and Working Conditions in the European Union", European Foundation for the Improvement of Living and Working Conditions, Dublin.

Lewbel, A. (1991), "The Rank of Demand Systems: Theory and Nonparametric Estimation," *Econometrica*, Volume 59, pp. 711–730.

(2008), "Engel Curves", in Durlauf, S.N. and Blume, L.E. (eds.), *The New Palgrave Dictionary of Economics*, 2nd Edition, Palgrave Macmillan, London.

Lewis, W.A. (1954), "Economic Development with Unlimited Supplies of Labour", *Manchester School of Economic and Social Sciences*, Volume 22, Number 2, pp. 139–191.

Lim, D. (1976), "On the Measurement of Capital-Intensity", *Review of World Economics*, Volume 112, Number 4, pp. 760–766.

Lotka, A. (1956), *Elements of Mathematical Biology*, Dover Publications, New York.

Lowe, G.S. and Schellenberg, G. (2001), "What's a Good Job? The Importance of Employment Relationships", Canadian Policy Research Networks Study Number W|05.

Lucifora, C. (1993), "Inter-Industry and Occupational Wage Differentials in Italy", *Applied Economics*, Volume 25, pp. 1113–1124.

Manna, G.C. (2007), "Precision of Estimates of Gross Value Added Per Worker", *Economic and Political Weekly*, September 15.

Mattoo, A., Rathindran, R. and Subramanian, A. (2001), "Measuring Services Trade Liberalization and Its Impact on Economic Growth: An Illustration", *World Bank Policy Research Working Paper Series*, Working Paper Number 2655, The World Bank, Washington, DC.

Mazumdar, D. (1975), "The Theory of Urban Underemployment in Less Developed Countries", *World Bank Staff Working Paper Series*, Working Paper Number 198, World Bank, Washington, DC.

Mazumdar, D. and Sarkar, S. (2008), "Growth of Employment and Earnings in the Tertiary Sector: 1983–2000", in Mazumdar, D. and Sarkar, S., *Globalization, Labour Markets and Inequality in India*, Routledge, Oxford.

Mckenzie, D. and Rapoport, H. (2007), "Network Effects and the Dynamics of Migration and Inequality: Theory and Evidence from Mexico", *Journal of Development Economics*, Volume 84, Issue 1, pp. 1–24.

Meghir, C. and Robin, J.M. (1992), "Frequency of Purchase and the Estimation of Demand Systems", *Journal of Econometrics*, Volume 53, pp. 53–85.

Melvin, J.R. (1989), "Trade in Producer Services: A Hecksher-Ohlin Approach", *Journal of Political Economy*, Volume 97, Number 5, pp. 1180–1196.

(1995), "History and Measurement in the Service Sector", *Review of Income and Wealth*, Series 41, Number 4, pp. 481–494.

Messier, J. and Floro, M. (2008), "Measuring the Quality of Employment in the Informal Sector", *Department of Economics Working Paper Series*, American University, Washington, DC.

Mincer, J. (1974), *Schooling, Experience and Earnings*, Columbia University Press, New York.

Mishel, L., Bernstein, J. and Schmitt, J. (2001), *The State of Working America: 2000–01*, Cornell University Press, Ithaca, New York.

Mitra, A. (1996), "Understanding the Informal Economy", *Economic and Political Weekly*, Volume 31, Number 24.

Muller, C. (1999), "Censored Quantile Regressions of Poverty in Rwanda", Centre for Research in Economic Development and International Trade, Working Paper 11, University of Nottingham.

Mukherjee, A. (2006), "India's Trade in Distribution Services" in Chanda, R. (ed.), *Trade in Services and India*, Wiley India, New Delhi, pp. 145–176.

Murthy, N. (2004) "The Impact of Economic Reforms on Industry in India: A Case Study of the Software Industry" in Basu, K. (ed.), *India's Emerging Economy: Performance and Prospects in the 1990s and Beyond*, MIT Press, Cambridge, Massachusetts.

Nagaraj, R. (2007), "Labour Market in India: Current Concerns and Policy Responses", Paper Presented at Seminar on Labour Market Issues in Brazil, China and India, Organisation for Economic Co-operation and Development (OECD), Paris.

(2009), "Is Services Sector Output Overestimated?", *Economic and Political Weekly*, Volume 44, Number 5, pp. 40–45.

National Sample Survey Organisation (NSSO) (1996a), Key Results on Employment and Unemployment, NSS 50th Round, Ministry of Statistics and Programme Implementation, Government of India.

(1996b), Key Results on Household Consumer Expenditure, NSS 50th Round, Ministry of Statistics and Programme Implementation, Government of India.

(2001), *Informal Sector in India 1999–2000: Salient Features*, Ministry of Statistics and Programme Implementation, Government of India.

(2002a), *Unorganised Service Sector in India: Salient Features*, Report Number 482, Ministry of Statistics and Programme Implementation, Government of India.

(2002b), *Unorganised Service Sector in India: Characteristics of Enterprises*, Report Number 483, Ministry of Statistics and Programme Implementation, Government of India.

(2006a), *Employment and Unemployment Situation in India: NSS 61st Round*, Ministry of Statistics and Programme Implementation, Government of India.

(2006b), *Level and Pattern of Household Consumer Expenditure: NSS 50th Round*, Ministry of Statistics and Programme Implementation, Government of India.

Nayyar, D. (1988), "The Political Economy of International Trade in Services", *Cambridge Journal of Economics*, Volume 12, pp. 279–298.

Nijman, J. (2000), "Mumbai's Real Estate Market in the 1990s: De-regulation, Global Money and Casino Capitalism", *Economic and Political Weekly*, Volume 35, Number 7, pp. 575–582.

Nitsure, R.R. (2003), "E-Banking: Challenges and Opportunities", *Economic and Political Weekly*, Volume 38, Number 51/52, pp. 5377–5381.

Nurkse, R. (1953), *Problems of Capital Formation in Underdeveloped Countries*, Oxford University Press, New York.

Ogburn, W. F. (1919), "Analysis of the Standard of Living in the District of Columbia in 1916" *Journal of the American Statistical Association*, Volume 16, pp. 374–389.

OECD (1999), *Employment Outlook*, Paris.

(2001), *Employment Outlook*, Paris.

(2005), Enhancing the Performance of the Services Sector, OECD Publishing, Paris.

Ofer, G. (2005), "Returns to Scale in Retail Trade", *Review of Income and Wealth*, Volume 19, Issue 4, pp. 363–384.

Oi, W.Y. and Idson, T.L. (1999a), "Firm-Size and Wages", in Ashenfelter, O. and Card, D. (eds.), *Handbook of Labor Economics*, Volume 3, North Holland, Amsterdam.

(1999b), "Workers are More Productive in Large Firms", *American Economic Review (Papers and Proceedings)*, Volume 89, Number 2, pp. 104–108.

Osberg, L., Apostle, R. and Clairmont, D. (1987), "Segmented Labour Markets and the Estimation of Wage Functions", *Applied Economics*, Volume 19, pp. 1603–1624.

Osburn, J. (2000), "Inter-Industry Wage Differentials: Patterns and Possible Sources", *Monthly Labour Review*, Volume 123, pp. 34–46.

Panagariya, A. (2002), "India's Economic Reforms: What Has Been Accomplished? What Remains to be Done?", Asian Development Bank, Economic Research Department Policy Brief Series, Number 2.

Planning Commission (2001), Report of Task Force on Integrated Transport Policy, Government of India.

(2002), *Tenth Five-Year Plan: 2002–2007*, Government of India.

Powell, J.L. (1986), "Censored Regression Quantiles", *Journal of Econometrics*, Volume 32, pp. 143–155.

Prasad, A. and Ghosh, S. (2007), "Competition in Indian Banking: An Empirical Evaluation", *South Asia Economic Journal*, Volume 8, pp. 265–284.

Pratap, S. and Quintin, E. (2006), "The Informal Sector in Developing Countries: Output, Assets and Employment", WIDER Research Paper Series, Volume 2006/130, World Institute for Development Economics Research, Helsinki.

Psacharopoulos, G. (1994) "Returns to Investment in Education: A Global Update", *World Development*, Volume 22, Number 9, pp. 1325–1343.

Qin, D. (2004), "Is the Rising Services Sector in the People's Republic of China Leading to Cost Disease?", *Economic Research Department Working Paper Series*, Working Paper Number 50, Asian Development Bank, Manila.

Raghuram, G. (2007), "Turnaround of Indian Railways: A Critical Appraisal of Strategies and Processes", *IIMA Working Paper Series*, Working Paper Number, 2007-02-03, Indian Institute of Management, Ahmedabad.

Rakshit, M. (2007), "Services-led Growth: The Indian Experience", *Money and Finance*, ICRA Bulletin, February.

Ranis, G. and Stewart, F. (1999), "V-Goods and the Role of the Urban Informal Sector in Development", *Economic Development and Cultural Change*, Volume 47, Number 2, pp. 259–288.

Ranjan, S. (2007), "Review of Rural Non-Farm Sector in India: Recent Evidence", *esocialscience.com Working Paper Series*, Working Paper Number 1215.

Rath, D.P., Nayak, P.K., Lakshmanan, L., Mandal, K., Rajesh, R. and Fanai, V. (2007), "A User's Perspective on the Database of Services Sector in Indian Economy", *Economic and Political Weekly*, September 15.

Ray, D. (1998), *Development Economics*, Oxford University Press, New Delhi.

Ritter, J. and Anker, R. (2002), "Good Jobs, Bad Jobs: Workers' Evaluations in Five Countries", *International Labour Review*, Volume 141, Number 4, pp. 331–358.

Rodrik, D. and Subramanian, A. (2005), "From 'Hindu Growth' to Productivity Surge: The Mystery of the Indian Growth Transition", *IMF Staff Papers*, Volume 52, Number 2, pp. 193–228.

Rosenberg, N. (1982), *Inside the Black Box: Technology and Economics*, Cambridge University Press, Cambridge.

Rosenstein-Rodan, P. (1943), "Problems of Industrialization of Eastern and South-Eastern Europe", *Economic Journal*, Volume 53, pp. 202–211.

Rowthorn, R.E. and Wells, J.R. (1987), *De-Industrialization and Foreign Trade*, Cambridge University Press, Cambridge.

Sabot, R.H. (1977), "The Social Costs of Urban Surplus Labour", *Development Centre Studies Employment Series*, Number 14, OECD, Paris.

Saluja, M.R. and Yadav, B. (2007), "Gross Domestic Product from Services Sector: Methodology, Data Sources and Limitations", *Economic and Political Weekly*, September 15.

Sampson, G.P. and Snape, R.H. (1985), "Identifying the Issues in Trade in Services", *The World Economy*, Volume 8, Issue 2, pp. 171–182.

Sapir, A. and Winter, C. (1994), "Services Trade", in Greenway, P. and Winters, A. (eds.), *Surveys in International Trade*, Blackwell Publishing, Oxford.

Sastry, D.V.S., Singh, B., Bhattacharya, K. and Unnikrishnan, N.K. (2003), "Sectoral Linkages and Growth Prospects: Reflections on the Indian Economy", *Economic and Political Weekly*, June 14.

Schultz, T.P. (1988), "Education Investments and Returns", in Chenery, H. And Srinivasan, T.N. (eds.), *Handbook of Development Economics*, Volume 1, Number 1, Elsevier, Amsterdam.

Schultz, T.W. (1961), "Investment in Human Capital", *American Economic Review*, Volume 51, pp. 1–17.

Shetty, S.L. (2007), "Status Paper on the Database Issues of the Services Sector", *Economic and Political Weekly*, September 15.

Singh, N. (2006), "Services-Led Industrialization in India: Prospects and Challenges", Stanford Centre for International Development, Working Paper Number 290, Stanford University.

Smith, A. (1776), *The Wealth of Nations*, Volume I, Methuen and Company Ltd., London.

Smith, A.D. (1972), *The Measurement and Interpretation of Service Output Changes*, National Economic Development Office, London.

Spence, M. (1976), "Competition in Salaries, Credentials and Signalling Prerequisites for Jobs", *Quarterly Journal of Economics*, Volume 90, Issue 1, pp. 51–74.

Srimany, A.K. and Bhattacharya, K. (1998), "Measures for Financial Services: A Review with Special Reference to Banking in India", *Reserve Bank of India Occasional Papers*, Volume 19, Number 1, pp. 1–38.

Subba Rao, K.G.K. (2004), "Estimates of Value Added Per Worker", *Economic and Political Weekly*, February 14.

Svendsen, S. (1981), "The Concentration of Capital in Shipping and the Optimum Size of Shipping Companies", *GeoJournal*, Volume 2, Number, pp. 163–174.

Tendulkar, S.D. (2007), "India's Growing Services Sector: Database Problems and Issues", *Economic and Political Weekly*, September 15.

Thurow, L.C. (1976), *Generating Inequality*, Macmillan, London.

Tilly, G. (2006), "Improvements to Timely Measures of Service Sector Output", *Economic Trends*, Number 630, Office for National Statistics, United Kingdom.

Tobin, J. (1956), "Estimations of Relationships for Limited Dependent Variables", *Econometrica*, Volume 26, pp. 24–36.

Triplett, J.E. and Bosworth, B. (2000), "Productivity in the Services Sector", Presentation at the American Economic Association Meetings, January 9, Chicago.

United Nations (1993), *System of National Accounts*, Inter-Secretariat Working Group on National Accounts, New York.

Uppal, R.K. (2007), *E-Banking in India: Challenges and Opportunities*, New Century Publications, New Delhi.

Verma, R. (2008), "The Service Sector Revolution in India", Research Paper Number 2008/72, UNU-WIDER.

Winters, P., Janvry, A.D. and Sadoulet, E. (2001), "Family and Community Networks in Mexico-U.S. Migration", *The Journal of Human Resources*, Volume 36, Number 1, pp. 159–184.

Wolfl, A. (2005), "The Service Economy in OECD Countries", *OECD Science, Technology and Industry Working Paper Series*, Working Paper Number 2005/03, OECD Publishing.

Wooldridge, J.M. (2002), *Econometric Analysis of Cross-Section and Panel Data*, MIT Press, Cambridge, Massachusetts.

Working, H. (1943), "Statistical Laws of Family Expenditures", *Journal of the American Statistical Association*, Volume 38, pp. 43–56.

World Bank (2000), *Beyond Economic Growth: Meeting the Challenges of Global Development*, The World Bank, Washington, DC.

 (2004), *Sustaining India's Services Revolution: Access to Foreign Markets, Domestic Reform and International Negotiations*, The World Bank, Washington, DC.

Wu, Y. (2007), "Services Sector Growth in China and India: A Comparison", *China: An International Journal*, Volume 5, Number 1, pp. 137–154.

Index

Printed in the United States
by Baker & Taylor Publisher Services